OUR VIETNAM WARS

As Told by 100 Veterans
Who Served

by

William F. Brown

PREFACE

This is not a 'war book.' Nor is it a book about the Vietnam War per se. And it definitely isn't fiction. Call them snapshots or vignettes, but it is a collection of 100 individual stories which I hope conveys the incredibly diverse experiences of the young men and women who served there. It focuses on who they were, where they came from, the jobs they held, their memories, and what they did after they came back home. Some of them are genuine war heroes, as you'll see, but most were simply targets and survivors. Like every other war our country fought, less than twenty-five percent of the troops "in theater" were actually in the field in combat units. The rest served in support units of one type or another, and Vietnam was no different.

Their stories are presented chronologically and cover the twenty years of American involvement in Vietnam, beginning with a twelve-year-old American boy who was in Saigon with his family in 1955-56, and ending with a Navy lieutenant who stood on the flight deck of an American aircraft carrier on "Yankee Station," as a forklift shoved Huey helicopters overboard into the South China Sea during the evacuation of Saigon in 1975. If you read carefully, you will see how the war changed, how our army changed, how Vietnam changed, and how "we" changed during those years.

January 30, 2018 will mark the 50th anniversary of the Tet Offensive. It was the defining event in a war that dominated my generation, and is still dominating the lives of too many who served there. It disrupted plans, jobs, college, careers, marriage, and every other part of our daily lives, both before and long after we went. For those who were killed or wounded, it disrupted much more for them and their families.

I decided to write this book because our children and grandchildren know so little about that place and time, and what most of us did there. What they do know comes largely from the Oliver Stone movie, Platoon, or the half-dozen good novels that have been written about the war. Unfortunately, most are set in 1968 in an infantry platoon in the jungle on the Cambodian border. I have no bones to pick with Oliver Stone. He was there, that was his war, and I respect him for it; but it wasn't my war or the Vietnam War most of us experienced. There were perhaps a hundred different Vietnam Wars depending on the year you were there, the service you were in, your branch, where you were located, your job, your race, your gender, and your rank. That is the diversity of experience I am trying to convey.

Those of us who served in Vietnam are now 70 years old, give or take. As you'll see from the photographs I've included, we've all grown a bit gray-haired and fat over the years, and probably look like cuddly Grandpas and Grandmas now. Trust me, that wasn't how we looked back then. And unlike any previous American war, when we came "marching home," we were reviled, insulted, spat upon, had blood thrown on us in airports, called war criminals by Jane Fonda, or simply avoided and ignored. Those were not isolated incidents, and they left scars every bit as real and painful as an AK-47 or an RPG, the infamous Russian- and Chinese-made Rocket-Propelled Grenade.

When we got home, no one wanted to hear about the war, and we quickly learned not to bring it up. We were the embarrassing "800-pound gorillas" in the room that everyone wished would fade away; so that's what we did. For many vets I interviewed, I am the first person they've spoken to about the war since they came home, including their wives or children. Neither the American Legion nor the VFW wanted us around, much less as members. So, we formed our own veterans' groups like the Vietnam Veterans of America, the Band of Brothers, and many others. They brought us together and have given us a new sense of pride, as you can see from the Vietnam Vet baseball caps many now wear.

Over 9 million of us served on active duty during the war; 2,710,000, or about one third served in Vietnam; 211,454 were wounded, and 58,220 were killed. Unfortunately, that last number does not include the tens of thousands who have died because of the indiscriminate spraying of Agent Orange, or had their lives dramatically shortened by the

myriad of diseases it causes. They are part of a growing list of names that are NOT engraved on the Wall in Washington.

My estimate, which is by no means scientific, is that well over 50% of surviving Vietnam veterans now suffer from PTSD or one of the many Agent Orange-related illnesses such as Type II Diabetes, Neuropathy, Heart Disease, Parkinson's, Prostate Cancer, Hodgkin's Disease, and other types of cancers. Most of those diseases struck as we approached 60 years of age, like so many ticking bombs. As someone said, "Vietnam—it's the gift that keeps on giving. If they didn't kill us over there, they're determined to kill us back here."

The irony is that we who served were patriotic then and, if anything, we are even more patriotic now. Still, I don't believe there was a single vet I interviewed who doesn't think the war was a monstrous mistake and that we were sold down the river by a long series of US Presidents and Washington politicians, few of whom ever served, fewer still let their own children serve, and none ever studied the history of the people and country where they chose to send us to bleed and die, because they were afraid to admit a mistake.

In the end, the truest words about those who did go and serve were written by the late Mel Tillis in his song, "Ruby," as sung by Kenny Rogers:

> "It wasn't me that started that old crazy Asian war,
> But I was proud to go and do my patriotic chore."

JOHN HIGBEE'S WAR

A Twelve-year-old Boy Scout and Schoolboy in Saigon, 1955-57

My dad was recruited from the State of Michigan to join the public administration part of Michigan State University's mission team to South Vietnam. It was early 1955 and I was only twelve years old, but off our family went on our two-year, great Southeast Asia adventure—my mother and father, my younger brother, my sister, and I. The second photo is a copy of our passport page when we re-entered the US in 1957. The State Department had asked the University to set up an Institute for Public and Police Administration in Saigon to help train the new South Vietnamese government, and my father went as part of that team.

The years 1954 and 1955 were tumultuous in South Vietnam. The French had been defeated at Dien Bien Phu, but that battle was way up north. They were leaving, the Geneva agreements had partitioned the country, and there were supposed to be national elections. Ho Chi Minh and his Viet Minh were consolidating their power in the north, while a half-dozen non-Communist leaders vied for power in the South. None of that made any difference to a twelve-year-old, nor did that turmoil show on the streets of Saigon, at least not at "bicycle level," while I was there. The US government had not yet decided to replace the French, and we weren't anyone's enemy, not yet.

Our family arrived in April, 1955, and moved into a classic French colonial mansion on the outskirts of Saigon. It was close to the US Ambassador's house—three-story, stucco exterior, surrounded by a high wall with barbed wire and broken glass on top. We slept on the top floor and there was a large steel grate that came down across the stairs that was locked at night. We had a cook, a maid, a driver, two garages, and a bomb shelter in the front yard. For a twelve-year-old kid from Mason, Michigan, it was really something.

Dad worked in a government building in downtown Saigon. Until we arrived, there hadn't been enough American kids to set up an American school, but that quickly changed as the American mission expanded. The State Department hired some teachers and a school was set up in a Quonset hut downtown. There were eleven students in my 7th–9th grade class. We had no guards around the school and there was little military presence in the city. The children of the project team members were chauffeur-driven to and from school each day.

As kids, we would ride our bikes into Saigon all the time. The club my family belonged to was across the street from the Presidential Palace. We would go to shows in Cholon, the Chinese neighborhood, and grab rides on "Cyclos." They were three-wheeled rickshaw/bicycles, with the driver pedaling in back. They cost almost nothing. The people were very friendly, and the only time I had any trouble with any Vietnamese was when I got punched by a Cyclo driver who thought I hadn't tipped him enough for a ride. He ended up getting arrested. In the two years I spent there, I managed to pick up quite a bit of Street Vietnamese, including how to argue, barter, and use most of their cuss words.

One of our teachers organized a Boy Scout Troop sponsored by the Embassy. The South Vietnamese Army loaned us some tents and camping gear, and we went out camping all the time. We did a summer camp up in the Central Highlands. There's a small river on the Cambodian border. We formed a chain and swam across, so we could touch the other side and say we were in Cambodia. We camped with a cook and a guard. He was someone's gardener who brought along a .22-caliber rifle, not because of any enemy soldiers, but to scare away the tigers. We also camped in Loc Ninh, Pleiku, Dalat, on the beach at Nha Trang, and a lot of other places that became bloody battlefields ten and fifteen years later. As the war and the devastation got worse and worse, I could only wonder what Vietnam might've been like if things had come out differently.

Rather than order expensive Boy Scout uniforms from the States, we tore some pictures from the catalog and took them to a Chinese tailor shop in Cholon. We got hand-tailored, hand-embroidered uniforms at a fraction of the US price.

When our family came back home to the States in March, 1957, my dad joined the faculty of Michigan State University. I finished high school in 1961 and went on to graduate from Michigan State. After a career in senior data processing and IT positions with Roadway Express, Blue Cross, and several other companies in the healthcare field, I am now retired.

In 2001, my wife Judi and I went back to Vietnam and Cambodia on a two-week tour, which took us to Saigon, Hanoi, and many other places in between. The countryside was beautiful and the people friendly. While I didn't have a chance to swim across to Cambodia, I was surprised at how much had changed and how much had not changed.

Author's Note—You can also read his wife Judi Higbee's account of her time as a Red Cross "Donut Dolly" in Vietnam later in this book.

ERNIE BURZAMATO'S WAR

US Marines, Corporal and Advisor,
US Military Assistance Advisory Group (MAAG),
II Corps, 1956 and 1961

I grew up in Brooklyn, dropped out of high school at sixteen, and joined the Marine Corps, as my older brother Chuck had done. In September, 1955, I reported to Paris Island for Boot Camp and went on to Recon and Demo schools. I did so well I was promoted to corporal and given an immediate foreign assignment to something called the US Military Assistance Advisory Group— MAAG, as it was called—in Vietnam. I was told I'd be helping organize the local militias and teaching basic weapons, defense, and tactics to the farmers and villagers. I was seventeen years old when I arrived and knew nothing about the country, its history, or its politics.

I was a member of the Advance Party of what would grow to be 350 US Advisors, most of whom were Army and Marine Corps. A quarter of the group worked in Saigon, and the rest of us went out to the villages, unarmed, and dressed in civilian clothes. For the next seven months, I worked the patchwork of rivers, swamps, rice paddies, and villages south of Danang. It was pretty country, but ten years later, we called it Dodge City, Hill 55, Go Noi Island, Operation Pipestone Peak, and Operation Meade River; and it kept two Marine Divisions busy. I didn't know it then, but this was the beginning of my 33-year career in the Marines and Reserves.

In 1956, there was no fighting going on. We got along with the villagers, or we thought we did; but we were out in the field. We had no knowledge of the big picture, or what was going on in Saigon, Hanoi, or Washington. What I remember was thatch huts, old men and women, a lot of rain and heat, eating strange food, and meeting a lot of wonderful people.

I was only there seven months before they quietly rotated me back to the States. The next year, 1957, the VC began to attack the US advisors. In 1959, Bien Hoa itself was hit, and several US advisors were killed. By 1960, the number of US advisors had grown from 327 to 685, and the Military Assistance Advisory Group—Vietnam became the Military Assistance Command—Vietnam or MAC-V. Soon the number of advisors increased to 3,400.

In 1961, I was sent back to Vietnam for my second tour, to the same area. This time, I was in uniform, carrying an M-14, and part of Force Recon, protecting Danang. A lot of the equipment we were giving the South Vietnamese came in through Danang, and the Marines were running sweeps outside the base. By then, the same villages where I had sat down and eaten roast pig, you couldn't go near. We were the bad guys, like the French, and it was all VC country. When we went through the villages, all we saw was old men and women, no young men. We all knew where they were.

One day I took a Force Recon patrol out south of Danang. I had two five-man teams and around dusk we were hit hard with mortars. I had two men killed, two men badly wounded, and a total of eight hurt, including myself, with shrapnel in my leg. We managed to get out of there, but back then we didn't have the backup, the helicopters, or the artillery support we had a few years later.

One of the sad facts of life is that neither the Pentagon nor the VA recognize any service, the wounds, or the men who were killed in action in Vietnam prior to 1962, before it was an official "combat action," even though we were in uniform, armed, and on orders. I always thought that was unfair to their families, not to at least get a Purple Heart.

After they took that piece of metal out of my leg, I could no longer run very well; and that got me bounced out of Force Recon. So, in 1963, after eight years on active duty with the Marine Corps, I knew it was time to get out. I tried to get in the Green Berets, but they didn't like my leg either. That was the end of my active duty, although I stayed in the Reserves.

I got my high school diploma by GED and went on to college. My family had been in heavy construction, so when I got a degree in Structural Engineering, I found myself being recruited by the Seabees. In 1972, I switched from the Marine Reserves to the Navy Reserves and joined a Seabee unit, rising quickly from Builder 2nd Class to Senior Chief. I was commissioned Lieutenant JG in 1987 and retired as a Lieutenant Commander in 1995. I was frequently called up to Active Duty and became one of the Navy's experts in unit and equipment mobilization and embarkation, working with the Marines in Vietnam, on the evacuation of US assets from the Suez Canal, and in Honduras, Lebanon, Somalia, Bosnia, Uganda, and in Desert Storm.

I'm now 79. During my thirty-three years of Active and Reserve Service in the Navy and Marine Corps, I received a Meritorious Service Medal, four Navy Commendation Medals, and five Navy Achievement Medals.

BOB CARELS'S WAR

US Army Special Forces A Team, C Company,
5th Special Forces Group in Gia Vuc, I Corps, 1963

In early 1963, I was a member of the 7th Special Forces Group at Fort Bragg and told to pack, because I was replacing a guy in an A Team at Gia Vuc in the mountains of Vietnam. An A Team has twelve members: a captain, a lieutenant, two operations sergeants, two radiomen, two medics, two engineers, and two demolition men. I was a radioman. I grew up in an Air Force family, had traveled around the world. After high school in Falls Church, Virginia, I worked for a year and then drove around Europe on a Vespa before I enlisted in the Army and qualified for Special Forces, back when that meant the Green Berets. I had a smattering of high school French, but I knew no Vietnamese.

The Gia Vuc Special Forces Camp was an old French Army base in the mountains of I Corps. It opened in early 1962 and was the most successful one we ran. It was in the Song Re River valley: beautiful, green, with terraced rice paddies and water buffalo, and home to 1,500 Montagnards of the Hre tribe and 300 Vietnamese. By 1969, there were 6,400 Montagnards and Vietnamese living there. The "Yards" were a distinct ethnic minority in Vietnam. They had dark skin and straight, short noses. The Vietnamese considered them to be a primitive, foreign people. The adults had their front teeth filed down or broken off, a tribal custom, and neither the North nor South Vietnam-

ese liked them. We did. We lived with them, ate their food, and fought side by side with them. They were very loyal to the Americans throughout the war. Some Hre had fought with the French in the last war and some fought with the Viet Minh. That was history. Now they were fighting for themselves.

The fortified camp was in the valley and blocked a main infiltration route from Laos to Danang. It had several barracks and storage buildings made of bamboo, with thatched roofs, woven mats for walls, and dirt floors. Our Special Forces team and an ARVN (Army of the Republic of Viet Nam) Special Forces team each had their own buildings. There was also an old stone building we used as a medical clinic. We were there to train the local militia and the ARVN Special Forces so that they could stop the infiltration from the north through Laos and defend their camp. This was all before the major escalation of the war in 1965. After that, they weren't just infiltrating; regular NVA regiments came marching down the Ho Chi Minh Trail.

While there weren't very many VC around in 1963, we were regularly probed and hit by mortar attacks, and they always disappeared before dawn. We had a "Mike Force," or reaction force, which we trained and took out on patrols. When we weren't patrolling, we were building, and I remember taking the truck and the water trailer down to the river to bring back loads of water and sand for construction projects many times.

There was an outpost on a nearby hill which we used as an observation post. One of the guys shot a deer from up there and we had fresh venison for a few days. One night when I was up there, I heard a tiger coughing and snorting in the jungle below, but he went away. Another night, we saw a line of flashlights coming down a trail on the other side of the river. To us, that was enemy country, so we fired off a few mortar rounds. After a few minutes, we heard a panicked call in English on the radio. It was an American advisor to an ARVN unit. They were moving through the jungle in the dark and got lost. Fortunately, no one was hurt.

We had a small airstrip near the camp. Sometimes, we'd get a Huey to fly over from the Special Forces Group at Nha Trang with parachutes. We'd use it as our "elevator," so everyone could get in a couple of jumps and we could keep our airborne status and pay.

Before I got there, it was the Special Forces who trained the ARVN troops and militias. Then the Military Assistance Advisory Group—MAAG—took that over and the Special Forces were given the mountain tribes to work with. I rotated home in 1964, but by 1965, with the help of the Australian SAS and the ARVN Special Forces, we had set up fifty Special Forces camps, half in VC-controlled areas. The hope was, if we could convert the local tribes to our side, we could beat the VC at the grassroots. The camps were isolated and had little conventional artillery or air support, but a Montagnard with a crossbow was a man to be feared. Giving him a modern rifle was even better. They were very effective soldiers.

After my deployment ended, I went back to Fort Bragg and was assigned to the Service Club, where I slept in a buddy's van, instead of the stuffy, coal-fired barracks. When my enlistment ended, I took night courses in computers, and was lucky enough to be hired at the Johns Hopkins Applied Physics Lab in Howard County, Maryland. I was an assistant computer programmer, from which I finally retired in 2002 after thirty-seven years. I'm now 78 years old, and live in Concord, New Hampshire.

MIKE SANNES'S WAR

**US Army E-4 and Radio Intercept Specialist,
the 8th Radio Research Unit, Army Security Agency,
Phu Bai and parts north, 1964–65**

I spent fourteen months in the hills and jungle of Vietnam very early in the war, before there was much of a war, in northern I Corps. I was assigned to the "8th Radio Research Unit" of the Army Security Agency. A Radio Research Unit? Whenever you work for something with a name like that, you gotta figure the CIA and NSA have their fingers deep in the pie.

I came from a military family in Oregon, where you weren't a real man until you'd been in combat. I tried college for a few months, and finally joined the Army. In Basic at Fort Ord, California, I did well on the signals and Morse code tests, and was selected for the ASA at Fort Devens, Massachusetts for cryptography and radio intercept training. I figured I'd go to an advanced communications center in Europe, listening to the Russians, not to the jungle playing infantry; but field intelligence is always one of the first units in, and the first casualty in Vietnam was an ASA guy named Davis.

After several stateside assignments, I spent six months on a spy ship off Havana, Cuba. When Kennedy was assassinated, the Russians and the Cubans sent missile boats out to chase us away. ASA then sent me to a small, secret communications center outside DC on a winding road with no sign and no name. That's when I volunteered for Vietnam.

When I arrived in-country in March, 1964, I was initially assigned to the 3rd RRU at Tan Son Nhut outside Saigon. That was fairly civilized, but two months later I was sent up to Phu Bai in I Corps and then to a series of remote firebases just below the DMZ, where I spent the rest of my fifteen months and twenty-six days in country. We monitored VC and NVA radio signals. At the company and regimental level, they used Chinese radios with small, hand-cranked generators. That was why we had to get close. And they used Morse code, usually encrypted, but they also used plain voice radio when they thought no one was listening. Very often when the VC and NVA got in a battle, their radio operators would get excited, their communication security would fall apart, and they would start broadcasting in the clear. That was when the good stuff came through, and we would earn our paychecks.

I remember a lot of things that happened in Vietnam, but my memory has holes in it. It's like watching an old black-and-white movie when part of the film is missing, like that old restored version of *Lost Horizon*. Scenes will pop up, but I can't remember what led up to them or what happened afterward.

Our firebase was on a hilltop surrounded by jungle. It was in I Corps, but there would be no Marines up there for almost a year. I was dropped off by helicopter and left standing in a dusty field by myself until two guys finally drove over in a Jeep. They looked me over, sneered, and then drove me to one of the tents in the compound. I went inside, put my gear on an empty cot, turned around, and some guy punched me in the face. I didn't understand it at the time, but this was a test to see how tough you were, to see if you'd fight back; because there was no place there for guys who couldn't hold their own on the perimeter. We had about one hundred men in the unit. Once they trusted you, you were admitted to the clique.

We operated two types of radio equipment. Some were inside a hut and some were on racks bolted inside an Armored Personnel Carrier, which had six antennas and three men working inside on twelve-hour shifts. In both the buildings and the APCs, there was a thermite grenade on top of each receiver to destroy everything in case we were overrun. One thing I picked up on as soon as I arrived, was that none of us signals guys were supposed to be captured alive. The guards were there as much to shoot us as protect us, if it came to that.

We lived in six-man tents, like the ones you see in *M*A*S*H*, but they weren't that nice. It was hot all the time and we had big fans, not that they accomplished very much. The tents had wooden floors. As soon as it was dark, there would be big rats all over the place. Someone brought in a dog to keep them away, but the rats ended up attacking the dog. One guy got a big python, which he put under the floorboards. That worked.

Like everyone else, I had to pull guard duty in a perimeter bunker. They were damp, smelled, had rats like everywhere else, and it was very loud inside when there was shooting going on. One night I heard movement out in front of my position. I yelled a warning three times, as we were supposed to do, and then opened up. In the morning, we discovered I had shot the hell out of a water buffalo.

There was a crude airstrip there, but we were always fogged in. The Army supply flights had trouble making it up there from Danang, but the Air America pilots in their black DC-3 never seemed to. Even when they made it in, we were the farthest north of any US base, and they were always out of whatever it was we wanted by the time they got to us. We always got ammo, more than we needed, and C-rations, old World War II stuff, which we would trade with the Special Forces guys when they came through.

The VC would hit us with mortars fairly often, always at night. We had burned and cleared a wide perimeter around the base for security, so it was hard for them to get close. But after you were there long enough, even when you were asleep in your tent, you could hear the mortar rounds when they came out of the tube with that distinct "Thunk! Thunk! Thunk!" as they walked the mortar rounds in on us. To this day, I can still hear that sound.

I remember one time when we were surrounded by the VC and cut off for three days. We had run out of food, were ordered to abandon the base, and had to fight our way east to a beach on the coast. We found a small lagoon that had a lot of crabs in it. We were so hungry that we caught them, ripped them open, and ate them raw.

When my year was up in 1965, I was more than ready to leave, until they told me I'd been extended indefinitely because of the big troop buildup. Things had gotten so bad that I never expected to return alive anyway, but this was the worst. I stopped counting the days. Three months later, the Sergeant called me over and said, "Grab your bag. There's a plane waiting for you." I was flown down to Tan Son Nhut, but rather than stay at the Repo Depot I took a cab into Saigon and checked into a hotel. Now that I was really on my way home, I was so paranoid that I locked the door and sat with my back against the wall with a pistol, convinced that the NVA would be coming through the door and window to get me any minute. The next day, I flew home, was discharged, and found myself standing on a street in San Francisco, cold turkey, with no transition. It was one of the cruelest things anyone could do to another person.

I had lived like an animal in the jungle for almost sixteen months. I wasn't a hero, just a kid trying to survive, and I had serious problems for a long time after Vietnam. I drank, got into drugs, and had problems with the law. I got rid of most of my things and traveled all over the US, Europe, South America, the Philippines, Japan, and Thailand. I even lived for a few years in Tokyo. Once, I went into a bar with a loaded gun. I had both survivor's guilt and a death wish, and you can't get much worse than that. There were other times when I couldn't leave the house. I had two 100-pound guard dogs and woke up screaming every night, convinced they were coming through the windows for me again.

Finally, I went to a Vet Center in San Diego and got some help. I had come home to a less than friendly reception in California in 1965, and I'd never talked about Vietnam to anyone. It was too painful. I don't think anyone can understand the savagery and horrors of war like that and what it did to guys, if you hadn't been there. I have been clean and sober for thirty-five years now, but it took me that long to feel comfortable in my own country.

In 1968, I went back to school for computer programming and got a job with the

Navy Weapons Program at the University of Rhode Island doing computer programming. That was the perfect job for me. I could sit alone in the dark in front of a computer screen and work with a machine, not people. Eventually, I became Vice President of a public software corporation with forty-two software engineers working for me, if you can believe that.

I'm retired and live in Southern California now. I have a 100% disability, and am being treated at Cedars-Sinai Hospital for a rare blood disease that I believe I acquired from Agent Orange, which was all over the place in I Corps. I've been on chemotherapy for over a year now, and have had a stem cell transplant that Cedars-Sinai arranged for me.

In 1995, I went back to Vietnam as part of a project doing relief work for disabled VC and NVA soldiers. Agent Orange messed us up, but the Vietnamese have had it much worse.

VIN MAULELLA'S WAR

**US Army, First Lieutenant and Recon Platoon Leader,
2nd Battalion, 2nd Infantry, 1st Infantry Division,
Lai Khe, 1965–66**

I grew up in Brooklyn and attended St. Peter's College, a Jesuit school in Jersey City, where I joined ROTC. Everyone was Gung Ho back then, but that was before Vietnam. I was active in Scabbard and Blade and Pershing Rifles and received a Regular Army commission when I graduated. My branch would be Military Intelligence, but a Regular Army Commission required a two-year assignment to a combat branch, which in my case would be the Infantry. After Officer Basic, I was assigned to the 5th Infantry Division Mechanized at Fort Devens, Massachusetts.

That fall, I completed the Officer Basic Course at Fort Benning, but then my orders were changed. I was supposed to go to Airborne and Ranger school, but they were canceled. Instead, I was sent back to Fort Devens where my unit designation changed to the 1st Infantry Division. Rumor was that our destination was Vietnam. Naturally, for our "Vietnam orientation" the Army sent us to the White Mountains of Vermont in the winter, where we ran around in the snow in white arctic camouflage uniforms and snowshoes. When we returned to Fort Devens, I was assigned as the Battalion Motor Officer and licensed to drive vehicles up to a 5-ton wrecker. After more pre-Vietnam spring training at cold and muddy Fort Drum, New York, I was assigned to be the Anti-Tank Platoon Leader. Since the VC did not have tanks, that gear was left behind, and I became a second Recon Platoon Leader, in charge of the Battalion headquarters security force. In August, 1965, we flew to Oakland and boarded a troop-ship. Twenty-one days later we arrived at Vung Tao and convoyed up to Lai Khe on Highway 13, where we established a base camp around a Michelin rubber plantation.

The 3rd Brigade was headquartered in former French Colonial housing, which was quite opulent. It was the first time I had seen a bidet. When we first arrived, the rubber plantation was still operating, and workers would come to tap the rubber trees. What we didn't know was that they were tilting the tree cups to mark our positions for the sappers when they came through the wire at night. When we figured that out, we broke their cups.

We went out on platoon and even company-sized sweeps, locally around Ben Cat and in the "Iron Triangle," and on larger multi-force operations throughout III Corps. Ap Bau Bang, Ap Nha Mat, and Cu Chi were memorable engagements. In Cu Chi, we secured the perimeter for the arrival of the 25th Infantry Division. Cu Chi sat on a maze of VC tunnel complexes. One time, I decided I would play "tunnel rat" and go down to see what it was like. I never did that again. It was pitch dark and you never knew what you might run into.

Those months are a blur now. We were out in the field and in combat continuously. I remember a lot of helicopter assaults, Air Force jets dropping bombs, cluster bombs and napalm, long marches hacking through the jungle, snipers in trees, gunfire, RPGs, and all the rest. And I remember we had an overly-aggressive battalion commander nicknamed "Colonel Smoke." But what I'm proudest of is that none of my guys were killed while I was in charge. Some were wounded, but none killed.

One day, we got ambushed. That's what we called it, anyway. Westmoreland quickly snapped that contact with the enemy should always be expected in combat; so by definition, it could never be an ambush. Thank you, General Westmoreland. We were ambushed.

Before I could volunteer for Long Range Recon Patrol, LLRP, training, my two years in the infantry were over and I was assigned to 1st Division Headquarters Military Intelligence at Di-An, where I worked as an interrogator.

I found that work very rewarding, and I proved to be good at interrogating prisoners. After 10 months in country and in the infantry, I had a decent understanding of the people and the terrain. Using ARVN translators was a challenge; they were like macho actors in a bad movie. Nobody listened. The VC we captured were mostly simple farmers and didn't know much. The NVA were hardcore, but I learned some tricks to figure out where they had come from by asking the right questions: "When you got up this morning and went down to the stream to wash your face, where was the sun? In your face, or on your back? How many hours did it take for you to walk here? And where was the sun in the sky?" From things like that, I could figure out where their base camps were, have them hit, and save a lot of lives.

When I rotated out in 1966, they asked me three places I wanted to be reassigned. I asked for three posts in California. Instead, they sent me to Fort Holabird in Baltimore,

Maryland, the Army Intelligence School. I was promoted to Captain by then and had been awarded a Bronze Star with V and an Oak Leaf Cluster. As it turned out, I was one of the few Military Intelligence officers there who had field experience, a Combat Infan-tryman's Badge, and who had actually interrogated a Vietnamese prisoner. Much of their theory dated back to World War II and Korea, so they had me teach and write a course.

As time passed, I knew I was headed back over for another tour in Vietnam; but my family couldn't take that. The Army offered to send me to Turkey first, but I was even less interested in that, so I resigned my commission and got out after four and a half years.

With my degree and my service completed, it wasn't hard to get a job. I went into office equipment sales, pharmaceutical sales, and then into bank operations in New York City with Manufacturers Hanover, Chemical, and Chase, specializing in international banking and foreign trade. In 2000, I was downsized as a Vice President and opened my own consulting practice, which I still do part time.

For almost fifty years, I never talked about the war to anyone. No one wanted to hear about it anyway. A couple of years ago, one of my men connected with me and stopped by. We talked a lot, and he kept bringing up this thing that happened and that thing that happened over there, but I couldn't remember any of it. All I could do was shake my head and tell him I guess I'd blocked all that stuff out. He had a lot of physical problems from Nam—cancer everywhere and a lot of other things, all Agent Orange-related. He was supposed to move to my area, but then I heard from his daughter that he had died.

In recent years, after not having talked about Vietnam for decades, I reconnected with that part of my life through the VVA. I was also diagnosed with Agent Orange-related prostate cancer, no doubt associated with the months I spent crawling around in the bush. Since then, I've undergone chemo and hormone therapy, and hope to be cancer free. I am Blessed.

PETE KARANGIS'S WAR

US Navy, E4 and A-5 Vigilante Jet Aircraft Mechanic, *USS Ranger*, Yankee Station, Gulf of Tonkin, 1964 to 1965

I enlisted in the Navy right out of high school in 1962, before the war started. I was only seventeen, but it was the best thing I ever did. I had graduated from Brooklyn Automotive High School, one of the best vocational schools in the city, so they sent me to the Naval Air Station in Sanford, Florida, to be trained as a mechanic on the A-5 Vigilante, the Navy's long-range carrier attack jet used for bombing and recon. It was the latest thing, made of aluminum and titanium with very advanced electronics for its time, like "heads up" displays, a nose TV camera, and an onboard computer. Unlike the Air Force or the Army, the Navy trained mechanics through OJT before they ever sent us to a school.

After that, I joined the crew of the *USS Ranger*, CVN-41, in San Diego. We were rushed out to sea on August 6, 1964, two days after the *USS Maddox* was supposedly fired on by the North Vietnamese in the Gulf of Tonkin. On the way, we made quick stops at Pearl Harbor, Subic Bay, in the Philippines, and at Yokosuka, Japan, before spending sixty days on "Yankee Station," as the Navy called that part of the South China Sea close to the coast of Vietnam. Our aircraft began attacking targets in the north and we worked twelve-hour shifts, 24/7. The guys got pretty feisty. The food on the ship was okay, but we ran out of fresh milk in two days. Our quarters were cramped, and we

slept in bunks, three high, maybe thirty guys to a section; but most of my time was spent up on the flight deck or down on the hangar deck working on my A-5s. We would be on station for forty to forty-five days, then break off and go to Subic Bay, Hong Kong, or Japan for four or five days to resupply. We did that for eleven months, until the next July.

The *Ranger* carried anywhere from seventy-two to ninety aircraft of different types. My section took care of six A-5s. We lost two planes on that first cruise. Both the pilot and navigator-bombardier were killed on one bombing mission. The other plane came in on fire and the crew bailed out just before it blew up.

I'll never forget when we made a port call to Hong Kong. We'd saved our garbage for a week, and off Kowloon a whole line of junks came up behind the ship. We'd dump our garbage overboard, right into their holds. They took it all back and ate that stuff. Another time, when we went into Tokyo, there were protesters on small boats trying to block our way. They had big banners that read "Yankee Go Home," but we didn't. I got to go to the 1964 Olympics for a couple of days, saw Bob Hayes run in the 100-yard dash, and met the Canadian basketball team. But Tokyo was incredible, even without the Olympics.

On April 13, when we were out at sea, we had a fire in a machinery room and had to go back to Yokosuka for major repairs. That took two months. They put the airplanes ashore, and moved us to barracks on the Navy Base. We had Japanese girls doing KP for us and doing our laundry, and I could look out the window at Mount Fuji.

When we stopped at Subic Bay in the Philippines, we'd ride into town on flatbed cattle trucks, hanging on a metal pole that went down the middle. In the bars, if you wanted to pick up a girl, you had to buy a beer; and they were expensive. I also remember there were pushcart vendors in town selling monkey meat on a stick. I came to like it. One of the vendors told me if anyone was bothering me, he'd kill them for me for five dollars.

Race was a big thing back then. Sanford, Florida, where I trained, was segregated. So were the Philippines, and so was the Navy. In Subic, they finally got buses to replace the cattle trucks, but one was for whites and one was for blacks. I went out drinking with a black friend one night, and we made the mistake of getting on the "black bus." He protected me, or I'd never have gotten off; but I didn't make that mistake again.

When my tour was over, I was reassigned to the *USS America*, another aircraft carrier, based in Norfolk, and went on an amazing tour of the Mediterranean. In Greece, I met my father's family. My uncle took me around Athens and other places and threw a big party with all the relatives. We went on to Italy and I did the same thing with my mother's family. Naples was filthy and really stunk, but they threw a huge family dinner for me and two of my friends in this little town. I'll never forget that. Like I said, I'd enlist in the Navy all over again. Where else could I see Japan, Hong Kong, Greece, Italy and all those other places.

I was twenty-one when I got out. I went back to my old job as a mechanic with the *New York Daily News*, and eventually ended up building houses on Staten Island. In 2005, I had a bad motorcycle accident on the way to a veterans' rally in Washington DC, had a traumatic brain injury and was in a coma. I couldn't talk, walk, read, or do any-thing. I did two years of physical therapy and worked out hard from eight to twelve hours every day. It took me two years to get my driver's license back, but I did, and slowly got better. I now play softball three days a week, stickball once a week, and keep in shape by working out.

DON DOHERTY'S WAR

US Marine Corps Captain, Fighter Pilot, and FAC
with the 3rd Marine Battalion, 3rd Marine Regiment,
3rd Marine Division, Okinawa and Da Nang.

There I was: A Marine Corps F-8 Crusader fighter-jet pilot standing on a mountain peak south of the DMZ in I Corps in 1964, looking at North Vietnam. I was a Captain serving as an Air Officer in support of a Marine infantry platoon, providing defense for a top-secret team of NSA spooks from Fort Meade. They had broken the codes and were listening to communications between the Chinese and North Vietnamese and other communist factions.

This was six months before the Gulf of Tonkin "Incident" that got us into a real war. Putting the pieces together years later, I now know I was caught up in high-level Defense Department politics. Secretary of Defense Robert McNamara and the White House were afraid the fledgling South Vietnamese government would soon fall to the Communists, and the next "dominoes" would be Laos and Cambodia. After the political backlash over the fall of Eastern Europe, it became "Not on my watch." They'd be blamed, and be out of jobs.

We had been funding most of the French war since the 1950s. With the French now defeated and gone, McNamara needed something to stir up US public opinion, so he could provide military support and advisors to prop up the South Vietnamese. The "alleged" attack by North Vietnamese torpedo boats on a US Destroyer in the Gulf of Tonkin did precisely that, and gave him his excuse.

The problem was China. What would they do? McNamara and Johnson didn't want another Korean War on their hands. They expected the Chinese to provide arms and advisors, but would they also send in their army? And what would the North Vietnamese do? Would they march their much larger army south, the one that had just defeated the French? Or would the South Vietnamese only have a civil war against the VC guerillas? The stakes were high, and McNamara and the Joint Chiefs needed answers.

After graduating from Santa Clara University in '58, I completed officer training at Quantico, and headed to flight school in Pensacola. After earning my wings in 1960, my first duty assignment was the Marine Corps Air Station, Kaneohe Bay, Hawaii flying the F8 Crusader in VMF-232. It was definitely a "hardship tour." The flying was great, and we were able to operate with many of the aircraft carriers that passed through the Islands enroute to the Far East. During this time, our squadron spent a six-month tour aboard the USS Oriskany, operating in the South China Sea. A great opportunity for a Marine squadron.

I was a Reserve Officer and was recommended for a Regular Commission in the Marine Corps. Had I remained a Reserve Officer, I probably would have continued flying, but, in the Marine Corps, Regular Officers are required to spend time with the ground forces. For pilots, that was usually as a Forward Air Controller, FAC, or an Air Liaison Officer, ALO, with an infantry battalion so we could learn the rifle and mud end of the business.

In late 1963, I was assigned to the 3rd Marine Battalion, 3rd Marine Regiment, of the 3rd Marine Division in Okinawa as a FAC. In March '64, I was tasked to coordinate logistics support for a "reinforced infantry platoon" from our battalion, which was to provide perimeter security for a highly classified mission. Of course, there's no such thing as a "reinforced infantry platoon." A machine gun and mortar squad had been added to beef-up a normal rifle platoon for this special assignment. It definitely made me wonder where we were going.

The answer was Vietnam. Technically, US military were noncombatants and only advisors back then, which didn't exactly square with the extra weapons; but off we went. We landed at Danang in early summer 1964, where we met a contingent of radio intercept and code people from NSA Headquarters at Fort Meade, Maryland and their very high-tech radio equipment. The Marine platoon's job was to protect them. I was not part of the platoon nor of the NSA group. As the battalion Air Liaison Officer, my job was to arrange helicopter lifts for the Marines or the NSA people from Marine Helicopter Squadron HMM-364 at Da Nang, and provide whatever other logistics support either group might need in the field.

Over the next few months, we moved around northern I Corps from one mountain-top to another. In addition to the Security Platoon Commander, Captain Bill Irwin, there was another Marine Corps officer in charge of the NSA team. He was Major Al Gray, who later would become a Four-Star General and the twenty-ninth Commandant of the Marine Corps. While the name meant little to me back then, you could tell that he was someone special, who had serious connections. One day, I asked him what the group was doing. He looked me in the eye and said, "Captain, if I tell you, you'll never be able to fly "in country" again. I decided I didn't need to know, but classified secrets don't remain secret for long in a small unit.

General Westmoreland was the Commander of US Forces Vietnam. He knew we were in country but not what we were doing. Apparently, we didn't work for him, and he threw a fit when he found out that we were there. Westmoreland wanted to know what the hell this NSA team was doing? Our in-bound and out-bound communication traffic went through Hawaii directly to DC, not through Westmoreland's headquarters, and Major Gray reported to the Pentagon. Even a simple fighter pilot from California could figure out that Gray must be working for people way above Westmoreland's pay-grade, and that was a very short list.

As the days passed, I found Vietnam to be a beautiful county, especially from the air, with lush jungles and beautiful beaches, large abandoned Buddhist shrines and temples, and rubber plantations. Outside Khe Sanh, which later became a major US firebase, another place where the French had been defeated, I met a marvelous French planter who had survived two wars and was still growing and harvesting his rubber trees, never losing them to fire. He too had the right connections.

Because no location in northern I Corps was safe for very long, we moved around a lot, relocating from mountain-top to mountain-top along the DMZ and the Laotian border. The VC followed us and were always probing.

Being the guy who coordinated the helicopter support, I managed to be back in Da Nang most nights, and never spent many nights on the ground. I had plenty of time on my hands and used the opportunity to fly an O-1B observation plane and a SNB small cargo plane to see the country and do some weather recon. We usually stayed above 3,000 feet, but did some low-level flying on our return to Da Nang one day. When we landed, my "plane captain" or lead mechanic, showed me a nick on the propeller blade. It was from a bullet. After that, I made it a point to stay above 3,000 feet and to sit on my flak-jacket!

By December, the NSA people and McNamara must have gotten the information they wanted, because we returned to Da Nang and soon left the country. In my case, I returned to the battalion in Okinawa. We eventually went aboard the *USS Princeton*, a helicopter assault carrier, as the Surface Landing Force (SLF) afloat. Soon we were relieved as the SLF by the 9th Marine Regiment, which was bound for Da Nang to make that photogenic, over-the-beach, "unopposed landing" on March 8, 1965, which began the US troop buildup in Vietnam.

I returned to Kingsville, TX where I served for three years as a flight instructor in the Advanced Jet Training Command. By then, Jann and I had married and had our first son. I did not like what was going on in Vietnam, so I got out of the Marine Corps in '68. Major Al Gray didn't need to worry, I never did fly again in Vietnam.

As a newly minted civilian, I had hoped to get a job with one of the airlines, but so did a lot of other, younger Air Force, Navy and Marine Corps pilots, just at the time the airlines were cutting back. That was when I discovered I was an "old man" at 34. We returned home to the San Francisco Bay Area and I got into real estate investment and development; but I never stopped private flying.

A few years ago, I went on a cruise in the Far East, and reluctantly agreed to go on a tour of Vietnam. Wow, it was a real eyeopener. The south was even more busy, vibrant, and entrepreneurial than it had been before the war. On the other hand, the north appeared old and gray, and the people were struggling. One of our guides said that the Vietnamese people in the south love Americans and believe that although we lost the war, they wouldn't have what they now have, if we had not been there.

I'm now 82. After flying for nearly fifty-nine years, I finally hung up my wings last year. Jann and I now split our time between Santa Rosa, California and Scottsdale, Arizona.

LARRY OWEN'S WAR

US Marine Corps, Lance Corporal and Machine Gunner, 3rd Marine Division, Da Nang, 1965–66

In 1963, my senior year of high school, I enlisted in the Navy Reserve, and then enlisted in the Marines that June. After Boot Camp in San Diego, I was trained as a machine gunner and stationed at Camp Pendleton, before going on a Far East tour, sailing on the *USS Breckenridge* to Okinawa for Guerrilla Warfare and Raider Schools. I was also trained as a cliff climber and I've got to say, I was never in better shape in my life than after I finished those schools. In March, 1965, I was a Lance Corporal E-3 assigned to the 3rd Marine Division.

They were about to send us to Mount Fuji in Japan for cold-weather training when our orders were changed, and they sent the whole Division to Danang in a landing ship. The ramps came down and we charged out of LSTs onto the beach, just like they did during World War II, to make some big dramatic statement I guess, although there was no shooting, only photographers and local fishermen.

We were placed around the perimeter of the airport and immediately began patrolling and expanding the perimeter until it went out several miles. My company area was very close to the airstrip, which had two runways. We slept in tents with dirt floors and cots. And I've got to tell you, when a pair of Phantom jets rolled down those runways, side by side, and took off in the middle of the night,

it was enough to blow you out of bed. We had a field mess set up in our camp, but as we were in the field expanding our perimeter, we mostly ate C-rations. I think it was three to four months before I saw clean clothes or a shower again. Every day, we were out on patrols and every night we set up listening posts and ambushes. We would surround a village in the dark, search it at daybreak, and then spend the next hour picking off leeches.

Outside our fence there would be locals selling bottles of "rum" for those dumb enough to drink it. One of our guys bought a bottle and chugged it. He went out riding a water buffalo and chasing people around camp before the other guys caught him and tied him down to his cot until he sobered up the next morning.

I was a squad leader and my squad developed a reputation for being a good place to collect one of those "million-dollar wounds" that was enough to get you sent back home, but not hurt too bad. When we were out in the field, I usually carried an M-60 machine gun, but I learned that the tracer rounds in the ammunition belts gave away your position at night. I took most of them out of the belts and replaced them with regular rounds. When I wasn't carrying the M-60, I would carry an M-14, which was then standard Marine Corps issue, and a .45-caliber pistol. At one point, I traded a case of C-rations to some Air Force guys for a sawed-off shotgun with 00 shells. In the bush, in close quarters, it worked great.

We took a lot of casualties. When replacements arrived, the Marine Corps merged them into the existing units. Unfortunately, promotion was slow. I had been in for two years and was still an E-3. Even though I'd been in-country for quite a while, the new kids frequently outranked me. However, once we got outside the wire, I took over, and no one objected.

Back then, Americans weren't too smart when it came to security. We would let the Vietnamese inside our bases to clean, do our laundry, and KP. There was even one guy who came on the base to give us haircuts. After an attack one night, we found his body in the wire. He had a rifle and a complete map of our whole compound.

On one operation, our battalion went into the hills for a 2-3-day sweep looking for a VC base camp and hospital. We saw Chinese officers in Chinese uniforms up there. Best guess is they were advisors. Out in the countryside, the Vietnamese could be strange. We were guarding a bridge that had a small village at one end. For days, the villagers shied away from us. They tolerated us, but not much more. Then Tet in 1966 happened. It was a big holiday, and overnight, when we walked through the village, they would smile, pull us inside their small houses, and feed us. But when the holiday ended, so did the smiles and the food.

I remember my last mission. We were up in the mountains on another sweep. We went down a steep hill. At the bottom was a stream with a crude log bridge. We started to cross it when, "Kerplunk!" Something landed in the water next to me. We all jumped and started looking around, expecting an attack from somewhere, when something else landed in the water with another "Kerplunk!" and then another! We looked up and finally realized we were surrounded by rock apes up on the cliffs, who were throwing rocks down at us. Even with the rock apes, the mountains were beautiful. In fact, if there wasn't a war going on, the whole country was beautiful, from the beaches and the rice paddies, across the Highlands, all the way up into the mountains in the west.

In February, 1966, I was wounded by shrapnel. We were charging up a hill when an IED went off. Most of it hit the guy ahead of me, but I caught quite a bit in my legs and lost a toe. We had been out in the field for several weeks and we all were filthy, unshaven, with long hair. I remember when I arrived in the hospital the Sergeant there kept complaining that we needed haircuts. We just looked at him. They sent me on to the hospital in Great Lakes, where the doctor in charge of the amputee ward was named Doctor Hacker. Hard to forget that.

I still had some time left, so when I was released, they sent me to El Toro in California, where I marched trainees around during the day and worked at the desk in traffic court. When my enlistment was over I stayed in Southern California and went to Santa Ana Junior College and then Cal Poly Pomona, where I got a BS degree in data processing, which got me a job with EDS. After that, I continued doing consulting with small businesses until I retired. I enjoy softball, golf, karaoke, dancing, and kayaking. Not bad for a 72-year-old. I also spend time working in the local food pantry and soup kitchen.

GEORGE L. RICH JR.'S WAR

US Army Captain, 2nd Battalion,
5th Cavalry Regiment, 1st Cavalry Division,
An Khe, 1965–66

When I graduated from high school in Washington, DC, in 1958 I wanted to go on to college. My mother looked at me and said, "You know, your high school grades aren't too good; and I don't know if we want to pay for all that." I told her I was going, one way or the other, even if I had to pay myself. I got in West Virginia State University, enrolled in the ROTC program, graduated as a Distinguished Military Student, got my degree, got married, and went on active duty in 1961 as a second lieutenant in the infantry.

After Officer Basic at Fort Benning I was assigned to the 4th Infantry Division at Fort Lewis, and then to the 31st Infantry at Fort Rucker. At the end of that tour, I received orders to the 173rd Light Infantry Brigade enroute to the Infantry Officer's Career Course and was promoted to Captain. Before I even got settled in, I was reassigned to the brand-new airmobile 1st Air Cavalry Division which was being organized to go to Vietnam in August, 1965. Our whole division went over by ship. I was on the *USS Buckner*. I was assigned to 2nd Battalion of the 5th Cav as the Liaison Officer to work with the villages and local militias. After a while, the 2nd Brigade Colonel brought me up to the brigade staff to become his new S-5, or Civil Affairs Officer.

The Division headquarters was at An Khe in the Central Highlands, and the Army didn't waste much time putting us to work. In November, we moved into the Ia Drang Valley west of Pleiku on the Cambodian border to relieve a Special Forces camp. It was the first big helicopter air assault operation of the war. That was an NVA base camp area and supply

33

route on the Ho Chi Minh Trail. You can ask anyone; the Ia Drang was one of the bloodiest battles of the entire war. I flew in with 2nd Battalion of the 5th Cav to LZ Victor and LZ X-Ray where the big battles were. More and more American battalions were dropped in, and the number of NVA regiments attacking us kept increasing too. The second and third days, the fighting was so heavy that the Air Force made B-52 strikes on the area. That finally broke the NVA. But I still remember seeing arms and legs and dead NVA lying all over the place. That still stands out in my mind. I was mostly on the staff, not in a line company, but we had a company commander and a lot of other officers killed in that battle, and the radio operator was killed right in front of me. I went out on patrols like all the rest, and I still have a scar on my leg from a punji stake. That's a bamboo shaft that has been sharpened to a razor edge with various poisons on the tip, and dug into the tall grass along a trail for us to step on or fall on. I probably could've got a Purple Heart, but I just cleaned it up. I knew it wouldn't sit right with all those guys who had been there from the beginning, if some headquarters guy had come in and gotten one like that.

I spent most of my tour working with the ARVNs and the militias. As part of that, I did a lot of aerial reconnaissance in one of those old H-13 "bubble" helicopters. In fact, I had so much airtime I got an Air Medal. The one day that I'll never forget was when my driver, a Vietnamese Captain, and I were out in one of the villages meeting with some of the locals. Out of the corner of my eye I saw a bunch of men with AK-47s coming out of the woods toward us. We jumped in the Jeep and tore out of there, narrowly avoiding getting captured. I think of that all the time, of what would've happened if I hadn't seen them coming.

Being on the staff, I didn't have it nearly as bad as the guys out in the field. I lived in a tent with other officers. It had a dirt floor, I slept on a folding cot with a sleeping bag, and we actually had hot food in a mess hall. We got mortared from time to time, but it wasn't as rough as a lot of the places.

This was 1965-66. Everything was a lot different two years later or four years later. The 1st Cav had trained as a unit in the states and shipped over as a unit. We were professionals, from the top right down to the bottom, and that time on the boat really helped everyone to pull together. You knew everyone, and they knew you. Drugs and race issues and all didn't happen until a couple of years later. Personally, I never had a problem. When I was a First Lieutenant back at Fort Lewis, I had a Second Lieutenant under me with an attitude, but I told him that my blood was red just like his was and we were both there to do a job. That was the way it was in the 1st Cav. Out in the field, everyone had everyone else's back.

In August, 1966, my tour was over, and I rotated back to the States, where I was assigned to teach ROTC at Ohio State. While there, I picked up my master's in education and got part way through a PhD. I knew I was due to get orders for another tour to Vietnam, and I had reached a career turning point. I wanted to stay in, but both my mother and wife were against it. We had one child, and my wife said she wasn't going to get pregnant again if I was going back. I had been lucky once, but she didn't think I'd be lucky twice. My mother was even more adamant. She said she knew if I went, I wouldn't come back. My mother was never wrong about things like that,  so I got off active duty in 1968 and went into teaching in the Columbus Ohio Public Schools. I stayed in the Reserves, joined a Special Forces unit as an A Team Leader and then its Executive Officer, made thirty-five jumps, and eventually left the Reserves as a Major.

In Columbus, I served as an Assistant Principal at a high school, and then as Principal of Linmoor Middle School from 1972 until I retired in 1994. I took great pride in that, and turned down several promotions to the school district staff. Like many urban school systems, the Columbus public schools have a lot of problems, and I believe that middle school is the last opportunity you have to turn some of those kids around. That's why I stayed there.

When I retired from the schools we moved to North Carolina. I'm 77 now, but in 2000, when I turned 60, I began to experience a series of Agent Orange-related illnesses that are all too common with many vets. I developed heart problems and had triple-by-pass surgery, which was diagnosed as Agent Orange-related; and in 2001, I went through treatment for prostate cancer, also Agent Orange-related.

AL SANCHEZ'S WAR

**U.S. Army, Spec 4, Personnel Specialist and
Headquarters Clerk, 11th Armored Cav Regiment,
the Black Horse, Xuan Loc, 1966–67**

I'm Puerto Rican-American, born and raised in the Bronx. I always loved numbers and wanted to attend one of the academic high schools in Manhattan, but my stepfather was "old school." He thought an honest day's work meant you got your hands dirty, so I enrolled in auto shop in Samuel Gompers High School nearby. After graduation, I worked in a cut-and-sew woman's sportswear factory. I was a jack-of-all-trades, batching pieces and distributing them to the sewers. I also fixed the machines, translated, and did anything else they needed, until I got my draft notice.

I was twenty years old in September, 1965, when I went in. They sent me to Fort Gordon, Georgia and trained me as a personnel specialist. A bunch of us came down on orders for the 11th Armored Cavalry Regiment, the "Black Horse," and we all thought, "Wow! We're not going to Vietnam after all, we're going to Germany!" which is where they were located. But no, they were coming back to Ft. Meade, Maryland, where they sent us, and then the whole Division was going over to Vietnam.

I was assigned to the regimental headquarters and worked for the Sergeant Major. I made a point of taking care of anything he wanted. He had a Mexican wife and thought I was Mexican too, but I didn't correct him. Then they flew us out to Oakland, where the whole Regiment went over in three troopships.

The troopship was bad. The ocean got rough and a lot of guys got sick below deck.

Three weeks later, on September 7, 1966, we landed and went up to Binh Hoa and Long Binh before we set up the regimental headquarters at Xuan Loc, twenty-two miles east of Saigon on Route 2. That was where I spent my whole tour. That next winter and spring, the Regiment was involved in four big "search and destroy" operations, as they called them, one after another—Cedar Falls in the Iron Triangle, Junction City, Manhattan, and Kitty Hawk. As the guys said, "We searched, and we got destroyed." A lot of them didn't come back.

I became the Regimental Personnel Clerk, and one of my jobs was to send out the Next-of-Kin Letters to families. They had to be typed on special paper and be perfect. No mistakes. No erasures. I was very careful and did them at night, when I wouldn't be disturbed. We also had to go through the lockers of the men who were killed and inventory their personal possessions. Two guys did that, to make sure nothing was sent home that might be embarrassing to the family, and we had to sign for everything. We probably had to do that two or three times a week, every week. It really got to me after a while, and left me with a lot of "survivor's remorse."

I lived in a four-man tent with a dirt floor, a cot, a metal locker, and mosquito netting my whole tour. Our tent was real close to the latrine, and one thing I'll never forget is the smell when they dragged those 55-gallon oil drums out from underneath every morning and burned them with diesel fuel. That smell's going to be in my nose forever.

After we'd been there a few months, we began hearing some strange noises at night. The Colonel finally sent some teams to look around. It turns out that the VC had been digging a tunnel for hundreds of feet under our perimeter wire and into our compound, and they were almost finished. Until then, we had been very casual about security. No one even carried a rifle inside the wire. They were all locked up, but not after that.

Once every week or so I took a truck down to Bien Hoa for supplies, and guys would give me lists of things they wanted. We were all set to go one day when one of the sergeants decided to go in my place. He outranked me, so I stayed back at base camp. Sure enough, on the way down, they got ambushed, the truck was hit by an RPG, and he lost both legs. That was the way it went over there. It was mostly all luck, good or bad.

When my tour was over in July, 1967, the Army tried to get me to re-up. They offered me another stripe, a $10,000 bonus, and a thirty-day leave, but I knew they'd send me right back to Vietnam, and I wasn't interested. When I processed out in Oakland, they gave me a first-class ticket home to New York. Like a lot of other guys, when I got to the airport in San Francisco I cashed it in, bought some civilian clothes to change into, and flew standby.

Back in New York, I got a job with Chemical Bank on Wall Street, in operations, preparing reports. I stayed with them and rose to Assistant Division Manager before I was cut loose in a big downsizing in 1995. I started helping a friend out in his deli, until a guy with a courier service came in and said he was looking for drivers. I ended up working for him in Staten Island for the next eighteen years until I finally retired. Now, I spend my time bowling, fishing, biking, and cooking for a private school that's associated with my church.

BOB PRZYBYLSKI'S WAR

US Army, 1st Lieutenant and Executive Officer,
Battery B, 1st Battalion, 7th Artillery,
1st Infantry Division, 1965–66

I grew up in a small town in central Wisconsin called Thorp, which had all of 1200 people. It was dairy country. After high school, I went to the University of Wisconsin in Madison. Two of my brothers and my uncle had served in the Army, so service to country, commitment, and joining ROTC seemed natural to me. Back then, particularly in the Midwest, people used that term, "service." They said they were entering "the service," not "the military." It's a little thing, but it meant something. And the times were different. This was well before the Cuban missile crisis, and nobody had even heard of Vietnam.

In 1963, I graduated with a degree in biology, was a Distinguished Military Graduate, and offered a Regular Army commission. I was assigned to Air Defense Artillery and trained in missiles, not to shoot cannon. I was sent to Fort Lawton, Washington, to the Missile Master Center, where we controlled seven batteries of Nike Hercules missiles that ringed Seattle. After all, this was the height of the Cold War. Army anti-aircraft missile batteries ringed most major US cities, waiting to shoot down Russian bombers as they came over the North Pole to bomb us. That was the big threat back then.

In September, 1965, when my two years in Seattle ended, I got orders to Vietnam, to be an advisor with MAC-V, the Military Assistance Command-Vietnam, which meant working with the South Vietnamese Army. I was a First Lieutenant and a missileman, trained to read sophisticated CRT radar displays and deal with electronics, missile fuel, and radar. I knew nothing about Vietnam and didn't speak a word of their language; so, I was sent to the "Snake Eater Course," which was a seven-week immersion into conversational Vietnamese, the country, and its culture. That's when LBJ announced we weren't sending anymore "advisors" to Vietnam. He was sending in ground troops. Too bad they didn't have an "immersion course" in field artillery. Instead of becoming an advisor to a Vietnamese unit, I became the Executive Officer of Battery B, 1st Battalion of the 7th Artillery in the 1st Infantry Division, which had just arrived in country and hadn't even finished digging its first foxholes.

In the rest of the Army, an Executive Officer handles paperwork and administrative duties. In the field artillery, the XO and lead NCO are responsible for "laying" the guns and for all fire missions. We had six 105 mm howitzers and around 200 men. Firing a 105 creates a lot of noise, smoke, and dust, and quickly makes you a target for enemy mortars and snipers. That was why we moved almost every day, relocating from one firebase or small clearing to another, to support the infantry as they moved around. We also supported ARVN units, truck convoys, and anything else in our area, which was mostly the III Corps, north and west of Saigon all the way west to Laos. It was September, 1965, and this was already a hot area.

Each time we moved, it would be a map and compass exercise. We would carefully "lay" the first gun, our most accurate tube, test fire a round at a known target, and then adjust the rest of the tubes for maximum accuracy, so we'd know we put each round exactly where it was supposed to go. The Fire Direction Center NCO and myself had to sign off on each fire mission, so if there was ever a "friendly fire" accident, the Army knew who to look for. In a little over six months, our battery of six guns fired 40,000 rounds, so accuracy was an important and time-consuming responsibility. I take pride in knowing we saved a lot of American lives with those artillery rounds.

We spent most of our time moving from one small firebase to another, almost every day, either by truck or helicopter. Breaking down the camp, sling-loading a Huey or a Chinook, moving everything, and setting up at a new place was hot, dusty work. After a while, we would be moving in and out of the same small firebases, usually on hilltops, and got to know the country well. A couple of times, we loaded up and flew back around to the same location, just to throw off the VC.

When my Vietnam tour was over, I was sent back to Fort Polk, Louisiana, and promoted to Captain. Polk was a big training area for troops going to Vietnam. I held many jobs there, including Company Commander and Supply Officer for a battalion of three companies. Like all the other jobs they had previously sent me to, I knew nothing about supply, but that didn't matter. You study, ask questions, learn the job, and do your best. As everyone who was ever assigned to Fort Polk will agree, Leesburg, Louisiana, wasn't fun.

After a couple of years there, married, with two children, I was due to be sent back for a second tour; so, I decided it was time to "get on with the rest of my life." I filed my papers to resign my commission, but the Army said, "Oh, not so fast." I was required to serve another eighteen months at Fort Polk, until I was finally discharged in January 1968, after five and one-half years of service.

Having been raised on a dairy farm, I knew quite a bit about that business and went to work for Carnation and then for a series of dairy co-ops, mostly running milk processing plants in New York and other states, finishing my career in Florida. I'm now 76 and I still get nightmares from my experiences in Vietnam. Twice, I've broken toes rolling out of bed and falling on the floor, thinking I was taking cover from mortar rounds that landed fifty years ago. Like many vets, I never talked to anyone about the war or my experiences until the past few years, when I began attending VVA meetings and talking to other vets.

BOBBY WALLACE'S WAR

**US Marine Corps Gunnery Sergeant, Crew Chief,
Door Gunner, Maintenance Section Chief,
and just about everything else with
VMO2 and VMO6, Danang and Dong Ha,
1965–66 and 1968**

My specialty was aircraft maintenance. I spent twenty-one years in Marine Corps aviation units in Opa-laka, Florida, Puerto Rico, Cuba, El Toro, Okinawa, and Japan. Most of that was working on fixed wing aircraft, such as the F3D, the R4Q "flying Box Car," which was a twin boom-tailed aircraft, the SNB, and the OV-10. From 1960 to 1964, I was assigned to a squadron in Japan that flew the R4D, a two-engine cargo plane that could carry men, equipment, and about anything else, drop parachutists, and land on very short airstrips. In the early years of the war, it was the perfect choice to resupply remote, top-secret units operating in Cambodia or Laos, which, of course, we never did... because they were never there... were they? The VC had no anti-aircraft guns at that time, and no one was shooting at us; but when they issued us rifles and bullets, we knew we were into something.

In 1965, I was sent to Advanced Aircraft Maintenance School, and was supposed to go to Japan again, when the big Vietnam buildup began, and I was sent to Danang in October to an Aerial Photo Recon Squadron. I was a Sergeant E-5 and we flew the Douglas F3D "Willy the Whale" and the F8U crusader. The F3D was originally designed as a carrier-based night fighter, but was now relegated to photo recon work. When the South Viet-namese Army was fighting among themselves over rival

leaders, they were located across the airfield from us. Several times a night, stray bullets came our way.

After a couple of months at Danang, they needed two guys to go down to Marble Mountain to be Aircraft Line Chiefs for the Marine helicopter unit down there. Half of the unit was based at Marble Mountain, where I spent five months, and the other half was up at Dong Ha in northern I Corps near the DMZ, where you could look into North Vietnam. Both sections flew the UH-1E, the Marine Corps version of the Huey, which had an M-60 machine gun in each door, and a pod of 2.75" rockets underneath. As Crew Chief, I was responsible for maintaining the aircraft and flying as the second door gunner.

After all these years, you remember bits and pieces, but not everything. I remember the monsoon. It rained so hard you couldn't see ten feet. When you're in the jungle, that's scary. I remember one of the pilots I flew with. He'd been an A-4 Skyhawk jet pilot and was doing a turn in helicopters. When he got excited, sometimes he forgot which he was flying, and he'd try maneuvers you don't do with a Huey without putting us into a blade stall. When you were coming in on a gun run, that could crash the helicopter right into the target. I sat behind him in the left door, and would shout into the helmet Mike, "Don't get us into a blade stall!" when he started doing it again, I'd say it again. That was worse than getting shot at.

At both bases, we lived in ten-man tents with wooden floors and slept on cots. One of our guys was an expert at scavenging and trading. He got us some lumber and we built bunk beds, which gave us a lot more room inside. We drew cards to determine who got the upper bunk and who got the lower one.

One day, one of the F3Ds had been shot up and couldn't get half of its landing gear down. It came in and tried to land on one wheel, but ended up flipping and losing part of the wing. We got the crew out, but the airplane was blocking the runway. We took a Huey and got a cable on it, lifted it up with an aircraft jack, got a wheeled vehicle under one wing, and slowly pulled it along the runway to the taxiway.

As far as our own Hueys went, we crashed a lot of times on lift-off. Most were not catastrophic, simply the result of overloading, usually on an extraction when we were pulling guys out. When they were under fire, it was hard to tell a Vietnamese to get off and that we'd come back for them later, or they could wait for "the next bus," but that was what we had to do. Another time, we had to move an entire ARVN unit. As we learned, that meant their families, all their possessions, and their livestock, including chickens and pigs, but it was hard to guess what all that stuff weighed.

One day I'll never forget was when an F3D came in to land and got too close to our four-hole latrine. When the jet blast hit it, it began to wobble. No one remembers the F3D, but everyone remembers Lopez running out the front door of the latrine with his pants around his ankles as the latrine tipped over backward behind him.

At the end of my twelve months, in October, 1966, I rotated back to El Toro, but I knew they'd be sending me back. Sure enough, nineteen months later, in May 1968 I reported in at Marble Mountain again. I was with a different squadron this time, but I did the same job in the same place. I was now an E-7 Gunnery Sergeant. I flew, and I was also the NCOIC responsible for aircraft support and maintenance in our section.

That tour lasted seven months, after which I went to a KC-130 squadron in Okinawa, then back to El Toro, and on to other assignments, including the Admiral's staff in Atsugi, Japan, conducting Air Wing inspections. I retired in 1977 after twenty-one years' active service, and fully retired after thirty years, in 1986. I received three Air Medals, a Meritorious Mast, and other awards, but no wounds.

Since I retired, I've been diagnosed with PTSD, Agent Orange-related diabetes and neuropathy, and I have a 90% disability. Agent Orange was all over the areas where I operated. None of us realized it at the time, but it was in the dust in the prop wash, in our tents and beds, all over the helicopters, and on our other equipment, even on the clothes of the guys we picked up on medevac flights. There was no avoiding it.

The Marine Corps is a small organization. If you stay in for a while, one way or the other you get to meet most of the guys in your specialty. In 2002, six of us formed the "Black Marine Heritage" group. We've now had our seventh reunion, in San Diego, and there were one hundred and twenty-five of us attending. I'm very proud of that.

WAYNE PAUL LOTSBERG'S WAR

**US Navy Lieutenant and Carrier Pilot with
374 Combat Missions on Four Cruises
Aboard the *USS Ranger, Constellation*, and *Midway*,
Earning Three Distinguished Flying Crosses
Flying A4's, A-7s, and F4's from 1965–73**

I grew up as a welfare kid in a tiny town in Minnesota. My father had polio and spent two years in an iron lung. When I graduated from high school in 1962, while in boot camp, I applied to the Navy NAVCAD pilot training program. It was a long selection process and I was competing against college graduates every step of the way. I had great eyes and pretty good flying skills. I not only passed the course, I was selected for jets. I was flying at nineteen, and a commissioned officer and naval aviator at twenty-one.

I'll never forget my first carrier landing. They had us fly in a big circle high above the ship waiting our turn.

You could look out the canopy and see that tiny flight deck sitting down there and think, "Oh, s**t! I'm supposed to land this thing on THAT?" But I did, and at the end, I was given a choice between the A-4 Skyhawk and the F-4 Phantom. I took the A-4, because I loved that little single-seater and didn't want to be responsible for anyone else. It was designed as a "pocket bomber" for low-level, under-the-radar, nuclear attacks against Russia and China. The F-4 flew higher and faster but it wasn't as nimble. To me, it was like driving a bus.

I remember the first time I flew supersonic in a jet. I was really keyed up, thinking it would be a big deal. I kept watching the airspeed gauge as it went from Mach .8 to .9, 1.0, 1.1, and 1.2, until I realized that nothing had happened. Nothing! No feeling, no boom, no nothing! It was just a gauge reading.

I went on four cruises to Vietnam. Each time, we went from a West Coast port to Hawaii, on to Subic Bay in the Philippines, and then over to Yankee Station in the Gulf of Tonkin. The first cruise was early in the war in the *USS Ranger* beginning in December, 1965. My squadron lost five of the twenty-two pilots we started with; but we learned from our mistakes, developed new tactics, and our loss rates went down. We only lost two or three pilots on the next three cruises.

On that first cruise, I was a Lieutenant JG in Attack Squadron 55, flying an A-4E. Even then, North Vietnam was "the most heavily defended real estate in the world." The AAA (Anti-Aircraft Artillery) was so thick you'd get bounced around by the percussion of the exploding AAA shells, even if they didn't hit you. That was when I got my first Distinguished Flying Cross, for bombing the Tho Trang railroad marshaling yards and hitting an important and heavily-defended railroad bridge, putting my six 500-pound bombs on it.

When we began a deployment, we'd "warm up" by doing close air support for the ground troops in South Vietnam for a week or two with bombs and rockets. For that type of work, we would usually carry bombs or six pods with nineteen rockets each. You could fire those individually or as a salvo, depending on the target. One day, a piece of one of the rockets I had fired came back into my air intake and damaged the engine, forcing me to divert to Danang for repairs. I stayed there for three days. To beat the boredom, I went up with one of the Forward Air Controllers, flying in the backseat of a Cessna Bird Dog. We flew down one of the valleys and came under some serious ground fire, at which point I asked myself, "What are you doing up here?" When I got back to Danang, I stayed there.

The next day, I saw a black F-4 come in and land. The pilot was wearing blue jeans and cowboy boots and acted like he owned the place. Somebody told me he was one of the Air America pilots working for the CIA. They were offering $50,000 per year plus $50,000 more in the bank for pilots who wanted to go work for them. In the mid-1960s, that was a lot of money, but it wasn't for me. After my airplane was repaired, I rejoined my squadron as the aircraft carrier steamed north and began attacks on North Vietnam.

My second DFC came during my second cruise. I was also part of Attack Squadron

55, but we were aboard the *USS Constellation* this time. I was the section leader in a division of A-4Cs bombing the important Loc Binh highway bridge. I placed all my bombs on target, destroying one span of the bridge. As we headed home, I heard a distress call and went to assist in the rescue of a pilot who had been shot down north of Haiphong. After an in-flight refueling I went to look for him, making low passes to draw fire and suppress the persistent ground fire until I found him, and the rescue choppers could pick him up.

Wayne Lotsberg in in primary flight training with the Navy at Saufley Field, Pensacola, Florida. He has all ready soloed up in the T-34 training plane. Seaman Wayne is the son of Mrs. Edmore Lotsberg of 133 Northeast 3rd St., Buffalo. —Navy Photo

On my third and fourth cruises in 1971, I flew the newer A7 Corsair II on 134 more missions, and was often designated to lead SAM suppression flights, which I got pretty good at. Two of us would fly ahead of the formation, armed with Shrike anti-radar missiles, baiting the enemy to fire their SAMs at us so we could lock on and take out their battery. The problem, of course, is that a SAM comes up at over 3000 feet per second, which is about three times the speed of a 30-30 bullet.

One thing we learned about the SAMs was that they could not correct down. So, the trick was to dive right at it as it came up, begin to climb, and when it did the same thing, to go nose down. If you waited and didn't break too soon, you could get them to miss. It was like playing chicken with an exploding telephone pole. To keep doing that, you needed what someone called an, "adrenaline sense of humor."

On 17 May, 1972, we were diverted to help rescue another downed pilot. Despite intense anti-aircraft fire, I rolled in and dropped my bombs on an active shore battery that was targeting the other planes. That was when we came under fire from a SAM missile battery. They fired five of them at us, but I got off one of my Shrikes and took the site out. With the anti-aircraft guns and missile sites eliminated, the helicopters rescued the pilot.

That November, I was shot down during a night recon mission over North Vietnam. It was about 1:00 a.m. on the 11th, foggy, with low visibility. My wingman and I were making a bombing run on a truck convoy when I was hit, probably from small arms fire. I tried to turn east toward the bay, but my controls froze. Normally when you lose hydraulics in an A-7, the nose pitches down, and you quickly lose altitude. That's not good; but next to flying it into the ground, what I didn't want was to bail out and end up a POW.

I was able to get the nose up a bit, enough for me to keep it in the air and pointed toward the coast. Over the radio, I heard that our people had a fix on my position, but I sure didn't. I had nursed it all the way up to 15,000 feet before I finally had to eject. When you're under stress like that, the brain seems to kick into "hyper drive" and everything slows down. What probably took about a second I perceived as taking about ten seconds, like watching a movie frame by frame. I saw the canopy release, the ejection seat fire and ride up the rails out of the airplane, and then began my descent in really, really slow motion.

I was about five miles inland; but I was high enough and there was enough wind from the right direction that I managed to make it all the way to the water. When I splashed down, the waves were running two to three feet. I turned on my beacon, got my raft inflated, and finally managed to get in. After several tries, the rescue helicopter picked me up in a "horse collar" harness, reeled me in, and flew me back to its ship, the USS *Truxton*. I was checked out by their doctor and flown back to the *Midway* the next morning. As it turned out, I was only four miles offshore when I came down. If it had been during the day, I'd have been picked up by a North Vietnamese fishing boat for sure.

Three days later, I was back in the cockpit. I ended up with 374 combat missions, 680 carrier landings, one "water landing," three DFCs, thirty-six Air Medals, and many other awards. I stayed in the Navy for a total of eleven years, and then got out. I had been recognized as the youngest, most highly decorated Lieutenant in the Navy in 1968. Over the next thirty years, I worked for a series of high-tech telecommunications firms such as ROLM Communications, Wang Labs, and Cisco Systems, eventually retiring and living the good life on a boat in South Florida. I am now 73 years old and am fortunate to have no service-related disabilities. I was always a fair athlete and play a vigorous game of golf and softball, trying to ignore my bad knees.

CONRAD FISCHER'S WAR

US Air Force E-4 Electronic Radar Jamming Equipment
Maintenance Technician on the F4 Fighter Jets,
Danang, 1967–68

I'm from Brooklyn. I enlisted in the Air Force right out of high school in January, 1966. They sent me to Lackland for basic and down to Keesler Air Force Base in Mississippi for electronic equipment maintenance tech school. That was a long, hard course that took almost a year, after which they sent me to the SAC base in Oklahoma, where I worked on B-52s.

After a year and a half, in July, 1967, they sent me to Danang to work on F-4 Phantoms. There were a lot of them based there. I worked on the flight line and repaired their electronic gear, mostly at night when they weren't flying, seven days a week. We got hit with 122 mm rocket attacks quite often, usually around 11 p.m. The Air Force decided to tear all the bunkers out around the base before I got there. I heard that was someone's idea of how to "beautify" it. I don't know where they thought we were. Omaha? As soon as we started taking more rockets, they quickly built them all back. We didn't have any rifles either. If they expected us to be attacked, what were we supposed to use to defend ourselves? We had M-16s and M-60s, but they were locked up in the arms room in their original crates, still packed in plastic with that thick cosmoline grease all over them. I asked whether it might be a good idea to get them out and clean them up, but nobody wanted to hear about that. I guess they figured we were Air Force, and we had all those Army and Marine Corps guys to protect us.

The VC and NVA knew exactly where everything was at Danang. A new mess hall was being built near our barracks. Every time they announced the work was finished and they were going to open it, it would be hit by mortar fire. Finally, they just passed the word around that it was open, with no announcements, and it didn't get hit anymore.

Somebody figured out that we were going to get attacked on the 4th of July, so the

49

Air Force set off a bunch of phony explosions the night before, on the 3rd, hoping to sucker them into thinking they had screwed up, were a day late, and should attack us right away. We had the C-47 "Spooky" gunships and the Cobras ready to pounce, but no attack ever came. The VC probably knew it was a fake.

In one of the rocket attacks, I went running out of my barracks, raced down the stairs, and had to dive on the ground when a rocket hit nearby. That was when I learned not to live on the second floor. It took too long to get out. Anyway, I got a lot of glass and shrapnel in my hand and foot, so they sent me over to the hospital. When I got inside, I saw there were a lot of seriously wounded guys in there, so I told them to just sit me in a chair and clean me up. When they were done, one of the nurses handed me a form for a Purple Heart. I wouldn't take it, not after I saw all those other guys. My father would have killed me. On the way back to the unit, I saw some Vietnamese laborers cleaning things up. They were dressed in black pajamas just like the VC. I started to go after them, but one of the guys grabbed my shirt and stopped me.

On January 30, 1968, my twenty-first birthday, a couple of the guys and I decided to go to the NCO Club for a few drinks of real booze. It was on the other side of the base, and there were three ways to get there. We could take a bus, walk the long way around the road, or take a shortcut along the fence, which is what we did. It was up against the Vietnamese compound, and we got almost there, when a couple of bullets hit the dirt right in front of me. Out beyond the fence, it was all dark, but I figured whoever shot at us couldn't be far away. Up ahead was one of those fortified foxholes with Vietnamese MPs. We had no guns or anything with us, so we lay in the dirt, figuring that when we saw the bus coming on the main road we'd make a run for it. The buses had rear opening and a wooden staircase hanging off the back. We finally saw the bus coming around the turn, yelled to the Vietnamese MPs to give us some covering fire, and started running for it. Three of us jumped on board, but the fourth guy was having a tough time catching up. I grabbed him and pulled him aboard, but the damned Vietnamese MPs never fired a shot. They just hunkered down and hid behind their sandbags.

When we got back to our hooch, I went to the refrigerator to get us some beers, but somebody had drunk them all. I slammed the refrigerator door shut just as a rocket came in and exploded not too far away. We looked outside and saw that it had destroyed the bus we came in on. Fortunately, it was empty by then, but that was only the first of a lot of rockets to hit the base that night. January 30, 1968, my twenty-first birthday, was the first day of the Tet Offensive, and the biggest battle of the war had begun. The rocketing and attacks continued for well over a week, and the other guys told me not to invite them to any of my birthday parties, ever.

My tour was over in July of that year and I rotated back to the States. What do you think the Air Force would do with a nice New York boy like me? First, they sent me to Oklahoma, then they sent me to Vietnam, and when I came home, they sent me to Columbus, Mississippi.

After I was discharged from the Air Force, I got into the electronics business doing parts distribution, and became a branch manager of the company. I'm completely retired now, but I stay active in vet groups, like the VVA.

JAN HORAK'S WAR

US Marine Corps Captain and Pilot,
the A-4 Skyhawk, the O-1C Birddog, and the F-4C Phantom,
Chu Lai, 1966–67 and 1969–70

During my two Vietnam tours as a Marine Corps pilot, I had the opportunity to fly three different aircraft: the A-4 Skyhawk, a small single-seat attack bomber, the even smaller O-1C "Bird dog" two-seat observation plane, and the heavyweight two-seat F-4 Phantom fighter bomber. Each had its uses.

I had been a very poor college student, but my best day on campus was when I ran into a Navy recruiter in the library who asked me if I'd like to fly jets. This was in 1958, and you could get into the Naval Aviation Cadet program with only a two-year Associate degree, so I applied. I started flight training at age 18 in the T-34 and in 1960 received my Navy wings and commission as a Second Lieutenant in the Marine Corps

When I arrived at Chu Lai in April, 1966, I was an experienced A-4 Skyhawk pilot. The base was still new and very primitive, with a short runway made of experimental AM-2 aluminum planking, the successor to the old WW II PSP. The metal planks might have been okay, but the base under them wasn't. When we landed, they had to use a wire to catch the tail hook to get the jet to stop, and the runway surface shifted a quarter inch each time a jet landed. Every few days, they would have us land in the other direction to move the runway back into place. And there was no taxiway, so an airplane had to get clear before the next one could land. Our accommodations weren't much better. We lived in tents stretched over 2 x 4 frames. During the monsoon, my tent leaked so bad that I had to curl up on my cot under an umbrella.

I loved the A-4, though. It was quick, maneuverable, and great for ground support. It could carry 250-lb bombs, 500-lb bombs, napalm, or rockets. Most of the bombs were "snake eyes," which had rear fins, and very accurate. That was critical for close air support. One night, several of us went up with an FAC, an Air Force Forward Air Controller, who was looking for an NVA truck convoy rumored to be near the Laotian border. It was a nasty night, with dense fog. The FAC marked where he thought it was with flares. We rolled in and hit the target, but saw no secondary explosions and assumed there was nothing there. I had several bombs left, so I swung back around, and decided to drop them long, beyond the mark. When I did, a huge fireball lit up the jungle. Both my wingman and the FAC assumed that was me, that I had flown into the ground, and blown up. They started screaming at each other and it took a few moments for me to be able to break in and tell them I was still alive. But if the explosion wasn't me, I must have hit a gasoline tanker, and that told us where the convoy was. We called in more support and pounded it.

By November, my squadron was due to rotate back to Japan, but I didn't want to go. I heard they needed O-1C "Bird Dog" pilots at Dong Ha, the northern-most airfield up on the DMZ, so I volunteered. The O-1C is a small, single-engine prop plane with a pilot in front and a rear seat for a FAC or passenger. It had a pod under each wing with three rockets in each. They could be smoke to mark targets, or high explosive. We usually flew low looking for bad guys, and my airplane got shot-up twenty-two times on various missions. Luckily, the North Vietnamese didn't know how to lead a target. Most of the hits were in the tail.

We worked all over I Corps, even at Khe Sanh, which at that time was a minor base with maybe 10-15 Marines. We would bring them their mail, and things like that. Another of our main jobs was to check on Marine Recon Teams that were operating in the jungle. We made radio contact with them several times a day, and always got one of two greetings. Usually, they were very quiet, whispering, and brief. Occasionally, we'd get a "Where the hell have you guys been? We're under fire and…" That meant we had to get them a quick pick-up.

Another time, we went to help a company of ARVN Rangers and their US advisors who had been hit hard and were being overrun by NVA. Unfortunately, the ARVN Douglas AD Skyraider planes that were providing their air cover had a different radio system than ours, and I couldn't communicate with them. I saw some NVA reinforcements headed for our guys and decided to mark their location with a smoke rocket anyway. That worked. The ARVN pilots figured out what I was doing, rolled in, and hit them with guns and rockets. Eventually, the NVA were beaten back. A week later, the American advisor looked me up and told me, "Thanks, man, I wouldn't be going home today if you hadn't shown up." That felt good.

One thing I realized flying the Bird Dog and getting "up close and personal" with the war was that the real heroes in Vietnam were the riflemen and the helicopter pilots. They bore the brunt of the fighting.

I left Vietnam in May, 1967, after thirteen months, completing 159 combat missions in the A-4 and another 155 in the O-1C. After a stateside assignment at Cherry Point, I returned to Chu Lai two years later as a Major, flying an F-4B Phantom and serving as the Squadron Aircraft Maintenance Officer. Chu Lai was completely different than it had been in my first tour. A full-length, concrete runway had replaced the metal strips, and solid, wooden hooches had replaced the leaky tents. We had two-man rooms, hot showers, and flush toilets. It made me think I was back home, or maybe in the Air Force.

The Phantom was a big beast, a two-seater, front and back, with two engines. It could carry a large load of bombs, making it perfect for our ground support missions. We also had the task of providing an Air Cap at night over any Navy ships operating off North Vietnam, in the unlikely event that the North Vietnamese decided to send aircraft out to attack our fleet.

One night, we had intelligence on an NVA position and made a run with cluster bombs. We hit them, and got lit up by a barrage of ground fire. Fortunately, neither I nor my co-pilot had been hit. However, since we had only dropped half our bomb load on that first run, I decided to go around again. This time, there was no ground fire at all. Either the CBUs I dropped had taken all their guns out, or we had sent them scampering into their tunnels.

I completed that second tour with 102 combat missions in the F-4B, plus twenty-four night missions in a C-117-D, bringing the two-tour total to 458. For my service, I had received a Silver Star, a Bronze Star with V, and a Navy Unit Commendation Medal with a V.

I remained in the Marine Corps for twenty-four years until I retired with the rank of Colonel. I could have stayed in, but elected to start a second career with Motorola. I stayed with that amazing corporation, in the Government Electronics Division in Scottsdale, for another twenty-four years, retiring at the age of 67 and now living the good life in Phoenix.

JAN SCHMEICHEL'S WAR

**US Army Sergeant and Infantryman,
1st Battalion, 26th Infantry, 1st Infantry Division,
Attached to the 5th Special Forces Group,
Phouc Vinh, 1966–67**

I'm from Tonawanda in upper New York, halfway between Buffalo and Niagara. After high school, I tried college part time, until the draft board came after me and I ended up enlisting. In October, 1965, I started Basic in Fort Dix, which wasn't too bad, so they sent me to Fort Polk, Louisiana, for AIT, Advanced Infantry Training, and Jungle School. I think we did our Final Exam in the Okefenokee Swamp with hills, rocks, pine trees, swamp, and snakes. I came out an 11-Bravo, Infantryman, qualified in light weapons, demolition, and as a medic.

In April, 1966, I landed in Vietnam as a replacement and was sent to the 1st Infantry Division in Phouc Vinh, forty-five miles northeast of Saigon. Years later, I found out that province was sprayed with more Agent Orange than anywhere else in Vietnam. Nice to know. We spent most of our time in the bush in the highlands and were in and out of Cambodia all the time. That was the worst-kept secret in the Army. Fortunately, my platoon had a great lieutenant. He had been enlisted and went to OCS. He told us if he didn't do something, then we didn't have to do it. He took his turn at guard duty, searching tunnels, and night ambushes, and he even carried the radio.

The area we worked was hilly and dense jungle. We would get dropped into an LZ by helicopters and then either sweep an area or be the blocking force. We did that over and over again. Our Base Camp was pretty much like everyone else's, with tents to start, and then make-shift wooden hooches with tin roofs and sandbagged walls. We had showers, a mess hall, and even a barber, when we stopped by once a month or so.

I lost a lot of weight over there. I was 170 when I arrived, and by mid-tour you could see my ribs. I ate a lot, but there was no helping it. You'd need to take in a million calories to compensate for humping up and down those hills in that heat. Still, it was a

beautiful country, if there wasn't a war going on and we weren't blowing it all to hell.

One night in base camp—we were in an eight-man tent at the time—we woke up to an incredible stench. We looked up and saw one of our guys standing naked, covered with... who knows what all over him. Turns out he was in the village visiting one of "the girls" when the MPs showed up. He jumped out the window and landed in a pig sty. She threw his clothes out and he ran back to the compound. We made him sleep outside, and he spent the next three days volunteering to wash trucks to try to get the smell off.

The Army was sending the 4th Infantry Division over, so they sent an advance team to work with us for a couple of weeks and see what Vietnam was like. We explained to them that when we swept a village and found any spider holes under the straw huts, you yell a couple of times in Vietnamese for whoever was in there to come out, and then drop in a grenade. We swept this one village, or "Vil" as we called it, and there were the normal grenade explosions every now and then, but when we went to leave, we couldn't find this one 4th ID guy. We went back through, heard some moans and groans under a collapsed hut, and found him lying under a heavy wooden door. Turned out what he thought was a hole was more like a shallow fire pit. He threw a grenade in, realized he'd screwed up, and leaned against the other side of the wooden door for protection as the grenade went off. He got peppered in his back with splinters, the door fell on top of him, and the hut came crashing down. "It worked in the movies," he kept mumbling.

From time to time, we would provide road security and set up observation posts and ambushes where someone thought the enemy might come from. The standard response was to send in a platoon, if you thought you were up against a VC platoon, send a company if you thought it was a company, and so on. Well, it turned out our OP had set up between two VC base camps. As our guys began to leave the next day, they noticed the VC, the VC noticed them, and we ended up in a battalion-sized fight that lasted for three days.

I was wounded in the leg by a sniper who couldn't shoot very well, and medevaced out to the 93rd Evac Hospital near Saigon. The damage wasn't all that bad, but I had a cast on my leg for a week and had to have the knee drained every couple of days. The hospital was great. I learned that rubbing coconut oil on a wound helps make the scar go away. One day we had a visit by two Generals, one US and one South Vietnamese, who went through the wards giving out medals. I got my second Purple Heart, a Bronze Star,

Air Medal, and South Vietnamese Cross of Gallantry along with a bunch of others. After the Generals left, the guys at the other end of the ward were laughing. Turns out the General gave a Purple Heart to a guy who was in there for a bad case of the clap. The next day they figured it out and took his medal away.

I was in the hospital for twenty-eight days. When I was finally cleared, I went back and finished my tour. I ended up staying in Vietnam twelve months, three days, and seventeen hours, but who was counting? I had made E-5 by then, but I still had six months left. So, where would the Army send me as a reward for a year in Vietnam? To Fort Ord, California to play war games, of course.

When I was finally discharged, I went back to work at a local natural gas company in upper New York State for nine years, but I began to have people problems. I didn't realize it at the time, but that was PTSD, which only got worse. I went on to work at a plastics plant, for DuPont, and finally Home Depot. When I was finally diagnosed properly and put on the right meds, part of our therapy from the VA was to visit the local schools and talk to them about Vietnam, its history, and the war. In the early years, we would almost always get the same five questions: What did you do? Was it as bad as they say? Were you in combat? Did you kill anyone? And what did that feel like? As the years passed, however, the last two questions changed. Instead of asking if I killed anyone, they'd ask what the country was like and what the people were like.

The thing about Agent Orange is you can run, but you can't hide. I had a quadruple bypass in 2010 due to Systemic Heart Disease, have been diagnosed with Type 2 Diabetes, and Prostate cancer in 2012, all from Agent Orange. From 1997 to 2009, I used to regularly compete in arm-wrestling contests to stay active, but I've cut back on all that. Now, I participate in Veterans organizations.

DEREK SMITH'S WAR

Australian Army, Sapper or Corporal,
and then Sergeant, 32nd Small Ship Squadron,
Vung Tao, Nui Dat, and Saigon, 1966, 1969, 1971

Australia began sending troops into Vietnam the same time you Americans did, in 1964. At its peak, we had almost 7,700 men there. By the time we pulled out in 1972, over 60,000 had served, 521 men had been killed, and over 3,000 had been wounded. For a country with a population of only 11 million, compared to your almost 200 million, that was a substantial commitment. Then again, Vietnam was in our "backyard." We had fought communist guerrillas in Malaya, and to us, the "domino theory" was all too real.

Our Army's structured a little different than yours. I grew up on the East Coast in Redcliffe, north of Brisbane in Queensland. In 1963, I enlisted at 16 in the Apprentice Program, which is how we train blokes, and came out as an administrative clerk and Corporal eighteen months later. I was assigned to an Army LSM, a Landing Ship Medium, and arrived in Vietnam in April 1966. The ship was about

200 feet long and had a crew of 50, and we lived on board. We were based in Vung Tau, a port southeast of Saigon, and our job was to supply material and equipment to our troops along the coast and up the rivers.

I was young, and it was my first time in a combat zone, much less out of Australia. The Captain of our ship was from the Merchant Marine and he wasn't one to share information; so rumors flew all over the place as to what was going on. We heard that the North Vietnamese Air Force had strafed Vung Tau and all sorts of

58

crazy things like that, which made things a whole lot worse; but after five months I rotated back home to Australia.

When I went back for my second tour in April 1969 it was for twelve months, I was a Sergeant E-5 and a lot older and wiser… or at least older. I was still a clerk, but had been transferred to the Combat Engineers at Nui Dat southeast of Saigon, inland from Vung Tau on Route 2, the road to Bien Hoa. The Australians were given Phuoc Tuy as our area of operations. I spent ten months there as the Orderly Room Sergeant and Troop Sergeant for the Engineers.

We would get rocketed and mortared, and we did a lot of patrolling at night. One of our big problems was land mines. Our own Army had laid a large "barrier" minefield to block the approaches to our positions. There were 20,000 mines out there and the regional militias were supposed to be watching them, but they didn't. The VC would come in at night, dig them up, and position them in the roads and paths to catch us.

That August, when I was on patrol I had my first contact and had to call in artillery for the first time. While I was reasonably confident I knew what I was doing, I was very concerned that I would get something wrong and have the artillery hit our own people.

During that tour, I spent a month in the hospital with what turned out to be an allergic reaction to the anti-malaria tablets they made us take. After ten months, I became a clerk at the Headquarters of Australian Forces in Saigon. I lived in an air-conditioned room in the Savoy Hotel and was glad to be out of the bush. Saigon was very different from Nui Dat, and the people were a lot friendlier.

When I rotated back to Australia, my service was over, and I left the Army. However, I had trouble getting a job and my romance broke up; so, I called up my old Sergeant Major and asked if I could get my job and rank back. He said sure, so I signed up again. When I said, "my job," I meant the one at our base in Sydney. He meant the one at Nui Dat, so in 1971 I found myself on my third tour, headed back to the same base doing the same thing as I had done two years earlier.

Again, we did a lot of patrolling. One night I took out a patrol of five guys. We had a PRC-25 backpack radio, like all the Americans carried. The area around the base was mostly rubber plantation—trees, brush, and scrub. We got out a "klick" or so, when the radio went dead. The backup battery wouldn't work either, so standard procedure was to stay where we were and send two guys back with the radio to get a replacement. We waited and waited, but they never came back. Again, standard procedure: we popped a flare to see if we could see anything. Nothing. Not even any reaction from the base. I pop a second flare. Still no reaction after which I really became "windy," and all three of us "stood to." We didn't know if there was an attack going on around us, if the VC had slit their throats, or what.

Sergeant Derek Smith and friend, South Vietnam 1969

We had "Rules of Procedure," which meant we had to challenge people before we could shoot them. So, there we were, all locked and loaded, and we heard some sounds. I yell, "Halt! Hands up! Who goes there?" A voice came from somewhere out of the bushes, "T... t... t... two f*****g soldiers! We're lost, and we don't know where the hell we are!" Our two blokes had gotten completely disoriented and had been wandering around in the jungle for an hour. We laughed about it, but it could've been real serious if someone had opened fire. By that time, the Australian forces were already in a drawdown, and the knowledge that we were leaving caused other problems. No one wanted to get hurt or be the last casualty.

I remained in the Army, and took the Administrative Officer Course. In 1975, I was commissioned as an officer, and eventually retired as a Major in 1986. Like many American vets, I have several Agent Orange-related disabilities from melanomas to various cancers.

I've made several trips back to Vietnam since the war. We became involved in fund-raising for several Montagnard orphanages in Kontum, which has become a major activity for me, my wife and a few of my friends. We now support over seven hundred kids at six orphanages in that area. I like to say that my wife Rhonda and I have two children, plus 700 Montagnard orphans. As anyone who served there knows, the Montagnards are dirt poor. They were our staunch allies in the war and both the North Vietnamese and the South Vietnamese hate them. They need a lot of help. Last year we raised $3,500 for the orphanages and that goes a long way.

Anyone who is interested in helping can find out more at our website www. askatvso.com or call me in Australia at +61 7447735104.

TOM KILBRIDE'S WAR

**US Army Spec 5 and Combat Medic,
1st Battalion, 327th Infantry Regiment,
1st Brigade, 101st Airborne Division,
Phan Rang, 1966–67**

I graduated from high school in Chicago in June, 1963, and enlisted in the Army. I was impatient and went in that August, when I was still seventeen. If I'd have waited another month until I was eighteen, I could have gone to OCS. Instead, after Basic at Fort Campbell, they sent me to Fort Sam Houston to become a medic. I arrived in Vietnam in August, 1966, in the sweltering heat of the summer, and was sent to the 101st in Phan Rang in southern II Corps. While it remained our main base, we were air mobile and operated all over from Dak To near the Cambodian border to Quang Tri in I Corps, Con Thien right on the DMZ, and about everyplace else. We even made a battalion parachute drop in Vietnam once. Why? Who knows, except to prove we could, or maybe because all the officers and NCOs needed it to keep their jump pay.

As everyone who served in Vietnam knows, every morning the cut-off oil drums under the four-holer latrines got pulled out and burned with fuel oil. They had the medics do it as a sanitation issue. The smell of burning fuel oil and s**t is something that stays in your nostrils forever; it's one of the aromas of Vietnam. On the other hand, that was the time you could smoke all the dope you wanted, right out in plain sight, because no one wanted to get close enough to find out what it was.

I'd been in the Army for three years and was a Sergeant E-5 when I got out in 1968. We spent all our time in the bush in one and two-company sweeps looking for a fight, with a medic assigned to each platoon. We would go in by helicopter in what they called a "Search and Destroy" mission with three of us on the rear seat and five sitting on the floor. The first time I went up, I swore I was going to slide right out the door, but that never happened. When we reached the LZ where I joined my unit for the first time, the helicopter never landed. We were maybe six or eight feet off the ground, when they screamed, "Jump!" I did, figuring I'd break my legs, but that didn't happen.

Once we were on the ground, we'd fan out on patrols until we reached a spot to dig in. Then, around dark, we'd move again, to a new place, always moving and never staying in the same place twice. We'd go out on night ambushes, set out listening posts, and hunker down. That was how it went, every day. One time, there were six choppers waiting to take us somewhere. I went to hop on one, but those guys screamed it was full and told me to take the next one, so I backed away. They lifted off, and immediately had mechanical trouble. Those guys started jumping out at treetop level, so I concluded I had taken the right one after all.

In addition to all the normal gear everyone had to carry, as medic I had my Aid Bag, which weighed another fifty pounds. It contained four canisters of serum albumin, which would stop a guy from bleeding out. Since we almost always got the wounded medevaced out in thirty to forty-five minutes, I never had to use one. I also carried morphine syrettes, all sorts of other pills, bandages, and tape. I carried a gun, like most medics who weren't conscientious objectors. At first, I was issued an M-16. With its ammunition, it weighed too much; so, I grabbed a .45 as soon as I could get one. I figured if push came to shove, there would be M-16s lying around on the ground; so why hump one?

When I first arrived, I stayed with the Company CO, Platoon Sergeant, and radio operators, RTOs, at night. It didn't take long for the sergeant to notice that I slept all night, and put me on radio response watch with the RTOs like everyone else. One night while on radio watch out in the bush, a big rat wandered behind my back. I sat very still until it wandered off.

We operated in triple-canopy jungle, barren prairies, big hills, rock fields, and rice paddies. In most firefights, you can't tell from which direction the shots came, much less who's firing at you. One time we came across a tunnel opening. I had never seen one, so I volunteered to go down with my .45 and a flashlight and see what it was like. Fortunately, it was empty, so I got the hell out of there and decided I'd never do that again.

We ate nothing but C-rations. One day, one of the guys shot a big hog. We had a

Hawaiian in the unit, who decided we'd have a Luau. I told him there was nowhere near enough time to safely cook pork, so we chopped off some meat and grilled it. Another time, we caught a chicken and cooked it up with some rice we liberated. One recipe we made up was rice with some of the canned fruit from the Cs. We called that "rice pudding."

The generals claimed we were the best-trained Army, ever. We were scared high-school kids with machine guns, who had no idea of what we were doing tactically. Every day, there would be some gunfire, some guy would get hit, and the rest would open up on full automatic. It didn't matter that they couldn't see anything, they thought we were surrounded. Then, they'd run out of ammunition and start screaming, "Medic!" and "Ammo!" The VC could have killed a lot more of us if they wanted to, but I think they just wanted us to go away. Our side was not fully  trained on what to do after a firefight starts, and poorly led by non-career officers who wanted to get their CIB, and get their asses back to a staff job. It was a hell of a war.

One time we were working our way through some rice paddies. Up ahead, a guy in black pajamas with a rifle began to run away. One of our guys, one of the few good shots, dropped to a knee on a dike and put the guy down. The radio man called it in: "One VC down." The battalion asked if we needed resupply. "Yeah," the radio guy answered. "One bullet."

Another time, we stopped for lunch on a big rock. I was out of food, but one of my pals offered to split a can of beef stew. That was one of the better meals. He carefully opened it and we began to heat it, when we were suddenly told we had to move out. Somehow, the can got knocked over. He and I stood there staring at each other. We were hungry, so we got out our spoons and ate the beef stew right off the rock. That became my personal culinary standard for restaurants. "Well, it beats beef stew on a rock."

One day we were on a sweep near Ban Me Thuot and came across a small village. As we were searching it, I was standing near a hut when one of the sergeants told one of the new guys to "Clear that hooch!" He tossed a grenade inside, but the walls were reed-thin thatch. When the grenade went off, I got shrapnel in my side. It was about the size of a piece of a paper clip, because US hand grenades have a tightly wound spring as shrapnel. I just pulled it out and made a note to self not to be that close to a grenade explosion in the future.

We set up an ambush one night and sure enough, toward midnight we saw a couple of guys walking down a trail with rifles, sacks of rice, and jugs of water, so everyone started shooting. Two of them ran off, but we caught one guy who was wounded. As far as we could tell, he was a farmer who had been dragooned into carrying rice for the VC. Typical.

Another day, in one of the few attempts of tactical planning I saw, we had taken a few rounds from a village. Half of us stayed at the wood line and set up a base of fire with our sniper, while the other half maneuvered to cut off the village. The idea was to get the gunman in the village to shoot at them and our sniper would get him. Good plan. I was watching this show through a pair of binoculars. Sure enough, the gunman took a few more shots at our guys and our sniper fired and missed. "Aim lower and right," I told him. "No, I can't," he answered. "I dropped the rifle in the rocks and the sight's broken." "Then let me shoot," I told him. "No, I don't want to kill anyone anymore," he answered. I stared at him, but it didn't matter anyway. The gunman had already run off.

When my time was up, I ended up with a Purple Heart from a punji stake wound, and a Combat Medic Badge that I'm proud of. The shrapnel got me in the door of the VA, which later diagnosed my hearing loss, some other things, and a 50% disability.

I went back to college in Chicago. Because I took the College-Level Exams (CLEP) and had credit from a few college courses I took while in the Army, I got a four-year degree in two and a half years. I made a career of a variety of law-enforcement agent jobs: US Customs, a Sky Marshall, a Postal Inspector, and worked in the DoD Inspector General's Office. I worked in offices in Chicago, Rock Island, IL, San Francisco, Jacksonville, New Orleans, Germany, and Guam, dealing with contract fraud and mail theft. The most amazing part of it all is that I've been married for fifty-one years to the same woman, my Maria, who married me just prior to my shipping out for Vietnam.

BILLY WEST'S WAR

US Army Spec 4 and Radio Repairman,
46th Engineer Battalion, 101st Airborne Division,
1966–67

I graduated from high school in Long Beach, California, in 1963 and the city junior college in 1965. I couldn't find a job I wanted, so I was going to enlist until someone told me about a little loophole. If you enlist, it's three years, but if you "volunteer for the draft" it's only two years. That September I found myself in Basic at Fort Bliss, Texas, followed by Radio Mechanic School at Fort Benning. In June, 1966, I arrived in Vietnam, assigned to the 46th Engineering Battalion at Long Binh, thirteen miles north of Saigon on Highway 1.

Our Engineer Battalion repaired roads, did general construction, and repaired a lot of different equipment in support of the 101st Airborne. When we weren't doing that, and I had no radios to repair, they had us fill sandbags, dig holes, fill holes, build buildings, tear down buildings, and string wire. We slept on cots in large tents that held twenty men. We had a mess hall and make-shift showers, but that was about all. The rest of the compound was full of storage, repair shops, heavy equipment, and a lot of dust, except in monsoon season, then it was mud. The monsoon was the heaviest rain I've ever seen, but at least there was no need to take a shower. We were wet to the skin all the time, and the rain was so heavy it knocked me down once.

The area around our compound was mostly flat scrub land. The French had been there before us and we were told there were still old "Bouncing Betty" mine fields outside the perimeter with rusty trip wires. No telling if they were still any good, but it wouldn't take much to set one off, if they were. I spent a lot of time on the road driving to Tan Son Nhut, Saigon, Bien Hoa, and Vung Tau.

The biggest thing that happened at Long Binh when I was there was when the VC blew up the ammo dump on February 5, 1967. It was the biggest ammo dump in Vietnam at the time, covering over 3,000 acres, but the VC probably knew the place as well as we did. Somehow, they cut their way through fence after fence of barbed wire and into the ammo dump, setting booby traps and charges in the middle of a bunch of pallets containing artillery shells. They were stacked three high, so there was a lot of high explosive munitions there. When the first shells began exploding, live shells got tossed in the air, setting off other stuff and starting fires. In the end, most of the dump went up and a lot of guys got hurt. They say it rattled windows in Saigon. Later, I heard the ammo dumps in Cu Chi and Cam Ranh Bay also got blown up. They always made good targets for sappers and rockets.

When I was discharged, I went to work for Southern California Edison and worked for them for 30 years in administration. I'm now 71 and I am 100% disabled by the VA with major Agent Orange-related respiratory problems, diabetes, neuropathy in my feet and hands, and congestive heart failure. Other than that…

CLIFF KIDDER'S WAR

US Navy E-4, A-4 Skyhawk Maintenance, *USS Franklin D Roosevelt*, on Yankee Station off South Vietnam, 1966–67

I graduated from Everett High School in Lansing, Michigan, in 1964 and started work on the assembly line at the big Oldsmobile plant the next day. If you lived in Lansing back then, that's what you did. I barely made it out of high school to begin with, and college was out of the question. For the next eighteen months, I worked swing shifts, with my father pushing me to join the Navy, which he'd been in. He and my mother were worried about the war, and they didn't want to see me "pounding the ground" in Vietnam. So, I enlisted in December, 1965, on my 20th birthday... in the Navy, of course. I signed a four-year enlistment to get aircraft maintenance. After Boot Camp that's exactly where the Navy sent me: to an A-4 Skyhawk squadron in Jacksonville, with whom I stayed for my entire enlistment.

The Navy didn't train aircraft mechanics like the Air Force or the Army. Instead of long, specialized courses, they throw you into a squadron where you dealt with only one model of airplane, nose to tail, and you learn OJT under a senior tech. I became a "Plane Captain," worked on the flight line, and performed maintenance and operational checks before and after every flight. We had a huge book with all the diagrams for the airplane and step-by-step instructions for every possible repair. They could literally ship the plane to me in parts, and with that book we could put it together again.

In mid-1966, our squadron deployed on the *USS Franklin D. Roosevelt* for a training cruise in the Caribbean, followed by a deployment to Vietnam. We were the first East Coast squadron to be sent, which meant a long sea voyage around Cape Horn into the Pacific and on to Yankee Station off the coast of Vietnam. It took a month to get there, and then a month to come back. While in the Western Pacific, called "West Pac" in the Navy, we used Subic Bay in the Philippines and Yokosuka, Japan, as our home ports. Our

Vietnam cruise began in June, 1966, and we were relieved in January, 1967. We had three A-4 Skyhawk Squadrons aboard, plus two fighter squadrons, four older A-1 prop planes, two photo recon planes, and some AWACs planes. The A-4 was a lightweight attack aircraft, a workhorse that was usually configured for ground support, but could carry the equivalent load of an old WWII B-17, if it were just loaded with bombs.

Mechanics were exclusively assigned to one airplane for the entire cruise. You see photos of jets with a pilot's name stenciled on the cockpit, often with a cartoon or aircraft name, but the truth was they flew the next plane available.

When we arrived on station, we would operate for four to six weeks, paired with another carrier, spend a week at Yokosuka or Subic, a week for refitting and leave, then go back to Yankee Station. One of the carriers would take the day shift and one the night shift, and the crew would work twelve on and twelve off. My duty station was usually the flight deck where we kept the operational jets. I would prep and inspect my assigned A-4 before it went out and tie it down and check it out all over again when it came back. Once a jet took off, we had an hour to an hour and a half before it came back. That was when we could go below deck and eat or do whatever we needed to do.

The Air Wing was separate from the ship's crew when we were at sea. Our maintenance section of thirty to forty guys had a compartment on the hangar deck below the flight deck. We slept in bunks stacked three high, had small lockers, and kept all our gear and tools in our shop next door. I liked the work, especially when we were out at sea. We did a lot of different things and it was never boring.

One of the more exciting things that happened every now and then during flight operations was when a jet would return with "hung" ordnance: a bomb that wouldn't release, or a jammed machine gun. Jets came in hard on the flight deck when they landed. That was often enough for the gun to unjam, and it would spray the flight deck with a burst of bullets. We did not have many casualties, but that fall our squadron lost our Skipper and our newest pilot. Both were probably hit by SAMs. We had another pilot wounded by ground fire. The cockpit and seat are armor plated, but that bullet managed to find a small seam in the armor and hit him in the hand. He nearly bled out, and was unable to land the jet on the carrier deck, so he and his wingman diverted to Danang where they landed. We had another pilot who was shot down, and became a POW for the remainder of the war. In general, though, our aircraft received relatively little damage from ground fire.

No one ever told us officially where we were operating, and after a while, no one cared. Still, we knew it was South Vietnam, and the A-4s were providing bombing support for the ground troops. Right after Christmas, the A-4s were taking off without supplementary gas tanks; so, we knew they were bombing North Vietnam, which was a lot closer. We could see the lights of their cities at night.

Toward the end of the cruise, we had a horrible accident when a sailor walked into one of the spinning propellers on one of the E1B radar planes that was parked on the flight deck in front of the island. Flight operations were shut down and the maintenance crews had to walk the deck with bags, picking up body parts. That was the most horrible thing I saw during the war.

After that cruise was over, we spent a month steaming back to Jacksonville. I took the Air Frame maintenance course, and returned to the squadron. I got an early out in October, 1969, to enroll in Emory Riddle Aeronautical University in Daytona Beach. After I finished, I was never able to get the kind of job I wanted, so I moved back to Michigan and got a job with Dana Corporation as a tool and die machinist, and Quality Manager. When that plant closed, I moved to a small, privately-owned forge plant in northwest Ohio, where I remained for twenty-six years.

BRIAN SANDFORD'S WAR

US Army, Spec 5 and Radio Operator, MAC-V,
Advisor to the 3rd Regiment, 1st ARVN Division,
Hue, I Corps 1967–68

I grew up in Newburgh, New York. It's on the Hudson, about one hour north of New York City. I had flunked out of Orange Community College in Middletown, New York, and was "in-between schools," as they say, when I got drafted. That was in May, 1966. I was twenty years old, sworn in, and at Fort Hood, Texas, by July. After Basic, they sent me to Fort Jackson, South Carolina, to become a radio operator, and then back to Fort Hood to the 1st Armored Division.

Armor? Tanks? In July, 1967, they sent me to Vietnam, to the Military Assistance Command headquarters in Hue. For the next twelve months, I was a radio operator working with the 3rd Regiment of the 1st South Vietnamese ARVN Division. That was one of their best. Out in the field, I was supposed to be working with an American major or a captain, or at least a sergeant. But most of the time I was alone, embedded in an ARVN battalion and calling in US artillery, naval gunfire, helicopter gunships, and even Air Force jets for them. I went out on four or five of their big Lam Son sweeps, and traveled as far away as Phu Bai, Khe San, and Quang Tri. I ate with them, slept with them, even dressed like them. Since I was small for an American, it helped me keep a low profile, which was a good idea, since the only time I ever saw another American was on my infrequent visits to the MAC-V compound in Hue.

I had no training in Vietnamese. Didn't speak a word of it when I got over there. At the radio operator school at Fort Jackson, we spent six weeks learning Morse code, which I never used, but not a word of Vietnamese. By the same token, we didn't use any of the radio equipment I had been trained on, either. I had never seen a PRC 25 radio until they handed me one in Hue. Most of the time in the field, I was standing next to the Vietnamese Battalion Commander, playing "advisor," calling in artillery and air support. That's a heavy responsibility for a twenty-year-old kid. If I made a mistake, a lot of the wrong people could get killed, including myself; so, I took it very seriously and was very, very careful with map coordinates. In the process, I grew up quickly and developed a lot of self-confidence I didn't have before. But whether I was with the Vietnamese or the Americans, I took my dad's advice, "Keep your eyes open and your mouth shut."

A lot of Americans didn't like the Vietnamese, but I came to really like the Vietnamese soldiers I worked with. They weren't as well-trained or well-equipped as American soldiers were, but they were fighting for their country and their families. And I didn't eat GI C-rations, I sat on the ground with them and ate what they were eating. Usually that was in a big pot into which you dipped your bowl and took some of whatever was in there. Usually it was rice with maybe some chicken, but it was hard not to notice odd body parts like claws, heads, eyeballs, and all the rest. They would be watching me, like a test, so I ate it just like they did. After a while I was accepted.

Most of the time I had diarrhea or dysentery. That went with the job. When you needed water, you put your handkerchief over the mouth of your canteen to keep the worst of the sediment out, and dipped it in a stream—sometimes I think that was the only reason they issued us handkerchiefs—and threw in a couple of iodine pills. That's what I drank for a year. And when you had to go, you squatted down at the side of the trail just like they did. Dealing with their sanitation was real culture shock at the beginning, but that was the way it was.

Then came Tet. Those thirty days will always be my most vivid memories of Vietnam.

I had been in the field for five months working in and out of hills, jungle, and rice paddies as my ARVN battalion fought small VC units. When the North Vietnamese struck on January 30, 1968, no one was prepared for the scale or intensity of the fighting. Hue was one of their major targets, as was the 1st ARVN Division.

A couple of days before the attack, we saw

hundreds of refugees streaming south on the roads. They said there were soldiers and fighting behind them, but nobody believed them. Then, two NVA officers flying a white flag walked up to the gate of our compound. No one had seen very many NVA uniforms before, certainly not in Hue. They expected the ARVN to surrender, and the city to rise up to support them. They were wrong. White flag or not, the ARVN didn't care. I was told to stay out of it when they marched the NVA officers down to the river bank and executed them.

When the NVA regiments poured into Hue the next day, I found myself trapped in the MAC-V compound inside the city. There was a big school maybe 100 yards opposite us, which the NVA had occupied, and we spent the next few weeks blasting away at each other. Hue had been a magnificent city before the attack. The Citadel and Palace were beautiful national monuments, and at first the American Army wouldn't allow artillery or airstrikes inside the city. Eventually, however, they realized that they'd never drive the NVA out without that, so we blew the whole place to hell. Even then, we had to clear the city house by house.

During Tet the fighting was incredibly intense, day after day. I told my wife later that I had a bunch of Guardian Angels looking out for me that whole time. I remember driving through the back streets and even backyards inside the old city in an ARVN APC with a lot of gunfire all around. At one point, we came to a patch of sugar cane. I was thirsty and got off the APC to cut some down and suck the water and sugar out of it. I bent over to pick a piece up, when a machine gun cut loose and mowed the cane down right above me.

Meanwhile, the 3rd ARVN Regiment that I was supporting had gotten themselves surround-ed south of the city and were running out of ammunition. I got a Chinook loaded, hopped in the rear, and flew down there to resupply them. We picked up a load of wounded and flew them back up to Hue. The fighting in the city lasted a month. When it was over, the ARVN chased the remaining NVA back up into the mountains to their base camps in Cambodia. My reward for living through Tet was to be sent into the A-Shau Valley with the ARVN on their next operation. That's another name that most American veterans remember, particularly those who served in the 101st and the Cav during the big battles in 1966.

My tour was over in July, 1968. I was discharged and went back to New York to finish college. It was strange, but I came back with a sense of loneliness and separation from other American vets. I didn't have the US unit affinity like most guys had, because I served with the Vietnamese, not the American Army. My "unit" was the ARVN 1st Infantry Division, and that isn't something you put on a baseball hat and walk into a bar with. That may be one of the reasons why I never talked about it to anyone until recently.

People sometimes ask me, with all the time I spent in Hue and working with the South Vietnamese soldiers, do I ever want to go back and see it again? I don't think so. I remember the city the way it used to be before it got blown all to hell. The Vietnamese have turned it into a tourist attraction in recent years, but I don't want to see it that way. And as for the South Vietnamese officers and enlisted men I worked with, I doubt they fared very well after North Vietnamese took over the country.

When I got home, I went back to Orange Community College in Middletown and met with the Dean. He looked at me and frowned. "Weren't you here before?" he asked as he stared at my grades. "Why should I even think of letting you back in?" I told him I had just gotten out of the Army and Vietnam. He looked me over again and finally relented. He said he'd let me back in, and if I could get a C average the first semester, he'd expunge all the old grades. I did. In fact, I did a whole lot better than that, and he did what he said he would do.

I ended up getting a teaching degree and taught high school English for thirty years in Newburgh and in Tri-Valley High School in Grahamsville, New York.

JOHN BYARD'S WAR

US Army Captain, and "Bird Dog" Pilot,
183rd and 185th Reconnaissance Aircraft Companies,
II Corps, 1966–67 and 1969–70

I grew up in Morristown, Tennessee, in "Davy Crockett" country in the eastern part of the state near Knoxville. After high school, I went to East Tennessee State, graduated from ROTC, and was commissioned a 2nd Lieutenant in June, 1963. I spent the next twenty-three years in the Army, with two tours in Vietnam as a "Bird Dog" pilot, retiring in 1986 as a Lieutenant Colonel.

When I went on active duty, the Army sent me to "Fort Benning School for Boys" for Infantry Officer Basic. I stayed for both Airborne and Ranger Schools, and went on to the 4th Infantry Division in Fort Lewis, Washington. I was a platoon leader and eventually the Training Officer, Long Range Recon Platoon Leader, and then the Company Executive Officer. In 1965, I volunteered for Flight School and was trained as a "Bird Dog" pilot. That aircraft is a small Cessna L-19 spotter plane, and our main job was reconnaissance, to provide direct artillery and aircraft fire support for the troops on the ground. The airplane was a two-seater used by the Air Force and Marines as well as the Army. The seats were front and back, not side-by-side, and the pilot sat up front. Sometimes a passenger or artillery observer from one of the units would sit in the backseat, but usually I flew alone.

I was part of the first contingent of sixteen Bird Dogs and thirty pilots that went into Vietnam in August, 1966. We picked up our airplanes from Cessna and flew them to the Oakland Army Terminal. The entire 183rd Reconnaissance Aircraft Company with its 150-200 people followed by train, and the planes and people went on to Vietnam by ship. That took sixteen days. We landed at Vung Tao and went up the coast to Cam Ranh Bay, but that wasn't our final destination. Across the bay was a big empty field at Dong Ba Tinh. A Navy Seabee company helped us get the place set up, but it was built from scratch. When the airplanes arrived in Saigon, some of the guys went down and flew them up. This was 1966. The company headquarters stayed at Dong Ba Tinh, but the aircraft were dispersed to wherever they were needed around the country.

I took a Section of four Bird Dogs up to Dak To to provide support for the 101st Airborne Division until they moved up to I Corps. As US troop strength increased and more aviation companies arrived in country, the geography was repeatedly divided up and rearranged. As we became familiar with our areas of operation, we did a lot of visual reconnaissance, were spotters for the artillery, forward air controllers, and did a lot of other things. We were in Dak To from April to August, and then moved to Tuy Hoa, to help protect the rice harvest from the VC.

We had flight sections scattered about at various small airstrips, from Phan Rang, to Phan Thiet, Dalat, Ban Me Thuot, and a lot of others, working for US units, the ARVN, Vietnamese provincial units, or whatever, doing what was needed to support ground troops. We also worked closely with the Air Force reconnaissance people. We taught them how to spot for artillery and they taught us how to call in airstrikes.

I remember my first mission. Several of us were sent to pick up three long-range reconnaissance teams. We got the first two out with no problem, but the third team was run off the LZ. I stayed in the air, covering them for four hours, which was a long time, until they were safely bedded down and out of danger. It was way after dark when I got back to base. None of the little airstrips we used had lights, but a Bird Dog doesn't require much runway to land. That night, I called ahead, and the Crew Chiefs drove a couple of jeeps over to illuminate part of the airstrip with their headlights. The next morning, we went back out and picked up that third LRRP team. One guy had stepped on a punji stake, but the others were okay. Getting them back safely is something I've always been proud of.

Dak To, our main base, had a paved landing strip, but most of the others were hard-packed dirt or sheets of PSP, Perforated Steel Planking. Some were 2,000 feet long, but they could be as short as 1,000 feet or even a dirt road, like the ones at some of the Special Forces camps. One of the courses we took in training was "short-strip landing," where we had to come in over a barrier and put the plane down. All in all, it was a fun job, most of the time.

In August, 1966, I was promoted to Captain. Two of the pilots in our company had been killed while I was there. One of them had transferred to a Mohawk unit and was killed in Laos. The other was a temporary replacement who was filling in for one of our guys who went on leave. Those were the only two pilots we lost while I was there, but the 183rd and its sister companies lost quite a few later.

The L-19 Bird Dog was a pretty strong aircraft. The first round I ever took was one day when I came in to land at Ban Me Thuot and felt the wheel pulled to the right. When I landed, the crew chief and I looked and saw little dimples on the aircraft skin, as if it had been hit by a shotgun. He accused me of flying too low, but I had been up at 1,000 feet. We finally saw a fragment of a .30 caliber bullet lodged in the landing gear. It must have shattered and that was what caused the little dimples. The tire was losing air, which is why it pulled to the right, but normally, when you took a hit, it was in the wing or the tail.

When my first tour was over, I rotated back to Fort Rucker. I wanted to be an instructor pilot, but they had a different idea. Since I was Ranger qualified, they said, "We have the perfect job for you." They put me in charge of the Escape and Evasion course for the aircrews. If you read any of the memoirs of the guys who went through it, they all hated it.

After seventeen months, I finally got into the instructor pilot course, moved the family to Hawaii, and was then sent back for my second tour. My intention was to get out of the Army after that and hire on as a pilot with one of the airlines. I interviewed with American and Delta, but they were full. I had made Major by then, so... I stayed in. I wanted to fly something else, like a Mohawk or helicopter for my second tour, but the Army sent me to a Bird Dog unit at Ban Me Thuot again, to the 185th Reconnaissance Aircraft Company. They had taken over half the area that my old company, the 183rd, previously had. I stayed there in Ban Me Thuot for a full year, from March, 1969, to March, 1970. We'd get hit with rocket and mortar attacks fairly often. The first week I was there, I think we got hit three times.

When I was promoted to Major, I became the Company Executive Officer. My main job was flight standardization, which involved checking out the new pilots, flying with them, and working with them on short strip landings and night flying. I also gave a reevaluation check ride to every pilot in the unit every ninety days. We were dispersed, working out of small airstrips all over the countryside, and flying on their own like that, pilots develop bad habits. When they came in for maintenance every hundred hours, I'd take them up on another reevaluation check ride. When I wasn't doing that and when things got hot somewhere, I would assign myself to those missions, to help the other guys out. I liked doing that.

The heaviest fighting I was in during either tour was around the Special Forces camp at Firebase Kate. It went on for five days, and I've never seen so much artillery fire and aerial bombardment in my life. The place had been hit by five NVA regiments, so we sent in helicopter gunships, Air Force fighter jets, even B-52s, and "Spookies," a DC-3, C-47 or C-130 loaded with rapid fire cannon and miniguns, sometimes called "Smokies," or

"Puff the Magic Dragon," depending on the area where they were used. A young Special Forces Captain named Albracht wrote a book about Firebase Kate, titled *Abandoned in Hell*. The base was overrun, but the Green Berets made it out. It was some story.

When the war began, the 74th Reconnaissance Aircraft Company covered all of Vietnam. Eventually, they put a company in each of the four Corps areas, and then broke those down even further with more companies as the war expanded in the late 1960s. Then, they began shrinking it all down after I finished my second tour in March, 1970.

SHERMAN FRANCIS'S WAR

US Navy Petty Officer Third Class
and Disbursing Payroll Clerk, USS *Kitty Hawk*,
Aircraft Carrier on Yankee Station,
Gulf of Tonkin, 1966–67

I was born in Evanston, Illinois, just north of Chicago, and my ill-fated college career ended after two years. The draft was getting close, so I enlisted in the Navy Reserves in 1964 but did not have to go on active-duty until 1966. Being from Chicago, I asked to be sent to San Diego for boot camp. They said, "Sure," and sent me to Great Lakes, north of Evanston, in January. Also, I wasn't supposed to go to sea. Naturally, they sent me to the USS *Kitty Hawk*, a new aircraft carrier, as a Payroll Clerk. At least it was home ported in San Diego. It was the biggest American carrier at that time, with 3,500 in the Ship's Crew plus another 2,500 in the Air Wing, which had its own staff. We used the Disbursing Office from 7:00 a.m. to 7:00 p.m., and the Air Wing guys used it from 7:00 p.m. to 7:00 a.m. The same was true of every other staff section on the ship.

I reported in over Labor Day weekend and they made me bunk in the Sergeant at Arms section until the rest of the crew returned, for fear that I'd get lost and wander around below deck forever. In fact, after serving on that ship for over two years, there were areas I never did see. And you can imagine the size of our payroll. When we were in port in San Diego, I had to go with our Ensign and several other enlisted men to pick up $150,000 or so in cash from a local bank. No one said anything, but with Tijuana and the Mexican border only a few miles away, I'm sure we were all wondering how far we could get before they caught us.

We went out to sea on two deployments of seven or eight months each. The first was from September, 1966, to June, 1967, which took us to the Gulf of Tonkin off Vietnam. We'd be on "Yankee Station" for sixty days, rotate back to Subic for a week, and then go right back out again. A ship that big consumes an unbelievable amount of fuel, supplies, and bombs.

Our Disbursing Section had twenty guys in it and we worked ten to twelve hours a day, seven days a week. We had our own quarters three decks below the flight deck. Technically the ship was air-conditioned and there was a small vent above each bunk, but it didn't do much. We also had closed-circuit TV that ran old movies and live feeds from the flight deck showing planes coming in and taking off, not that we needed it. Fighter jets come in at a very steep angle when they land on a carrier deck. It's not like landing on a runway. So, when flight operations were going on, even three decks down, we could feel the pounding. And in my bunk, right above my head, ran one of the jet fuel lines that went up to the flight deck. That was a comforting thought.

Mail call was the most important event of the day. We had no cell phones, no online chats, no laptops, no e-mail, and no Facebook, just pen and paper. When we got mail, you could see three kinds of reactions—the happy guys got a letter, the unhappy guys didn't, and the very unhappy ones got a "Dear John letter" from their wife or girlfriend.

At the height of the bombing of North Vietnam, things never slowed down. At one point, there were four carriers working on "Yankee Station." We lost ten to twelve planes on each of my deployments, and you could watch the damaged ones, A-6 bombers and Phantoms, on the closed-circuit TV as they tried to land. One plane was so badly shot up that he bounced on the flight deck and missed the wire. It finally stopped, teetering on the edge of the deck.

Back then, all payroll and personnel records were on paper, kept in the finance and personnel offices, and hand-carried to the next duty station—no computers, fax machines, scanners, or electronic documents. No one in his right mind ever pissed off a payroll or personnel clerk, because of the power they had over those documents. We had a great Ensign in our section. There was a Lieutenant Commander aboard who was rude and obnoxious and gave the Ensign a lot of grief for no reason. Surprise! When that Lieutenant Commander was due to rotate out, no one could find his payroll records, anywhere. No one said anything, but we all knew that our Chief had dumped them overboard with the garbage. It was going to take that Lieutenant Commander six months to get his pay straightened out, if he was lucky.

One of the scariest things you can ever have on any ship is a fire. We were in port at Subic Bay, scheduled to deploy, when a couple of drunken sailors decided that a small fire would keep the ship in port for a while. They poured some kerosene in the tire locker and set it on fire. However, burning tires are very hard to put out, and the smoke can be very dangerous. We were confined to our workstations and could see smoke coming under the door. Eventually they got the fire out, but I'm sure those two guys ended up in Leavenworth.

In 1968, as my enlistment was coming to an end, my Ensign told me I could get an early out if I got accepted to college; so, I applied to Eastern Illinois, got out, and got my degree. All in all, going in the Navy was the best thing I ever did. At one point, I went down to the VFW Hall and tried to join, but they wouldn't let me in. They said Vietnam wasn't a real war. A lot of vets got that same reaction, which is why we formed our own Vietnam Veterans Association, which I joined some 40 years ago.

WALTER SZWEDA'S WAR

US Marine, Corporal E-4,
Hawk Antiaircraft Missile Batteryman
and Air Controller,
Monkey Mountain and Danang, 1966–67

Monkey Mountain is a tall, rocky outcrop that sticks out into the South China Sea east of Danang. The "Island in the Bay," as it was called, is connected to the mainland by a narrow causeway and a steep road uphill. It was the perfect place for the radar dishes and radio towers to control not only the big airbase at Danang, but all of Vietnam. The Marines built it and put a Hawk Missile anti-aircraft battery on top, in case the North Vietnamese Air Force ever tried to attack the place, which of course they didn't, but who knew back then?

I graduated from Foreman High School in Chicago, spent an "academically indifferent" year and a half at UCLA, and enlisted in the Marines in June, 1965, rather than get drafted. While they say that every Marine is an infantryman, I went to 29 Palms in California and they trained me to operate a Hawk battery and be an air controller.

I arrived in September, 1966, and remained there until Christmas, 1967. During my sixteen months, the only time I came down off the rockpile was to work at the Danang air base as an air controller for two weeks, and a few days at the in-country R&R center at China Beach. My first night on Monkey Mountain, I was put on guard duty. That meant taking a shift in one of the bunkers on the perimeter. They were fortified foxholes, with logs, sandbags, shooting slits, and a corrugated steel roof with sandbags holding it down. The place was called Monkey Mountain for a reason. It was overrun with rock apes. At night they would get in the trees and throw stuff down on the metal roofs. To a newbie, it sounded like a gunshot. There was a rule that we weren't supposed to fire or throw grenades without calling the Duty Officer for approval, but Marines aren't built that way. If you think you're under fire, rock ape or not, you shoot back. That woke everyone up, and we got a lecture. The longer we were there, however, the rock apes lost their humor value and became a major nuisance.

Around the base of the hill was jungle. There were 150 Marines up top, and we took turns going out on patrols down there. That meant ten to twenty guys went into the jungle for two or three days each twice a month, but the only real threat we faced was from the sea, from infiltrators who would come in from the north by boat. They would make landfall and try to climb up the mountain; but that wasn't easy, and we were well protected.

On top, we lived in Quonset huts and ten-man wood barracks. It beat the bush, and at least we had a mess hall and showers. Because we were near Danang, we got to see a few USO shows too, like Nancy Sinatra; but the town of Danang was off limits, at least for Marines. Our rules were different than the Army. No fraternization.

It was during Tet, 1967, that we were sent down to the Danang Air Base for a few weeks. On my time off, I hooked rides on six or seven Forward Observer flights to look for bad guys, coordinate artillery and air support for the infantry, and see the country-side. Several of those flights were in the backseat of a small Cessna "Bird Dog" and others were in an F-4 Phantom. Both were fun.

Naturally, that Danang visit also included guard duty. American airplanes rarely came back with live bombs; but when they did, the bombs were immediately taken off the planes and defused. The ARVN Air Force was also there, but they were too stupid or too lazy to do that. They simply parked their airplanes with live bombs hanging on them. One night, the Sergeant of the guard told me to check all the guard posts. I was near the ARVN area when mortar rounds started coming in. One of our guys screamed, "Hit the deck!" I jumped into a concrete culvert just as mortar rounds hit a couple of ARVN planes, bombs and all. Everything went up and I got shrapnel in my ass. The good news was, if I'd been standing, I'd have been dead. The other good news was that they sent me to China Beach for two weeks to heal.

Later, back on Monkey Mountain and on patrol again, the guy walking point ran into a booby trap and was killed. Some of the others were wounded, and I caught shrapnel in my knee. The VC loved to use American grenades, sometimes slipping them into a can with the pin pulled out, at the end of a wire. We figured that's what it was. Of those ten guys I went out with that night, I'm the only one still alive today. The others have all died from a variety of diseases, many of which were Agent Orange-related.

One of the fun things that happened on the rock was when we fired a live Hawk Missile at a Continental Airlines passenger jet as it was leaving Danang, flying a bunch of GIs on R&R. The stupid pilot took off and turned the wrong way, north, out over Danang Bay, where he was not supposed to be. He suddenly popped up on the radar screens and we had no idea what he was or where he came from. When we got no response from his transponders or the radio, our orders were to fire, which we did. An airplane that big near Danang couldn't be ignored. Fortunately, the pilot finally respon-ded to the radio calls and we were able to destroy the missile in flight before it reached him.

I rotated back home just before Christmas, 1967. The big Tet Offensive came a month later, but I was stationed at Yuma, Arizona, by then. I was a pretty good baseball player, a pitcher. I got to play on the Marine Corps baseball team, got a tryout with the San Diego Padres, and played on one of their minor-league teams for three years. After the dream of the Big Leagues faded, I went back to Chicago and worked in banking and health insurance sales and distribution, retiring at sixty-two. I have two Purple Hearts, have been diagnosed with Agent Orange-related Myasthenia Gravis, and am currently working my way through the VA claims process.

My wife and I are going back to Vietnam in December as part of a cruise. It stops in Danang and I have hired a driver to take us up to Monkey Moun-tain. The big rock that you see in the pictures is called Boom-Boom Rock. When I was stationed there, my ten friends and I buried a metal container up there with personal remembrances on the backside of the rock. As the only survivor, if I can find it, I want to dig it up and try to share that stuff with the families.

After I retired, I worked part-time and then full-time as a park district police officer. I still like to play golf and referee high school and college basketball games.

ROB STEVEN'S WAR

**US Air Force Tech Sergeant and C-130 Flight Engineer,
463RD Tactical Airlift Command,
Anywhere In-Country with a Runway 1966–68**

I graduated from high school in northwest New Jersey in June, 1965, and got my draft notice, so I enlisted in the Air Force in July. My older brother was in the Army and he told me to get in the Air Force or the Navy, because I didn't want to get drafted into the Army. After Basic and a one-year tech school, I became a Flight Engineer on a C-130. It was the workhorse of the Air Force in Vietnam, because it could land and take off on short runways almost anywhere. And during my eighteen months in-country, that's where we went: almost everywhere.

Most guys who served in Vietnam rode in the back of a C-130 at one time or another. They were loud, noisy rattletraps with four big engines, a drop-down rear hatch, pulldown seats along the sides of the cargo area in back, and room for pallets down the middle. We had a crew of six on board: the pilot, co-pilot, navigator, flight engineer, crew chief, and load master. The load master was responsible for securing and offloading the cargo, and the crew chief for the maintenance of the plane. The flight engineer sat in the middle between the pilot and copilot. He operated the panel that controlled heating, started the engines and motors, and the jet assist takeoff units. The C-130 was a good plane, and I loved my work.

Technically, the 463rd Tactical Airlift Command was headquartered in the Philippines and operated out of Udorn, Thailand, but we were there only once or twice a month. We were always in-country and flying troops and supplies in and out of Tan Son Nhut, Cam Ranh Bay, Danang, Pleiku, An Khe, Kontum, Khe San, and many other places. Very often, we would carry supplies in and carry body bags out. The first time we did that, I puked my guts out, but eventually I got used to it. I was there during Tet in January, 1968. We made runs into Khe San, and our unit carried supplies to the 1st Cav when they went into the A-Shau Valley. We were shot at plenty of times and hit, but nothing serious. The 463rd lost nine planes during the war, five shot down and four destroyed on the ground.

I flew in the same plane with the same crew the entire time. Our missions took us almost everywhere and we stayed in whatever accommodations were available. If it was an Air Force base, we knew we'd get a nice billet with air conditioning, hot showers, and good food. Not so much at the Army or Marine bases. Whichever, there was always a lot of drinking going on. During my tour, I made a lot of money by picking up and delivering things to guys on some of those bases—liquor mostly, steaks, or anything else they couldn't get where they were. Not drugs, that was available everywhere and they didn't need my help to get any of it.

Most of the days were repetitious, and my memories of Vietnam have a lot of blank spots. As someone said, war is long periods of boredom punctuated by moments of stark terror. One of those times was when we were at either Pleiku or An Khe, I can't remember which, waiting to take off. We were third in line, when the runway came under fire. The lead plane was hit with a rocket or mortar shell, caught fire, and rolled off the runway into a rice paddy. It was loaded with troops. The ramp jammed, they couldn't get out, and they all died in the fire. Minutes later we took off right over them. It was one of the worst things I ever saw. Another time, we were on the runway waiting to take off and a mortar round came down and went right through our wing. I almost crapped my pants, but the mortar round must've been a dud. It didn't explode. Our pilot gave the airplane full power and we got the hell out of there.

I extended six months and stayed in Vietnam until April, 1968, to get an early out. After a short stateside assignment, I was discharged in 1969. Thank God, I was never wounded and have developed none of the illnesses or Agent Orange things that a lot of other guys have. When I got home, I got a job work-

ing construction, working in some of the big tri-state tunnel projects, and operating the very tall tower cranes, the kind used to build high-rise buildings. I did most of my work in New York City and over in New Jersey, and continued doing that for forty-five years.

HENRY KOK'S WAR

**US Army Spec 4 Supply Clerk,
180th Assault Support Aviation Company,
"The Big Windy," 1st Cav Division,
Dong Ba Thin, 1966–67**

I was nine years old when my family emigrated from Holland and settled on Long Island. My father had been a professional waiter in Holland and spoke no English, so it was hard. I graduated from the City's Aeronautical High School, a very good school. To celebrate, I went to Europe with a friend and was trekking across Europe the next winter when my Draft Notice arrived at home. By the time they located us, the FBI was looking for me, but that blew over.

So, I was drafted. In January, 1966, I arrived for Basic at Fort Gordon, Georgia, and then went to the Logistics and Finance AIT course at Fort Knox, Kentucky, before I was sent to the 180th Assault Support Helicopter Company which was being formed in Fort Benning, Georgia. We had 186 men and a flock of Medium Lift Chinook C-47C helicopters. I was put in the company headquarters in charge of records and reports. In August and September, they shipped the men and machines to the West Coast and then on to Vietnam by C-130, hopping across the Pacific. I arrived on November 15, 1966.

After some "in-country" training, we were packed off to Dong Ba Tin as part of the 10th Aviation Battalion. It was across the bay from Cam Ranh Bay and hosted several different aviation companies, from our Chinooks to Hueys and Bird Dog spotter planes. There had been a small airstrip there, but we had to build everything else from scratch. We routinely flew to Tuy Hua and Bien Hoa carrying material for the US 1st Cav, the 9th Korean White Horse Division, which was protecting us in the hills to the west, and three ARVN Divisions. We even carried the Bob Hope Christmas Show to Cam Ranh Bay.

One day at company formation, the 1st Sergeant asked who had a driver's license. A couple of guys raised their hands, and he pointed to some wheelbarrows. "Drive those, and follow me," he said as he led the work detail away. Somebody asked me why I didn't raise my hand. I told him I grew up in New York City. My family was too poor to have a car, so I never got a license. Not wanting to drive a wheelbarrow or go out in the bush, I made myself as useful as I could in the company office, taking over payroll, allotments, and officer flight records, all of which had been screwed up. Believe me, those documents were  very important to the people in the food chain above me, like the officers, the pilots, and the NCOs. Getting them right got me in good with the First Sergeant, who directed that I was not to stand guard or go out on patrols. That was fine with me. After that, the closest I got to getting hurt was when I fell off a bar stool and banged up my leg. Having at least a modicum of honor, I did not ask for a Purple Heart.

Our base was very rough in the beginning, but we had the best enlisted man's club in the area, with a bar, stolen furniture, and music, and that was all that really mattered. We were good scroungers. We even traded with the priest for some paint.

One of my funniest memories was when the First Sergeant threw me the keys to one of the jeeps and told me to make a run up the coast to Nha Trang to deliver something. Not only did I not have a license, but I had only driven a vehicle once or twice in my life, and I had never driven a jeep. Somehow, I figured it out, but on the way back I got stopped by some MPs who gave me a speeding ticket. In Vietnam? What a joke.

On more than a few occasions, we would take chairs out at night, sit, drink beer, and watch "Puff the Magic Dragon" attack some targets in the hills to the West. It was a C-47 that had been converted to a serious gunship. They carried four miniguns and would circle a target. When they opened up, the tracer rounds looked like a stream of red light from the airplane to the ground. It made quite a show.

One thing that really bothered me over there was the old people and children who were always foraging for food in the trash dump. We were told to burn it, but I refused. After a while, I wouldn't go there at all. People shouldn't be subjected to things like that. It was terrible.

I was a Spec 4 most of my tour and rotated out in November, 1967.

When I got home, I found it was much easier to get a job when you don't have a Draft Notice hanging over your head. With my Aeronautical High School training and the Army schools I attended, I got a job in purchasing with Swissair in New York. Eventually I became Chief Stores Coordinator for them, and went on to work for Lockheed, Raytheon, Booze Allen Hamilton, and the Henry Jackson Foundation in Maryland. I have been diagnosed with PTSD and Agent Orange-induced Type 2 Diabetes. It was everywhere over there, at Dong Ba Thin, on the helicopters, everywhere. I'm now 72. I enjoy photography and remain active in the Vietnam Veterans of America, where I serve as Chapter Membership Chairman.

BILL SCHMIDT'S WAR

**US Army, Sergeant E-5 Squad Leader,
1st Battalion, 12th Infantry Regiment,
4th Infantry Division,
Pleiku and Dak To, 1967–68**

I grew up on a small farm near Riverside, Iowa, and was a 4-letter athlete in high school. I went on to play football at the University of Iowa for two years, but had to drop out and run the family farm when my father became ill. As soon as I left college, I was drafted. In June, 1967, I went to Fort Campbell for Basic and Fort Polk for AIT, coming out as an 11-C, Light Mortarman. After a month's leave, in December, 1967, I landed at Cam Ranh Bay.

Everyone arrives in Vietnam with a certain amount of innocence. My unit was up at Pleiku and I was put in a 250-truck convoy headed there. I remember we drove through a village and swarms of kids came running up to the trucks with their hands out. Some other new guys and I tossed them C-rations. The older guys threw the cans at them, hard. I asked what they were doing, and one of them warned, "You never know what them kids have underneath their shirts."

I was assigned to the 1st Battalion of the 12th Infantry, the "Red Warriors," part of the 4th Infantry Division in the Central Highlands. Our base camp was at Pleiku, but we were always in the field, operating out of "forward base camps." I saw they had mortars at most of them, so I was optimistic that I might not end up in the field. Unfortunately, we had a battalion commander who decided each company should take an .81 mortar to the field with them, and that meant me. We normally carried an M-16 and ten magazines with 200 rounds of ammunition, but I would always carry fifteen to twenty magazines, plus four

to six canteens of water, food, and all the rest. Plus, the mortar squad had to carry the tube, tripod, and rounds for the mortar, divided between us. When you added it all up, I know I carried 100 to 120 pounds on my back.

I had been there a little over a month, when the CO sent for me and he told me to grab my stuff. This was January 6. A kid I grew up with who was in the 1st Cav had just been killed. His father, who was like a second father to me, requested me for escort duty. That's a solemn thing in the Army. I was sent back to Cam Ranh Bay and loaded into the back of a C-130. It had a big, open cargo bay with pull-down web seats and canvas straps along the sides. We were given a blanket and a packet of gum and rode like that all the way to Hawaii. When we got there, I was frozen, my ears were plugged up, and my eyes were swollen shut from the exhaust fumes. In Oakland, we cleaned up, got fitted with new khaki uniforms, and given a day of training. After that, I met up with the casket and was with it each step to the cemetery. Doing that was the hardest thing I've ever done. My friend's bunker had taken a direct hit, and it was a closed casket. We came from a town of six hundred. Everyone knew everyone. There was a National Guard Colonel supervising, but my friend's father had taken it very hard. I was only supposed to be there for seven days, but after fourteen or fifteen, the Colonel finally told him I had to go back.

During my return flight to Saigon in late January, 1968, the Tet Offensive began. Fighting was raging all around Saigon, and even Tan Son Nhut was attacked. I found myself in the replacement depot for a day and a night in khakis with no weapon. No one could tell me anything. My unit didn't even know I was there. Finally, I took matters in my own hands, went out to the helipad, and caught a ride up to Ban Me Thuot and then on to Pleiku.

The way the 4th Division operated, we normally maneuvered as a company, sometimes several companies or even the whole battalion. We would have four artillery bases in the hills around us, and we would work between them, so we had artillery support from four directions, but all we did was move, move, move. It was usually 120° during the day, and it got cold at night in the hills. We maneuvered through dense triple-canopy jungle and hills covered with trees and bamboo, which gave great cover for snipers. We often humped a mile or so up and down the hills to cover a quarter-mile on a map.

That summer, particularly July and August, was terrible. We were in contact all the time. On August 17, we were in a major battle with an NVA Regiment. Poor intelligence again. No one told us that one of the batteries that usually supported us was being moved, and that the company that was supposed to reinforce us had been sent someplace else. When it started, we were hacking though the bush and I was the third man back from the point. The gunfire was so heavy we had to call in artillery. When it was over, of the two hundred men I started with, only forty-seven of us weren't killed or wounded. I always felt bad about that. Call it survivor's remorse, but it took the Lord, my Guardian Angel, and all my luck to come out uninjured.

When I arrived in country I was a PFC, but was soon promoted to Spec 4, and then Sergeant E-5. Normally I'd command a squad of ten to twelve guys, but on August 17, we were hit so hard that I ended up as Platoon Sergeant and then Platoon Leader. When we got back to the base camp I stopped by one of the artillery batteries that had been firing support for us with their 105s and 155s. They had fired so many rounds that the tubes were warped. One of the artillery guys told me that they had been peeing on the barrels to try to cool them off.

We were air-mobile. They would fly us around and drop us off at different LZs all the time. If it was a longer distance, they would take us in Chinooks. For closer operations, we'd be taken by Hueys, usually six, with twelve men and all their gear crammed inside or hanging on outside. We were told to jump when we got within three feet of the ground, because the helicopter wasn't waiting around.

On a typical day, once we were on the ground, we would then hump up and down hills through the jungle, and then stop around 3:00 p.m, and set up camp. We would put out trip flares and Claymores, dig three-man foxholes, and fill the sandbags we carried to add some height. We cut down the small trees and bushes in front of us and covered our holes with the brush. Unfortunately, that whole area was covered with red ants. We carried air mattresses. In the middle of the night you'd hear a hissing sound and some guy swearing because the ants had chewed a hole in his. It would be weeks before he could get a new one.

I don't think anyone can imagine the filth we lived in. I still can't. During the monsoon season, it would rain all morning and we would be covered with mud. When the sun came out it would all crust up, but we had no spare uniforms. By the end of a month or six weeks in the field, we'd be wearing tatters. But our biggest problem was feet and fungus infections. Every week, a fair number of guys would have to be sent back to the hospital to get their feet treated.

When we were working down south around Ban Me Thuot, we were fighting the Viet Cong. We would maneuver through the jungle in three columns, staying in sight of each other. Our air cover would tell us if we were approaching a village. When we did, one column would swing around the other side of the village as a blocking force, and the rest of us would sweep through. We had interpreters, but it was always the same story. The villagers always said there was no VC around, but when we searched we would find caches of rice and weapons. Of course, if they cooperated with us, the VC would come back and kill them, and we knew it. In VC country, we would find booby traps, punji stakes, and never be sure who to trust. Up north in Pleiku and Dak To, we were mostly fighting regular NVA main force regiments. If we saw them, they would be in uniform, well trained, and outnumber us. So, I'm not sure whether we were better off fighting the VC or the NVA.

Two weeks before my year was up, a couple of days before Thanksgiving, I was about to go out on patrol again when the CO called me over and told me to grab my stuff. I was getting an early out and the helicopter was waiting for me on the pad. We shook hands and I found myself at the personnel depot in Saigon before the sun set. They told me if I extended my tour by another two months, leaving me with five, they'd give me a discharge when I got home. But I wasn't spending one more night over there than I had to, especially over Christmas.

I was lying on a bunk in Saigon, staring at the ceiling, unable to believe it was over, when a Lieutenant came in and saw my stripes. "Sergeant," he said, "I want you to be Sergeant of the Guard tonight." I looked up at him and shook my head. "With all due respect, Sir, I've been in the bush for almost twelve months and I'm not going out and have some desk clerk with a loaded gun get spooked and shoot me my last night in this country." I could have gotten in real trouble, but the Lieutenant looked at me, nodded, and told me he'd find someone else.

I played football at Iowa at 212 pounds. When I got home, I weighed 162. The Army sent me to Fort Hood. Since I had two years of college, I became the Legal NCO for the Battalion. I worked in an air-conditioned office and even had my own jeep. When June 29, 1969, came, I was out. I went back to college, got a degree in accounting, and went to work for John Deere in international tax for the next twenty-four years, until I retired. I don't think anyone there knew I'd been in the service, much less in Vietnam. We never talked about it, no one ever brought it up, and it probably wouldn't have been good if they had. I knew other vets who tried to join the VFW, but they never wanted us, and I never even tried.

I've been diagnosed with both Type 2 diabetes and prostate cancer, both Agent Orange-induced, with 100% disability and PTSD. The results of that stuff on us vets are bad enough, but new studies by the VA are showing that the effects of Agent Orange are passing down to children and grandchildren. My VA doctor insisted, for the third time, that I see one of the shrinks. I finally did, and began to realize how much I had been blocking out all those years.

I remember almost nothing about August 17, and don't want to. One of my old machine gunners visited me in Florida, and brought up this thing that happened and that thing, and I couldn't remember any of it. Finally, I asked him whether I had done anything to get any of our guys killed that day. He said absolutely not, and I had to take his word for it. I'm now 71. Despite my physical ailments, I stay active swimming, playing golf, visiting family, and in church activities.

JOHN CASIANOS'S WAR

US Army, Spec 4 and Combat Medic,
4th Battalion, 39th Regiment, 9th Infantry Division,
Bearcat and Dong Tam, 1966–67

I was a City kid from Washington Heights in Manhattan. After graduating from high school, I went to CCNY and studied biology. Unfortunately, my hours dropped below twelve one semester, and the Draft Board gobbled me up. They told me I was going to Fort Riley. Where the hell's Fort Riley, I asked? In Kansas, they said. Where the hell's Kansas? Whatever, on April 25, 1966, I was twenty years old, and I was there.

Toward the end of Basic I was told I'd be going to Fort Sam Houston to be a Medic. It wasn't my choice. The class was ten weeks long, after which I was sent to the 9th Infantry Division. It had been activated that spring and was going to Vietnam by ship, which we did, arriving at Vung Tau on New Year's Eve, 1966.

We were based at Bearcat east of Saigon, but we worked all over III and IV Corps, even down in the Delta. Medics are assigned to the company, and one is sent to each infantry platoon when they go to the field. I worked with A, B, and E companies but you get to know all "your boys." You take care of them, they take care of you.

We were air-mobile, but once we landed in an LZ, we operated like any other infantry unit and even the medics weren't exempt from guard duty, patrols, ambushes, or listening posts. Some of the worst action we saw in those first months was in the "Rung Sat Special Zone," a big tidal mangrove swamp and an awful place to maneuver. The rest of the areas we worked in were mostly flat with rice paddies and dikes, mud, and water. We'd be out in the field for two to three months at a time, wearing the same clothes, sleeping on the ground or wherever, eating C-rations, and getting resupplied once or twice a week. Most of the stuff we got: the Cs, my medic bag with all its bandages, tourniquets, and medicines, even the hand grenades—were old WWII stuff. You could tell from the packaging and dates on the boxes. Even the cigarettes in the C-ration boxes were old Lucky Strikes in a green package.

When we were in fire fights or out on night ambushes, I fired my M-16 like everyone else. I went through Basic and knew how to shoot, but it wasn't a high priority. I have no idea if I ever hit anyone, but it wasn't for lack of trying. When we weren't in combat, as medic, I'd hold my own sick calls every day, dispense malaria pills, making sure everyone took them, and treating the accumulated cuts and infections. Some of the nastiest wounds were from punji stakes, which were razor-sharp bamboo shafts that the VC would leave around for us to step on or fall on. They had some really bad stuff on their tips. If you got cut by one, you could almost watch the infection grow right in front of your eyes.

In the field, the days were all the same. So were the nights, because I couldn't sleep. In fact, in the whole twelve months, I don't remember sleeping, not out in the field or at base camp. If I didn't have a "Short-Timer's Calendar," I'd have lost all track of the days or how long I'd been there. They were all the same, except for the very bad ones.

My worst day was when eight of my guys went down within a half hour. My job was to do a quick triage to keep them all alive until we could get them medevaced out to the Battalion aide station or the EVAC Hospital. After the guys started going down, I heard people yelling, "Medic!" and I began running from man to man, quickly determining the damage, treating the most serious wounds, stopping the bleeding, and then moving on to the next guy, until I got back to the first ones again. I was so focused on them that I wasn't aware of anything else that was going on. There's what's called "The Golden Hour." If you can get a man stabilized and back to the field hospital in less than an hour, they usually survive; so that's what I tried to do.

Medics are issued five morphine syrettes, and they're closely accounted for. One day I was staying in camp, but another medic was going out and found himself short, so I loaned him two, which we did all the time. Sure enough, the First Sergeant inspected my bag, found me short, and accused me of using. He was going to bring me up on charges, until my buddy brought mine back. I told the First Sergeant to look at my arms if he thought I was using. Maybe he thought I was high because I smiled all the time, but that was my nervous reaction to everything I was going through.

One night we set out a platoon-sized ambush and caught seventy-five VC with torches going down a trail carrying weapons and big bags of rice. Our old battalion commander said we had to radio in and get permission before we could open fire; but we had a new commander. We called in to get approval and he started screaming over the radio, "Why are you calling me? Why aren't you killing them? Kill them!" So, we opened up. We hit some of them, and the others dumped the rice and ran away.

When it got light, we went out and found a seven-year-old girl among the wounded. My platoon sergeant told me to patch her up, but I refused. "She's the enemy, just like the others," I told him. He looked at me and told me that he'd beat the crap out of me if I didn't take care of her. So, I went to work and patched her up. It didn't take long for me to feel very guilty about what I thought and said. Even today, I feel bad about that, guilty as hell.

Funny things happened over there too. One day we were on a sweep, we took fire, and had casualties. I ran low on bandages, so I yelled, "I need bandages!" Next thing I know, I'm getting pelted with a dozen of those canvas bandage holders that guys wear on their web gear.

After six months in the field, a medic is usually rotated back to the division's medical battalion, because six months out in the field was about all a guy can take. The medical battalion was in Dong Tam in the Delta, where we lived in tents with wood floors, slept on cots, had a shower, and a mess tent. It was an improvement, but we did get regular rocket and mortar attacks. I worked twelve on and twelve off and my job was to man the emergency radio and dispatch medevac helicopters to where they were needed.

I was in-country 360 days when they finally sent me home at the end of my tour. My proudest possession is the "Combat Medic Badge" I was awarded for serving in a line outfit under fire. They can keep all the rest. I had broken both of my wrists from a fall out of a helicopter, but they wouldn't give me a Purple Heart because they said there was no blood.

When I got home, I went through several jobs and finally became a carpenter in Northern New Jersey, which I did for the next twenty-nine years. I've been diagnosed with Agent Orange-related Diabetes and PTSD. The areas we worked were covered with the stuff. After I retired, I served as an EMT in town, and now enjoy golf, battalion reunions, and veteran's gatherings.

DENNIS O'ROURKE'S WAR

US Army Spec 5 and Artillery Fire Direction Chief,
B Battery, 1st Battalion of the 77th Field Artillery,
1st Cav Division, An Khe, 1966–67

I grew up on Long Island. After high school in Nassau City, I got a job as an apprentice printer at *Newsday* until I was drafted into the Army in December, 1965. I was nineteen years old and they sent me to Fort Hood, Texas, and the artillery. I had always been good with numbers and maps and was trained as a Fire Direction Chief, who's the one who does the geometry and math to aim a field piece. I was then sent to the NCO Academy. I finished second in my class, was promoted to Spec 4, and spent a few months training Basic Recruits before they sent me to Vietnam and the 1st Cav.

On December 6, 1966, almost one year to the day after I was drafted, I arrived at An Khe, assigned to a 102 Howitzer battery. The Cav and airborne divisions used the 102, which was a lightweight version of the 105. We had six of them in the battery, five to six men on each gun, and five to six more in the battery's Fire Direction Center where we plotted the fire missions. Firing artillery was serious business. If we screwed up the numbers, shells could go long or short and hit our own people with "friendly fire." I'm proud to say that we never had a "mishap" like that while I was there.

Except for a one-week R&R to Bangkok and a three day in-country R&R to Vung Tau, I spent the entire year in the bush, right to the end. I never wanted to be at base camp. Things were more formal back there, and I didn't like it.

We moved around constantly, firebase to firebase, depending on where our infantry units were working. I figure we were at 12 to 15 different firebases that year, some for a month or two, like LZ English, and some for only a couple of days. Several times, the bulldozers had just finished leveling the LZ as we landed with a platoon of infantry for security. We did not get mortared or rocketed all that much. Sometimes, they'd send us a

"Quad .50-caliber" machine gun for protection. It was an old WWII anti-aircraft weapon, with four barrels. It put out a lot of fire and was devastating against an infantry attack. Around sunset, they would turn it loose on the surrounding wood line, just to let the bad guys know it was there. We were rarely bothered after that. If pressed, we could also depress the barrels on the 102s and fire high-explosive or "Bee Hive" rounds, which were like really big shotgun shells and were equally devastating. If that didn't work, we could always call in our own Cav gunships, and the NVA knew that.

Even still, we were scared silly for the first two weeks after we arrived in country, somewhat resigned to it for the middle eleven months, and then scared all over again for the last two weeks. The last thing anyone wanted was to get killed with only a couple of days left after you'd suffered through a tour in Vietnam.

At a firebase, we usually slept in tents, and would lay our air mattresses on top of wooden ammo boxes to get off the ground. That really helped during monsoon season. It was cold in the mountains at night, and being wet and cold for weeks on end was miserable. When it rained like that, we often had a small river running through the tent at night; not that it mattered, because I rarely got more than three hours of sleep at a stretch. We stood two-hour watches on the guns, and we took turns getting up to fire pre-arranged H&I, or "Harassment and Interdictory" rounds, in the areas we had infantry units operating. Even after I got home, it took me six months to be able to sleep for more than six hours.

Food was pretty good. The Cav took pride in that, and they had a lot of helicopters. No matter where we were, we could usually count on a hot breakfast and a hot dinner being sent out to us in Mermite cans. Lunch, of course, was C-rations, but that's better than a lot of guys had. I always got "care packages" from home, too. That's probably why I gained weight, while most guys lost.

I went flying as an artillery observer, or AO, quite often. We were looking for targets, but we were also there as bait to draw enemy fire for the gunships above us, waiting to pounce. We were shot down once playing that game, but the pilot put the helicopter down in a rice paddy. Still, I got a different view of the war up there. One time I flew over where an "Arc Light," or B-52 strike had taken place. The target was usually an NVA troop concentration, regimental headquarters, or a bunker complex. After the B-52s were done, the area looked like a lunar landscape, all torn up with craters and shattered tree trunks lying around like pick-up-sticks.

When my year was almost up, and they hadn't sent a trained replacement for me, I was afraid they might hold me over; so I looked around the unit, picked out a smart kid, and trained him myself. I needn't have worried. My orders came down early and they let me go home on November 27. When I reached Fort Lewis, they processed me out in four hours, which must have been a record; but when we reached the Seattle Airport, in uniform after a year in Vietnam, I could not believe how unfriendly the people were. I'll never forget that.

I went back to *Newsday* in Long Island, New York, finished my printer apprenticeship, and stayed with them through all the ups and downs and automation of the newspaper industry until I retired in 2008. I have been diagnosed with and am being treated for Agent Orange-induced Neuropathy and Type Two Diabetes. I'm now 71, serve as Treasurer of our local VVA Chapter, play golf, spend time with grandkids, and proudly wear my Cav Stetson with a red cord for the artillery.

STEVE MCKINZIE'S WAR

**US Navy, E-2 and Surveyor,
the 7th Mobile Construction Battalion, "The Seabees,"
Phu Bai and Dong Ha, Two Tours 1965–68**

After I graduated from high school in Indianapolis, I got a job as a tool and die draftsman for several years; but the draft was getting closer and I enlisted in the Navy in September, 1965. The Seabees have one advantage in that they always rotate whole units in and out of places. The 7th Mobile Construction Battalion was coming back from an assignment in Spain, and I joined them at Camp Lejeune before we were sent over to Vietnam, just before Christmas.

We were based at Phu Bai near the coast on Highway 1, with Hue to the north and Danang to the south. There was nothing there when we arrived, and we built the place. At first, I drove the gas truck and refueled the heavy equipment. Driving a gas truck in a war zone isn't the safest thing to do. Thankfully, I was switched to receiving the gravel and sand trucks from the Vietnamese, and gave out the voucher tickets they needed to get paid. After a while, I became a surveyor.

The whole time we were at Phu Bai, we lived in squad tents and slept on cots. We built the officer, NCO, and enlisted clubs, but never had time to build barracks for ourselves. We had a mess hall, but the food was so bad that we ate C-rations by choice, cooking them on little cans of sterno. To this day, I hate the smell of sterno. We also built the first latrines there—four-holers with sawed-off 55-gallon oil drums underneath. They were enclosed on three sides, but ours were open to the rear and backed up to rice paddies. We'd be sitting there while the Vietnamese were working the fields. They'd wave, and we'd turn and wave back. One lesson I learned over there was that your most prized possession was your own roll of toilet paper.

There were little kids everywhere around the base and out on the roads. Some of them were Catholic and some of them were Buddhist, and they didn't like or trust each other much. There was one little girl who always came around with the others, and I would try to talk to her. I always wondered what happened to her. When we drove our trucks up to Dong Ha on Route 1, the Buddhists would build little shrines in the middle of the road as a protest, to try to stop us. We would barrel right through them. I felt bad about that, but the first thing you learn about a truck convoy was you never stop or slow down; and we didn't.

The Seabees also provided direct combat support for the Marines. That meant we were armed, pulled guard duty on the perimeter, and were ready to rein-force them if needed. Every now and then, we would see Marine sniper teams waiting to be picked up by a helicopter. They carried special, long barrel rifles and had a look about them that told you they were the real infantry, not us. The Marines protected us, and we made a point of taking care of them. We built them some hooches that at least got them off the ground at night. In return, they brought over a tank with a flamethrower. They called it Zippo, and it could shoot fire a long way outside the base to burn off the scrub brush where the VC liked to hide.

One day, I was flown with a five-man team to Khe Sanh to survey a potential rock quarry site. We had to do that to estimate how much sand and gravel we could dig out if we were given a road project up there and needed a quarry. Wherever we went in the country, after we surveyed a construction site, we went looking for rock quarries, because nothing got built without a good base. When we were surveying at Khe Sanh, I met a guy in black clothes with no patches, who watched us work and smiled, apparently amused. I found out later he was CIA. That was another first, and I suspect he already knew that Khe Sanh wasn't going to be a very good place to work in the near future.

When we went out surveying in the bush, the bane of my existence was elephant grass. I'm short, and it was way over my head, so I usually carried the survey pole in one hand and a machete and the other. I still have that old machete.

There were a lot of Montagnard tribes living around Khe Sanh. They were very dark-skinned and primitive. They had several NVA prisoners locked up in bamboo "tiger cages," which were about two and one-half feet square. There was no "Geneva Con-vention" between the "Yards" and the NVA. They didn't like each other. We were only there a few days when we were told to leave. There was a lot of enemy activity in the hills and things were getting hot. Shortly after we left, the base was overrun.

We were at Phu Bai for eight months before we were shipped back to the States and another Seabee battalion took over. Eleven months later, in July, 1967, they sent us back to Vietnam, to Dong Ha this time. It was Northwest of Quang Tri, only eleven miles from the DMZ, up at the very top of I Corps. Our job was to build a small runway, and we were hit with rockets and mortars all the time.

I was working in a building one day when a piece of a nail from a nail gun flew back and hit me in the eye. That got me sent to the hospital ship USS Repose, where they had an eye surgeon. I didn't enjoy the surgery, but it was nice to see "round eyed" women and eat ice cream. We rotated out the second time in mid-January, 1968, only days before the big Tet Offensive, when both Dong Ha and Quang Tri were hit hard. While I received most of the normal I-was-in-Vietnam medals and ribbons, the one that I am most proud of is my Marine Direct Support Badge, which means that we fought side-by-side with them.

I was discharged after my four years were over, and I went back to school for a BA and MBA. I then reenlisted in the Navy, was commissioned, and went into the Supply Corps, where I ran fuel depots and became a contracting officer. I retired from the Navy after twenty-three years as a Commander, with 4 years enlisted time and nineteen years as an officer. In the process, I became somewhat of an expert on incorporating per-formance standards into high-tech purchasing contracts, and have continued to teach that subject in several Navy procurement schools.

In addition to hearing loss, I developed Agent Orange-related prostate cancer. I'm now seventy-two, but remain active with my consulting business, golf, pool, and general-ly enjoying life.

KEVIN McCABE'S WAR

**US Army, PFC and Radioman,
Recon Team, 2nd Battalion,
502nd Infantry, 101st Airborne Division,
Phan Rang, 1966–67**

I grew up in the town of Iselin in central New Jersey and dropped out of high school to enlist in the Army in July, 1965, when I was seventeen. After Basic, I became a Supply Clerk, got in Airborne School at Fort Benning, Georgia, and was assigned to the 101st Airborne. After more training, in 1966, half the Division was going to Vietnam and my half was sent to work with the 199th Light Infantry Brigade to help them get ready to go. That fall my half went over to Vietnam.

I was with the 502nd Regiment of the 101st, who were famous for dropping into Normandy on D-Day and the Battle of the Bulge. They were based at Phan Rang, where I arrived in December, 1966. The place was packed. I couldn't even find a bunk to sleep in. Everyone was in tents and every bed was full. I finally laid down under a tree and in a couple of hours found myself covered with red ants.

After ten days of in-country training, I was sent to Headquarters Company, 2nd Battalion of the 320th Artillery in supply. That only lasted three months. I wasn't cut out for headquarters work and didn't get along with the First Sergeant. He was old school and wanted us to spit shine our boots. That wasn't me, so I was sent to a line company, C of the 327th Infantry, for four months to be the radio operator for a forward observer team.

We operated in the Central Highlands, were involved in some big battles, and I got pretty good at calling in artillery. The 101st, being airborne, used the new light-weight 102s, but from time to time I called in 155s and even naval gunfire—whatever was available.

I carried this badly damaged photograph of me in my wallet all the way through my tour. It's wrinkled and water damaged, but somehow it survived, like I did.

Our forward observer team usually had three men—a Captain or Lieutenant, a Sergeant, and me. One day we ended up in a big firefight. I had the radio and looked around for the Captain for orders, and found him hiding behind a tree. I called to him several times, and then called in the artillery myself. When the fighting was over, he called me over and wanted us to leave, but I told him I wasn't carrying a radio for a coward. That got me put on charges in front of the Battalion CO. I told him what happened, he thought about it, and reassigned me to a different Recon Team. That was the last I heard about it.

The best part of that time was going on R&R to Bangkok. That was in July. When an Op started, they would fly us out to a LZ and we would walk for the next month. Then they'd pick us up, fly us back to base for a few days, and it would start all over again, and again, and again. That took a terrible toll on the body. We were wet all the time from rain and fording streams, filthy, and covered with cuts and sores. Nothing healed. All we ate were C-rats, which were the big racial divide out in the bush. The white guys liked peaches and pound cake and the black guys liked ham and lima beans. Other than that, we were equally miserable.

We worked all over the Highlands as far up as Chu Lai. In the south and the low-lands, with the rubber plantations and rice paddies, we usually faced the VC. In the mountains, it was NVA. The difference was that the VC would normally run and disappear, while the NVA were the aggressors and would stand and fight.

On September 26, 1967, we were on a small firebase on the edge of the A-Shau Valley. It was the second time the 101st had gone in there. The first time, we evacuated the Vietnamese out of the villages. They were resettled someplace else, which got the "civilians" out of the way. By then, my body was falling apart with sores and jungle rot. I had been in-country for ten months and twenty-six days and I had already been told I was going back to base camp the next day, where I'd stay for a couple of weeks until they sent me home.

When I was back there and was waiting to leave, one of our night patrols captured an NVA Lieutenant. After some interrogation and "persuasion," he told our guys where an NVA base camp was. Our guys wanted to follow up and go find it, but they needed an

RTO, a radio operator, to go along. I was short and didn't want any part of it, but I wasn't given a choice. We tied the NVA Lieutenant's hands and I held the rope as we went down into the valley. It was all jungle trails, until we came to a small bridge over a creek. Sure enough, we found their camp up ahead. I began to cross the bridge and pulled on the rope for him to follow; but as I stepped forward, he pulled back, and I stepped on a mine. The radio I was carrying saved my life. It and my legs took most of the blast. Surprisingly, the radio still worked, and I had the honor of calling in my own "dust-off" medevac chopper.

I was flown to one of the big EVAC Hospitals. I had damage from shrapnel in both legs, but the wounds to my left leg were so bad that it had to be amputated below the knee. I stayed there for six weeks, before I was transferred to a hospital in Japan, then to the Philippines, and finally to Fort Dix. The hospital there was so full that by Christmas I was sent home and treated out-patient for physical therapy until June, 1968, when I was finally discharged with 100% disability. They promoted me to Spec-4, but wouldn't give me a CIB, a Combat Infantryman's Badge. Even though I carried a radio and served with line infantry units, I couldn't get a CIB because my MOS, the Military Occupation Specialty or designation for the work I was trained for, was in supply. That still irritates me.

I was nineteen years of age when I was wounded and lost my leg below the knee, and twenty when I was discharged and became a civilian again. In the months that followed, neither the Army nor the VA were much help with my benefits. Eventually, I got in to see the right doctors, who diagnosed me with PTSD.

When I got out, I got married to the sister of a buddy of mine from Basic, and got my high school diploma by GED. We bought a 150-acre farm in West Virginia and raised horses, then moved to Colorado and Pennsylvania before we moved to Florida in 2014. I've had a lot of physical ailments and PTSD, but I haven't been diagnosed with any of the Agent Orange diseases. They said I was there a little early and the areas where we operated hadn't been sprayed all that much, so it was all luck. While the prosthesis on my left leg limits my physical activities, I stay active with veteran's groups, and do volunteer work with a lot of clubs and organizations.

JIM NEUSTADT'S WAR

US Army, Sergeant,
Cargo Movement Specialist and Cook,
1st Logistics Command, Cam Ranh Bay, 1967–68

I graduated from John Jay High School in Brooklyn in 1966, and enlisted in the Army. After Basic at Fort Bragg, they sent me to Fort Eustis in Virginia for Transportation School, where they taught us cargo handling for airplanes, helicopters, and boats. On January 23 of the next year, I was on my way to the port at Cam Ranh Bay. As the airplane came in to land there, I thought, "Oh my God, I'm going to spend my next twelve months here? It's going to seem like twelve years."

They had built some big floating piers, but what my unit did was unload big cargo ships directly onto smaller LARCs. That's Army talk for a "Lighter-Amphibious Resupply-Cargo." It was like a big barge with a motor. They came in different sizes, but they all had front ramps. They could ride right up onto the beach, drop the ramp, and be unloaded at Cam Ranh Bay or go on to other places nearby, like the Air Force Base a few miles to the North, the little Navy base down to the South, or the Dong Ba Tin airfield across the bay. Cam Ranh Bay was the big port that served the central coast and most of II Corps and III Corps with ammunition, gasoline, food, and everything else.

At that point in the war, everything was coming in. We had about 250 men in our company and we worked 24/7 in twelve-hour shifts unloading boats. Every few weeks we would switch shifts. That might sound easy compared to being out in the bush, but it was hot, sweaty work, and it could be dangerous too. We worked around big boats, big equipment, big cranes, and forklifts, and sometimes they didn't send us the brightest guys to operate them. We had two men killed in a forklift accident. Another time, a 2 ½ ton truck ran over someone.

What we mostly did was hook up cables and cargo nets to the pallets on board the big boat. Then the crane operator would swing the load down into the LARC where we'd unhook it. One day, someone wasn't minding one of the cables and I was knocked off into the water. I almost got crushed between the LARC and the ship. That was enough for me. I wouldn't do that anymore, so they put me up in the mess hall as a cook, which was just fine with me. I knew how to cook. It was just as hot and sweaty, but I liked it. Unfortunately, that was when I started putting on weight. Maybe I cooked too good.

To help pass the time, I joined a choir. We would sing at the hospital and up in Nha Trang, and we had the chance to sing for some Korean diplomats and some South Vietnamese government people, as well as some of the schools. That was nice.

When I got out, I had a couple of jobs and then got hired by the New York Transit Authority and worked as a clerk in Manhattan and Brooklyn for the next 29 ½ years. Now that I'm retired, I stay busy with some charities like Operation Shoebox and the DAV, veteran's groups like the VVA and our local Band of Brothers, and the Knights of Columbus.

TERRY SHERMAN'S WAR

US Navy, Petty Officer Personnel Clerk,
USS Bon Homme Richard, **CV-31, Aircraft Carrier,**
4 Deployments, 1966–67

At the beginning of my senior year of high school in Ionia, Michigan, three of us joined the Navy Reserve. By the time we graduated, the number was up to seven, and we all enlisted together on June 14, 1964. We went to Great Lakes, which was very cold that winter, but three weeks later I was in San Diego for the rest of my training. That was much better.

I was trained as a Personnel Clerk for enlisted records. I stayed in San Diego for thirteen months before being transferred to Norfolk with 200 others in October 1965, to fill out the crew of the *USS Arlington*, an old aircraft carrier that was being converted to a communications relay and intercept ship. Fortunately, it was delayed, so they shipped us back west to the *Bon Homme Richard*. It was home ported in Long Beach, and I stayed with that ship through the rest of my enlistment.

We left port for the Pacific in September, 1966 and returned at the end of June, 1967, going from Long Beach to Pearl Harbor, Yokosuka, Japan, and Subic Bay in the Philippines before going on station in the Gulf of Tonkin off North Vietnam, which we called "the Gulf of Tonkin Yacht Club." *The Bon Homme Richard* was one of the older World War II Essex Class carriers commissioned in 1944, but I really liked it. Unfortunately, as the airplanes kept getting bigger and heavier, the old carriers couldn't handle them. Soon, they would be replaced with newer ships.

I was with the Air Wing. We had a mix of F-8 Crusaders, which downed more MiGs than any other kind of plane, and A-4 Sky Hawks, which were attack jets with stubby Delta wings that fit perfectly in the old carriers. They had been refitted with newer, faster engines, and could carry a lot of bombs. We also had a squadron of old A-1 single seat propeller-driven planes, which would soon be phased out.

After we left Pearl Harbor, we were practicing air operations out at sea, when one of the new guys wasn't careful where he was walking. He stepped behind one of the jets just as it tested its afterburner. He got blown off the side of the ship and we never did find him. Another time, someone was repairing something on deck and backed into the propeller of one of the A-1s. That was terrible. You really hated to see accidental deaths like that.

Typically, we would be on station from thirty-two to thirty-six days and then rotate back to Subic Bay or Hong Kong for five to six days for leave and re-provisioning before going back out to sea again. On this trip, our deployments were off North Vietnam. The first day we were in the Gulf of Tonkin, the seas were very rough. One of the helicopters coming in to land had problems and bounced off the side of the ship. We lost four pilots from the air wing, plus the helicopter crew.

Perhaps it was because our aircraft were older, or perhaps because the North Vietnamese were shooting a lot of missiles and anti-aircraft guns at our guys, but we lost seventeen planes on that deployment, and a lot of Commanders and Lieutenant Commanders. Homer Smith, the commander of our air wing, was shot down on one of those missions. It's believed that he was captured alive and later died in captivity. One day we sent out 77 sorties, but the next day only 20 planes were airworthy enough to fly. The rest were so badly shot up that they needed major repairs.

My enlistment was over a week or so before the ship's deployment was over, so they flew me to Japan and from Japan back to California. I spent my last month at Treasure Island, across the bay from San Francisco, and was then discharged.

After I got out, I spent two years working at TRW making auto parts and then got a job with the Michigan Department of Corrections. While working full time, I also attended Michigan State University full time on the G.I. Bill and got my degree in Criminal Justice. After 35 years with the Department of Corrections, working at several state prisons, in 2005, I retired as the Warden of the Ojibway Prison on the Upper Peninsula near Lake Superior.

I consider myself fortunate to have no service-related disabilities, and like to spend my time playing golf, swimming, walking, traveling, and hanging out with veteran's groups.

BOB WESTFALL'S WAR

US Army, Spec 4 Radio Operator,
A Battery, 2nd Battalion, 20th Aerial Rocket Artillery,
1st Cav Division, I Corps, 1967–69

I grew up in Newburgh, New York, and enlisted when I was about to be drafted in October, 1966. I had a scholarship offer to Northwestern College in Kansas, but ended up attending the University of Vietnam. After basic at Fort Jackson, they trained me as a radio operator for the artillery. I arrived in country in March, 1967, and was assigned to an experimental artillery unit that was part of the 1st Cav. They hung large pods of 2.75-inch rockets under Huey helicopter gunships to provide close-in support for the infantry. Basically, I was a forward observer and would be dropped in ahead with a radio, sometimes alone, into areas where they expected to send the infantry to plan rocket strikes. The tactic was highly effective. We had the highest kill rate of any artillery unit in the Army.

I ended up spending twenty-three months doing this, and most of it was a blur. They moved us numerous times from the Central Highlands all the way north to Quang Tri, about 15 miles from the DMZ. I was in all the "fun spots"—the Ia Drang Valley, LZ X-ray, LC Albany, and almost everywhere in I Corps west of Danang. I even spent thirty-five days alone in the A-Shau Valley in a hole in the ground, under some canvas, at the bottom of "Hamburger Hill." That was as dangerous as it could get in Vietnam. I was maybe nineteen or twenty years old then. In the end, I was amazed that I didn't get killed or injured, because I was in almost continuous contact with the VC or NVA.

On November 14, I'd been in-country two months when they sent us into the I

Drang to provide fire support to the 101st Airborne and the 4th Divisions, who had run into a strong NVA regular force. That became a major battle with heavy casualties on both sides. That was where I saw what real war looked like, the devastating effects it had on people, and what was expected of me. That was when I matured quickly.

One day they dropped us off in a clearing just as the sun was coming up. We had just put our gear on the ground when we came under fire. It was obvious that this spot wasn't going to work, so we ran back to the helicopter which had not yet taken off. We got halfway there, when I remembered I had left a bag sitting on the ground that held our top-secret crypto book. I ran back, grabbed it, sprinted back to the helicopter, and dove through the door just as it lifted off. Unfortunately, the deck inside was slick from the morning dew. I slid across, out the other side, and onto the ground. I jumped up and dove back inside again, as the Crew Chief and the Door Gunner cracked up laughing.

In February, we moved up to Quang Tri. Our Commanding General was a character. He wore cowboy boots and a set of pearl-handled revolvers, like that Kilgore character in *Apocalypse Now,* and he was just as aggressive. I happened to be at the headquarters one day and witnessed a shouting match between him and Westmoreland. They were nose-to-nose and swearing at each other.

That might've been the trip when I got a speeding ticket at Quang Tri. I'll never forget that. You've got to understand, we were right up at the DMZ, and never knew when we might get shot at. I was driving like hell through some mud, when an MP Jeep chased me down with its flasher on. This guy starts writing me up, so I asked him how long he'd been in country. It hadn't even been a week. We laughed and asked him if he had any idea where he was? He gave me the ticket anyway. What a crazy war.

Most vets will recognize a Chu Hoi pamphlet. "Surrender with Peace." They were invitations for the enemy to surrender. We were in a big battle one day, when some headquarters guy showed up with cases of them and ordered us to take them up and drop them on NVA positions. We dropped them, but we got shot at the whole time. A month or so later he showed again, but this time we just pitched the boxes out the door as soon as we got out of sight.

In April, I was sent back into the A Shau Valley, but

the mountains were so high and the air so thin our helicopters couldn't come in with a full load of rockets. Instead, they sent the rockets ahead on pallets in a C-130 to LZ Stallion. A C-130 is big and slow and it could be seen coming in from a long way off. When that happened, an LZ was a dangerous place to be. The NVA would open fire with machine guns and artillery, so the Air Force would come in low and shove the pallets out the back with a drag chute.

On May 15th, my luck ran out. I kept a diary, and here's what I wrote:

"Sitting in the doorway of the Huey, I heard the whistling of incoming artillery. One landed close and the aircraft started to take off. I jumped out and I began to run. When I got to the top of a dirt pile, an artillery round landed fifty feet away and blew me up into the air. Shrapnel hit me in the chest, arm, stomach, and leg and the blast blew me down the other side of the dirt pile. Rounds were hitting all around me and I thought I was a goner. I asked for the Lord's acceptance, and had a feeling that things would work out. I got in a hole when a round landed ten feet away. I dreamt of the beauty of life and how my dream would come true, of Les and I getting married. This helped lift my spirits, but I was still scared. When things began to slow down, I crawled about seventy-five yards as fast as I could until I found a safe place. My mouth was dry, so I took a drink. Out of nowhere, I heard a scream and I looked up to see a guy falling out of the helicopter, about 100 feet up. One of the medics who later treated me told me the guy didn't make it. Finally, one of our choppers picked me up and flew me back to base camp at Quang Tri. I wasn't there long before they sent me back out in the field again."

During Tet in 1968, we hid out in a Vietnamese cemetery. Another time, the enemy artillery shells got so close that one of the rounds blew the antenna off my radio and I had to borrow one from an infantry unit. That was the second time I took shrapnel in my legs. I never did get medevaced out. A medic showed up, pulled the shrapnel out of my shin with a pair of pliers, and bandaged me up. Years later, they were still finding little pieces of steel in me.

The reason why I spent twenty-three months in country was I had extended to get an early out. On 19 June, my last day in country, I was leaving Tay Ninh in a Jeep, headed for Bien Hoa to fly home when the convoy got attacked. One of the trucks was blown up and four guys were killed. Twenty-four hours later I was home. How can anyone reconcile that?

We flew back into Oakland and I left through the San Francisco airport, where we were greeted by the usual "Berkeley Welcoming Party," screaming insults at us. There was a whole bunch of 1st Cav guys in the bar that afternoon. If the Berkeley clowns had come inside, there would've been real trouble. I did, however, have coffee with Tommy

Smothers in a restaurant. He was flying somewhere and had two big wooden swords that were props for some show he was going to. We had a friendly swordfight, and then some coffee. He said he wasn't opposed to us, but opposed to the war, as he hoped everyone would be, when the truth came out.

Anyway, I went back home to New York, went back to school, got my degree, and went to work for Verizon. For the next 35 years, I did new construction, repair, instal-lation, and finally troubleshooting for telecommunications equipment. Almost all that time I spent on the road by myself, much as I did in Vietnam, like that 35 days I spent in a hole in the ground at the foot of Hamburger Hill. I'm now 70 and retired. Now, I paint landscapes and still lifes in both oil and watercolors. Sometimes, when my wife sees me off by myself painting or reading, she wonders how I can stand to be alone. It's because I've had a lot of practice.

Other than attending some veteran's functions, I admit I've become "somewhat of a recluse." Like so many other veterans, particularly ones who lived out in the bush as long as I did, I've suffered the long-term health effects of Agent Orange, including cancer. I have a photo of the six guys who had been in my squad. Three are still alive, all with cancer and diabetes, and three are already dead.

RON WYGONIK'S WAR

**US Army, Spec 4 Tank Driver, A Battery,
5th Battalion, 2nd Artillery, 1st Infantry Division,
from Phu Loi to Cambodia, 1967–68**

I grew up in Dearborn, Michigan, near Ann Arbor. I was out of high school for a year when I got drafted in February, 1966, and sent to Fort Knox, Kentucky, for Basic and AIT. I extended for a third year to get Supply and Administration. Naturally, when I was sent to Vietnam in March, 1967, I was sent to an artillery battery of the 1st Infantry Division at Phu Loi, 26 miles north of Saigon.

I did get the supply and administration job I thought I wanted, but it turns out I didn't like that very much. I asked for something else, so they had me pouring cement pads and doing a lot of other things. One day they were looking for tank drivers, so I volunteered for that. Even though I'd been at Fort Knox, I'd never driven a tank. They took me out to this open area and had me drive one around for a half hour. That's how I became a tank driver.

Well, it wasn't really a tank. The M-48 Patton Main Battle Tank was too big and heavy for the soils in Vietnam. What I drove was an M-42 "Duster," which was an old M-41 Walker Bulldog light tank with a Bofors WW II twin-barrel, 40-millimeter anti-aircraft cannon mounted up on top, like they had on ships back then. I think the cannons were anti-aircraft weapons they took off old World War II ships, but they could put out two hundred and forty rounds a minute, and were perfect for Vietnam. That's why everybody liked to have us around, except the VC. It had some armor, so it was perfect for perimeter defense, or to go out and protect convoys. The only prob-

lem with a Duster was that it drank a lot of gas, so we couldn't run up and down the road with a truck convoy. They'd park us at trouble spots as a reaction force.

The countryside around us was flat, mostly scrub with red dirt, not thick jungle until you got further north and west. Our main job was to protect the perimeter of our Phu Loi base camp and truck convoys on Highway 1. We also spent a lot of time in Cam-bodia, and on "Search and Destroy" operations in the rubber plantations, working with the 1st Infantry, the 1st Cav, and the 11th Armored Cav Regiment, the "Black Horse".

In the field, pretty much, all we ate were C-rations. As they said, the menu always varied. We either had pork and chicken, or chicken and pork. We'd heat it with a little sliver of C4, but the can got real hot, and you had to be careful. We were almost never in our Phu Loi base camp. When we were, I became friends with the cook. He made good doughnuts.

In the M-48, the driver sat up front. The rest of the crew was behind me and the gunner was up top, with thick armor plate around the cannons. Driving it was easy, but you learned to stay in the middle of the road to avoid mines, which the VC usually planted along the sides. The driver didn't have much visibility, so I learned to line up one of the hinges on the right side of the front hatch with the edge of pavement, and that would put me right down the middle of the road. I remember the first time I drove through a village. The street was narrow, and I hadn't quite figured out how to stay in the center of the road. I was driving along, almost halfway through town, when the Sergeant up top started hitting me on the head and shouting for me to stop. There had been big rolls of concertina wire laid alongside the road. I had snagged some of it on the track and was dragging a whole bunch of barbed wire behind us through town. We got out and it took us quite a while to cut it all free.

We never hit a mine while I was driving; but we had that stupid Sergeant, who thought he knew everything. One day he insisted on driving. I kept telling him to stay in the middle of the road, but he didn't, and sure enough he hit a mine. That blew a track off and put us down for almost a month for repairs.

It was a crazy war. One of my friends was killed in base camp when he was fixing the torsion bar on a track. We heard this explosion. Somehow a hand grenade had come loose, exploded, and killed him. That was just the way it was over there—all luck.

On January 30, 1968, we were out on a search and destroy operation when the North

Vietnamese attacked. That was the beginning of Tet. Our base camp at Phu Loi was hit, so they called us back to reinforce the perimeter. As soon as we arrived with the "Dusters," the attack stopped. I don't think they wanted to take us on.

My tour was over, and I rotated back to Fort Campbell the next month, into a job in my original supply MOS. When I was discharged, I went back home and got a job with General Motors as a set-up man in the gear division of their Willow Run plant. We made the Hydramatic transmission, and I retired 37 ½ years later. I now spend my time in the color guard of the local VVA Chapter, and on its Board of Directors.

ALAN WILENKIN'S WAR

US Army, Infantry Sergeant,
5st Battalion of the 7th Cav, 1st Cavalry Division,
An Khe, 1967–68

I never thought I'd live through my 21st birthday. It was February 16, 1968, two weeks into the Tet Offensive. We were dug in outside Hue in the toughest battle we'd faced since I got there. We were trying to retake the city, and getting shot at from all sides. Someone told me there were two battered US Marine Corps battalions, eleven South Vietnamese ARVN battalions, some of the 101st, and our two battalions from the 1st Cav surrounding the city, going toe to toe with the 10 NVA and VC Battalions inside. I'd been in Vietnam for eleven months when Tet hit. It was the worst, but only one of many battles we fought during my tour.

We were 100 miles to the south in a serious fight of our own, when we were told to mount up; they were flying us to Hue. The NVA had grabbed the old city and the Citadel, were well-armed and dug in, and stuff was flying everywhere. Most of our hardest fighting was outside the city, in the suburbs. By the time we fought our way inside, it was pretty much a mop up. Except for a few snipers, most of the NVA and VC were dead or had run away.

The Marines were the ones who really had it the toughest, though. They were sent in as soon as the NVA attacked on January 30th, during what was supposed to be a Tet truce. The Marines are light infantry to begin with, and the Pentagon wouldn't let them use artillery or bombs inside the city, because both Hue and the Citadel were ancient national shrines. Nobody wanted to destroy them. The NVA knew that, and took advantage of it. They massacred a lot of civilians and didn't give a damn what happened to the city. Without artillery or air power, the Marines lost a lot of men that first week or two. Finally, the Pentagon turned loose the big guns, the fighter bombers from the carriers and Danang, and the B-52s. They leveled the old city and the Citadel, and some of the rounds came damn close to where we were. All we could do was dig deeper and keep our heads down. When we finally got inside, there were so many bodies and body parts lying around that they were using front-end loaders to push them into mass graves. The brass wouldn't let the UPI reporters inside the city until that was finished. They said it was because there were too many snipers around; but the truth was, they didn't want that kind of publicity.

I grew up near Ellenville, east of Liberty, New York, in the "Borscht Belt." I got drafted in October, 1966, right out of high school. They sent me to Fort Jackson, South Carolina, where I became an 11-B, an infantry rifleman, or "11-Bush," as we called it. Naturally, they sent me right over. Six months later, in March, 1967, I was at An Khe in the 5th Battalion of the 7th Cav in the 1st Cav Division. I say I was at An Khe, but I only saw the place twice. The rest of the time we were in the field. My battalion had come over as a unit from Fort Carson, Colorado, the August before. They were a pretty tight group and I was one of the first replacements. As the unit went from original members to all replacements, it completely changed.

The Cav was the first air-mobile division, so they sent us all over the place. We were mostly in the Central Highlands from Bon Son to Pleiku, Kontum, and all the way up to the DMZ, along the Cambodian border, and in the A-Shau Valley. We did air assaults all the time, into one LZ or another. I slept on the ground, slogged through triple-canopy jungle, up and down steep hills, and did sweeps through villages. We ate nothing but C-rations, and drank filthy rice-paddy water. They could never supply us with enough water, so we drank the water from the rice paddies and dropped in a couple of iodine pills. Do that month after month, and it really screws up your thyroid gland and didn't do much to prevent Dengue Fever, which I ended up catching. That's what I did for 365 days.

For the first six months I was there, we operated below Quang Tri. I remember Friday, October 13. We were doing a sweep, approaching the village through a rice paddy and I saw a six-inch-wide plastic pipe sticking up a couple of inches above the water. A couple of us rocked it back and forth, twisted it, and pulled it out. Suddenly, it was like pulling the plug in a bath tub. A big hole opened, and half the rice paddy suddenly ran down into the hole. It must have been an air tube from a cave or tunnel under the paddy and we had just flooded it. Further on, we found a lot of NVA in bunkers. One of my friends caught a bullet in the head. It didn't kill him, but he spent a lot of time in the hospital. We blew the hell out of that place.

Later, when we were up north on another sweep, my friend Ed and I took a break. We went to the top of a hill and were sitting on some rocks having a smoke. Really stupid. We were talking, and as Ed raised his hand to his helmet, an NVA sniper's bullet went right between us. It ricocheted off his helmet and took off the tip of his right index finger. We hit the dirt and low-crawled out of there. He got medevaced out. It was his trigger finger, so he never came back. Not a bad trade.

One night, our company had dug-in in the "Ti-Ti" woods south of Hue. It was raining, and our stupid Captain had us dig in on a direct line between our artillery and the area we would sweep through in the morning. You could hear the rounds going over us, and I told him that wasn't a good idea. Back then, the gun-powder bags the artillery used were silk. When they got wet, they didn't burn right, and you could easily get a "short" round. Sure enough, I heard one coming right at us and yelled for everyone to get down just before it hit.

We often worked with the ROKs, the South Korean Marines. They were tough and nasty. The US provided them with Korean food—green bags of rice, fish heads, and Kimchi. They loved it, but it really stunk. One time, I saw one of their officers find a guy sleeping on guard duty. He just pulled out his .45 and shot him dead on the spot. I asked him why he didn't kick him or something and wake him up? He said this way, the next guy wouldn't fall asleep. That was how they operated. They never took any prisoners and never let Vietnamese inside their compounds. They thought we were the ones who were stupid.

After I got out of the Army, I got a job with the New York State Department of Corrections, working as a corrections officer mostly at the Eastern Corrections Facility in Ulster County. It was a Maximum-Security Prison with about one thousand prisoners inside. I retired from Corrections after thirty-five years. In 1977, I joined the Army Reserves, the 854th Engineers. They kept going places like Fort Drum, in the winter, which was crazy, so I switched to the Navy Seabees and retired as an E-6 twenty-five years later. I'm now 70 and retired to Florida. In addition to two badly damaged discs in my back from falling out of a helicopter, I've been diagnosed with various Agent Orange-related disabilities, PTSD, malaria, and dengue fever.

BOB PISONNEAULT'S WAR

US Air Force, Senior Airman E-4,
37th Security Police Squadron,
Phu Cat, 1967–68

I spent my year in Vietnam as an Air Force Security Policeman at Phu Cat Air Force Base. Security Police? I was on the night shift, guarding the base perimeter, and it felt like I was in the Infantry. We spent our nights in bunkers, up in guard towers, patrolling inside the perimeter, or patrolling outside in the bush. As I said, like the Infantry.

Phu Cat was located twenty miles Northwest of Qui Nhon near the coast in Bin Dinh Province. That area was flat and wide open, with scrubby underbrush. It was dry and dusty in the summer and wet and muddy in the winter. Outside the base there were rice paddies with water buffalo, farm fields, and Buddhist temples, and vendors along the side of the road who made sandals and anything else they could sell us.

I grew up in Pittsfield in western Massachusetts and enlisted in the Air Force in March, 1966, after one year of college in Kansas. I volunteered to go to Vietnam. I must admit it had its moments, but I'm glad I went. I grew up quick over there. The first day I arrived, I was walking to the armory to be issued my weapons when I passed a line of VC bodies in open body bags lying along the side of the road. I'd never even seen a body bag before, much less a body or a line of them. Each had a bullet hole in its forehead. I was told that was compliments of the South Koreans. The ROKs planned to take the body bags out to the village in the morning, dump them on the ground, and see who would pick them up. No one did, but by the next morning the bodies had all disappeared.

Another day, I saw a VC who had been caught in the wire. He was naked, hand-cuffed to a flagpole by the headquarters building, covered with axle grease, and had a rope tied around his neck like a scarf. The axle grease was to help him slip through the

120

wire and confuse the dogs. The rope was so the other VC could pull him back and hide his body if he got killed.

The Phu Cat airbase was new. It had been built the year before I got there, and the full 10,000-foot runway opened the month I arrived. We had four squadrons of F-100 Super-Sabre fighter-bombers, four AC-47 "Spookie" gunships, and a bunch of other aircraft based there. The F-100s were replaced by F-4 Phantoms right after I left, but they flew more missions than any other jets during the war. We had new, two-story wooden barracks, an NCO and Officer's club, mess halls, paved roads, grass, even palm trees, so it wasn't bad duty.

When the base was built the previous autumn, a ROK battalion protected the contractors. They lost three men doing that, and didn't take it kindly. One day they captured a VC outside the perimeter and questioned him. He wouldn't talk, so they took him up in a helicopter and threw him out. When they landed, he was still alive; but he still wouldn't talk. I saw them take him back up and throw him out again, from a higher elevation this time. They were tough.

As a Sergeant and squad leader, I worked nights and slept days, so there wasn't much time to do anything else. Other than the body bags on my first day, the guy handcuffed to the pole, and VC tossed out of a helicopter, I didn't see a whole lot of action. A couple of times, we went into Qui Nhon and hit the bars and the beach; and I got to take a nice R&R to Taiwan. Mostly, though, I stayed in the barracks and didn't spend much time outside the base.

When I was on perimeter duty, I spent several nights outside the fence sleeping on one of the APCs. We would park them out there as a deterrent, but there was nothing going on. Every now and then we would go on alert when a flare was tripped, but that was mostly water buffalo wandering around the rice paddies. Besides, we had F-100s taking off and landing all night long. The whole North Vietnamese Army could have been marching around out there and we wouldn't have heard a thing anyway.

The Bob Hope show came to Phu Cat around Christmas, which was a very big deal. They invited in troops from all over the area, and our security guard company was on duty the whole time. I remember looking up and seeing a Huey come over that had a sign on its side that read "Merry Christmas." As it got close, flying over some rice paddies, one of its rotor blades flew off. It started spinning, and guys jumped out or were thrown out. The helicopter crashed, but most of the guys landed in the water and mud, cushioning their fall. Those who weren't too badly hurt were brought to the show anyway, but we were stuck guarding that chopper all night until the maintenance unit could come and haul it away.

At the end of January, I was lucky enough to go on R&R just as the Tet Offensive started. The VC and NVA had already attacked Qui Nhon in the days before; and if the full extent of Tet had been known, they'd have never let me leave. No one knew that when I left, though. The VC came in and blew up the ammo dump, but the Air Force had just moved most of it to a new location. The destruction would've been much worse if they knew that. But my R&R in Taiwan was great. When I was due to come back, the base was still receiving mortar and rocket fire, so they wouldn't let me return for two extra days.

I stayed in Vietnam two more months, for a total of exactly twelve. I came home in March, 1968, spent a year at Griffiss Air Force Base in New York State in the Security Police, and was discharged two years later, in March, 1970. I went back to Pittsfield and did some construction work before getting a job as a security guard with General Electric. After that, I went to work as a Court Officer in Pittsfield providing security for the local District Court, and stayed there until I retired eight years ago.

I'm 70, but I stay very active playing softball, kayaking, walking, hiking, biking, and playing golf. Other than a loss of hearing, I have no other serious service-related disabilities.

ED LAWHON'S WAR

US Army, Captain, 3rd Brigade,
4th Infantry and 25th Infantry Divisions,
Maintenance Companies,
Dau Tieng and Cambodian Border, 1967–68

I grew up as an Army brat, and traveled around the world as my father's assignments took him to various places, including Japan and Libya, where I graduated from high school. I attended Ouachita Baptist College in Arkansas, graduated from ROTC, was commissioned a second lieutenant, and went on active duty in May, 1963. All of this was before Vietnam blew up.

I was in the Ordnance Corps, which repairs and maintains equipment, and my first assignment was in Korea for two years. I had commanded two different maintenance companies, and had made captain by the time I arrived in Vietnam in April, 1967, assigned to the 4th Infantry Division. When the new 25th Infantry Division arrived, they reorganized, and my brigade was switched to the 25th and one of their brigades was switched to the 4th. Except for changing shoulder patches, it didn't alter what we did. I commanded a maintenance company, an S&P truck company, and a refueling point, among other things, near Dau Tieng, between Saigon and the Cambodian border. It was located at the foot of the mountains in an area that had once been the large Michelin rubber plantation. That was where the NVA infiltration routes came out of Cambodia.

I flew to Vietnam through Travis Air Force Base in California with another captain. When we arrived at Long Binh, they told us we were both being assigned to the 25th Infantry Division, since they were short on captains; and to wait out at the helipad, because there would be a helicopter coming to pick us up. When it arrived, only one seat was open, so I told the other guy to go ahead and I'd take the next one. I arrived twenty minutes after he did. He got assigned to Saigon as a liaison with the headquarters and lived in an air-conditioned hotel, while I ended up in the bush on the Cambodian border. Sometimes it doesn't pay to be polite.

The area we operated in that whole year had steep mountains, thick jungle, a few rubber plan-tations, scrub forest, and rice paddies scattered around on the flatland below. It was very difficult country to try to get around in on foot. In the hills, on the muddy trails, you couldn't get any traction. In a column, the fourth guy would slip and slide, and it was impossible for the ones after him. I later served in Nicaragua, and it was the same down there.

When we went back to base camp, the NVA would shoot rockets at us from time to time. One night, a mortar round landed against the building outside my hooch and blew a hole in the wall right behind my desk. Another night I won't for-

get was when we came under attack. I was hunkered down in the bunker just outside my bunk, certain that the next round was going to come right in there on top of me. The bunker had a big opening at the top, and I couldn't see how they could miss.

Every unit at Dau Tieng took their turn going out on patrol. When it was our turn, I had maybe seventeen guys, all maintenance and supply clerks. We geared up with rifles, machine guns, claymores, over-and-unders, radios, ammunition, and everything else. The rule was, if you could stand up, you weren't carrying enough.

When we went out beyond the perimeter at night, the jungle came alive. It was very dark under triple-canopy jungle, and you can't see a thing when you're walking point. You're always walking into spider webs, and you don't know if there's a big one in there waiting for you. When you finally do reach a spot to set up an ambush, the rule was to walk past it and then loop back around before you set up. And when you lay down on the ground, you don't know if you're on top of an ant hill or if there's some snake nearby. I carried a starlight scope, so I could see a little bit in the dark, but it was pitch black.

When we were lying in our foxholes inside our perimeter at night, we told our machine gunners not to shoot unless they really had a target, because our tracers would give away our positions. The NVA used them too, so if a fire fight started, there would be ribbons of red and orange going out and green ones coming in. One time I had an RPG fly right past my head. It probably wasn't all that close, but I sure thought it was at the time. Once our position was exposed, we had to get up and relocate to secondary positions quickly before the NVA zeroed in on us. I put tracer rounds in my .45, and I'd use those to mark the targets. The joke among the guys became, "Don't shoot there, wait until you hear them laughing."

Another thing I remember, was what was called the "90-day letter." When a guy's wife or girlfriend back home decided to leave him, she'd write him a letter, ninety days before he was due to come home, while he was still in Vietnam, rather than face him later.

My maintenance company supported one of the mechanized infantry battalions. They had M-113 personnel carriers, M-48 tanks, and vehicles like that. In January, 1968, we knew something was up because intelligence reported that the NVA and VC were buying a lot of rice bags. They'd lay them over the barbed wire when they attacked. Sure enough, as soon as the Tet Offensive began, we were hit hard. We were in the rubber plantation then and the fighting went on for two weeks. With all those rows of trees and underbrush, it was very easy for them to move around without being seen. When the fighting was finally over, there were places around our perimeter where there were so many NVA bodies that we had to bring in a tank retriever—that's a bulldozer with a big blade in front—to push them back from the barbed wire. They were then stacked in a big pile in an open area and burned with napalm. By that time, I was so exhausted I couldn't sleep. My battalion commander finally told the medics to give me one of the "little red pills" they had to make you sleep. They should've told me to have my head on the pillow before I took it, because I was out like a light. Guys would come in and out of the hooch, but I was lying there with no idea what was going on.

After my tour was over and I rotated out, I remained on active duty until 1975. I was promoted to Major and moved into intelligence work for what had to be the NSA and some other people. Eventually I ended up in Nicaragua as the unrest there unfolded. That pretty much ended my career after the things that happened down there. I joined the Army reserves in 1975, and stayed in until 1991, retiring as a Lieutenant Colonel.

I'm now 75. During my twenty-nine years on active duty and in the reserves, I received the Bronze Star, Army Commendation Medal, and other commendations for my service in Vietnam. I stay very active in the color guard for Chapter 1036 of the Vietnam Veterans of America, the largest VVA Chapter in Florida, and the 9th largest in the country. Our color guard participates in dozens of flag ceremonies each year.

ANGELO FIORENTINO'S WAR

**US Army Corporal, C Company,
2nd Battalion, 3nd Infantry,
199th Light Infantry Brigade,
Long Binh, 1967–68**

I graduated from Flushing High School in Queens and tried college for a year or two, but got drafted. They sent me to Fort Gordon for Basic and then Fort Jackson for Infantry AIT and Jungle School, coming out an 11-B Rifleman. I was on orders for Korea until I got pneumonia in AIT. By the time I got out of the hospital and recycled, they were sending the next batch to Vietnam. That was how I ended up in the 3rd Regiment of the 199th Light Infantry Brigade in April, 1967.

We were a specialized, three-battalion, air-mobile infantry unit based at Long Binh, kind of a "fire brigade" for the Saigon area. We worked the jungle to the north and east, the rubber plantations to the north and west, and the rice paddies and Delta to the west and south, and even in the city itself during Tet, but always around Saigon. That meant we fought the VC in the south and the NVA in the north. I spent the whole year jumping on and off helicopters at one LZ or another, and I never had a clue where I was.

The entire 199th had been shipped over to Vietnam by boat before I arrived, and I was the first individual replacement. All the other guys had trained and been fighting together for months, so I was the new guy. The day I arrived, the First Sergeant sent me out on a patrol. "Throw him in the mud," he said. I had no idea what that meant until we began a sweep through some rice paddies. It was spring. I was carrying a full pack, and the thick, muddy water was waist-and chest-high at times. It was like

trying to hike through deep snow. I think I got a hundred yards before I passed out from heat exhaustion. They dragged me out and gave me a couple of IVs. The other guys were all laughing, because it had happened to them, too. I guess that was my initiation to the club.

I started out carrying an M-16, but it kept jamming, so I found an M-79 grenade launcher. It's like a short shotgun, but it shoots high explosives or a "beehive" round that's like a gigantic shotgun shell. I loved it. I wore a vest that held the shells plus six hand grenades. I didn't like the Army .45, so I bought an "unofficial" snub-nose .38 off a guy and carried that. Because we were the machine gun squad, our section had to divide up the machine gun, the tripod, the baseplate, and several belts of machine gun ammo, which is what I took, slung around my neck. That was in addition to my own pack, water, food, bullets, and all the rest.

We would always find sniper pits and tunnels when we found a VC or NVA base camp. Because I was the smallest guy in the company, I always got picked to be the "tunnel rat" to search them. When I did, the .38 was a much better choice down there. We'd roll some hand grenades in, and after the smoke and dust cleared, I'd be sent in with a flashlight and my .38 to see what I could find. Usually it wasn't much, but one time I found five Chinese rifles. I'd never seen any of those before.

We were out in the field all the time, patrolling during the day and setting up ambushes at night. Sometimes we'd ambush them, and sometimes they'd ambush us, but we were in combat all the time. We would put out Claymores, post guards, and wait. We had night vision scopes. If we saw movement ahead of us, we'd open up on it and check it out in the morning. One time we went out and found dead NVA soldiers and a huge Chinese version of a Claymore. If they'd set that thing off, we'd have been in big trouble.

Several times, we worked with the Australian Army. They had a couple of battalions that operated south and east of Saigon, their SAS commandos, mechanized infantry, and even some tanks. They were the best—professional, crack infantry, and a lot of fun to be with.

We were out on Operation Uniontown, another large sweep, when the Tet Offensive began. At 2:00 a.m., we heard a lot of explosions, stuff we'd never heard before. They were Russian 122-mm rockets aimed at Bien Hoa, one of which blew the hell out of our helicopter pad. They pulled us back to defend Long Binh and we ended up in a battle with a dug-in NVA unit. When we finally took their positions, they were all dead, chained together in their trenches. I also thought some of them were not Vietnamese.

They were too big and did not have the same facial features as the Vietnamese. They looked Chinese to me, but nobody wanted to hear that.

The next day, we were walking on a railroad track when the VC blew up the ammo dump in Long Binh. The explosion was so powerful, it knocked me down; and we were nowhere close to it. We all saw a huge mushroom cloud rising in the sky, and a lot of guys thought the VC had set off a nuke. Later, they picked us up and rushed us to Bien Hoa, where the VC 275th Regiment was overrunning the Air Force Base. It was touch and go. We landed on the edge of the runway and had no trenches or bunkers. All we could do was drop to the ground and start shooting, but we finally stopped them.

After that, they asked for volunteers to go into Saigon, where there was fighting everywhere. I decided to go, because I figured it was the only way I'd ever get to see the city. Some of our guys were going house to house in Cholon, the Chinese quarter. I ended up on the roof of a hotel with my machine gun squad, manning a .50-caliber. I loved that! There was a 7:00 p.m. curfew in the city. Our orders were to shoot anything that moved after that. Later, a VW Beetle came driving down the street toward us. I opened up on it with the .50 and blew it to pieces. We stayed in Saigon for five or six days before they pulled us out.

I consider my time in Vietnam to have been pure hell. I didn't have a good time in the service to begin with, and when you're in the infantry you never have a good day, especially in those conditions. The worst day of all was the first time one of the guys in my unit was killed. I threw up. After a while, you'd think you'd get used to it, but I never did.

My father became very ill in March, 1968, and passed away. I was given a compassionate leave to go home and because I already had eleven months in-country, they didn't make me go back. I was assigned to be a Drill Sergeant at Fort Dix and was discharged the next November.

I returned to New York, worked at Pitney Bowes for a while, and then in furniture sales and management. In 2005, I retired. I have since been diagnosed with PTSD and with a Leukemia-like form of blood cancer, but I still try to play golf and attend veteran's meetings.

RON IRWIN'S WAR

US Army Specialist 4th Class Clerk Typist,
MAC-V Headquarters,
Cholon, Saigon 1967

On April 2, 1967, I arrived in Vietnam and my Vietnam War lasted exactly fifteen days, at least the in-country part did; but its effects continue to bother me, even today. I was assigned as a clerk typist at the Headquarters of the Military Assistance Command, or MAC-V, with some other Americans who were advising the Vietnamese Army, the ARVN. We were located in a small Vietnamese Army post in Saigon and were billeted a short distance away in a hotel in the Cholon district. The hotel is still there. It's now called the Coliseum Hotel, but it was more like a cheap American Brand X motel back then. It didn't have a restaurant or any other facilities, and there was no mess hall in the South Vietnamese compound either. For lunch, we would usually leave the compound and walk down the street to the USO. They had hot dogs and hamburgers. For dinner, we would take a taxi into Saigon where there were some clubs and other places where we ate.

I grew up in Vandergriff, Pennsylvania, a steel mill town, twenty-five miles northeast of Pittsburgh; but my family moved to Hershey, where I finished high school in 1964. I enlisted in the Army in December, 1965, rather than be drafted. After Basic Training at Fort Gordon, Georgia, I was sent to Fort Jackson, South Carolina, where I was trained as clerk typist.

Saigon wasn't a particularly safe place back then, as I soon found out. When we went out walking, we learned you never stopped, even at a street corner. You kept moving. One day we were having dinner in a hotel and we saw a helicopter attack taking place in the city. The VC had apparently attacked a police station, and the ARVN were firing machine guns with tracer rounds, which you could see streak across the sky. That was followed by an explosion big enough to shake the water glasses on our table. There was a small American Country and Western band playing, and they would flinch and jump every time something went off, probably wondering who got them this booking. The hotel food was okay, but the funny thing was, my stay in country was so short that I never had a chance to eat any Vietnamese food until I got back home.

There were usually fifteen or twenty of us staying at the hotel, and every morning at 6:00 am a bus would pick us up at our hotel and drive us to the ARVN compound. It was a Vietnamese driver. The hotel had a chain-link fence around the outside with big rolls of barbed wire on top, and a front gate on the street. That was where we caught the bus. On April 17, my second week on the job, we were standing at the curb and saw the bus coming down the street towards us. This was one of those moments in life when things slow down, and you see an event unfold one frame at a time for the rest of your life. For no apparent reason, the bus stopped about 100 yards short of the hotel. Some of our guys began yelling at the driver, and waving for him to come the rest of the way. Meanwhile, I turned my head and saw two Vietnamese men pushing a motor bike past us on the other side of the street. That was when I felt something hit me in the foot. I glanced down and saw what looked like a soup can with a fuse, just as it exploded.

The MPs later told me it was a Russian hand grenade, and the two Vietnamese on the motor bike had thrown two or three of them at us. Thirteen of our guys were wound-ed and three killed, but the MPs said we were lucky. If they had thrown American hand grenades, we would have all been killed.

We were taken to the 3rd Field Hospital in Saigon, which wasn't very far away. I had taken a lot of shrapnel in my legs, in both knees, and in my left side. It also blew my glasses off. For the next month, I was in a cast from my waist down. Everyone was very nice there. Even the Colonel I worked for would stop by every few days and drop off cigarettes and stuff for me. When they finally took the cast off, I was sent to the 249th General Hospital in Osaka, Japan for rehab. When I could walk, one of my tasks was to push other vets around who were in wheelchairs. I stayed there for about six weeks more, until late June, when I was flown to the Valley Forge VA hospital near Philadelphia. By that time, I could walk, but I remained there until the end of October continuing with the rehab. All in all, I was in Vietnam for two weeks and various hospitals for the next six months.

When I was in the hospital in Saigon, two young Vietnamese girls were brought in. One was only three or four years old. One day I noticed her bed was empty and I asked the nurse where the little girl was. She had died. Apparently, she had inhaled Napalm fumes from a bomb, and had serious damage to her lungs. That one has always stuck with me.

I still had over a year left on my enlistment, so I was assigned to be a clerk at Fort Monroe, Virginia, which was a big headquarters back then, but now it's a museum. In November, 1968, I was discharged and went back home to Hershey. After trying several jobs around town, in 1977 I got a job with Roadway Express and drove a truck for the next twenty-eight years, until I retired in 2005.

The damage to my knees kept bothering me and by 2007 I had them both replaced. I also had my left hip replaced in 2012, which the orthopedic surgeon said was a result of favoring one leg, and the shrapnel wounds in my upper thigh. I'm still fighting the VA over compensation for that one.

My Vietnam service was rather strange. Because I was only in country for two weeks, I never served in an American unit and have no division or battalion or company affiliation to identify with, I feel kind of alienated or isolated. On top of everything else, I was only a Spec 4 at the time. Most of the guys who worked at MAC-V were officers or senior NCOs; so, the only Army friends I had were the guys I knew from Basic.

I'm 70 years old and retired now. I like to play golf, and I'm active in the Vietnam Veterans of America as a member of their color guard and managing the chapter store.

MARC MEYER'S WAR

US Navy, E-5 and Corpsman,
Sangley Point NAS in the Philippines
and Khe Sanh, 1967–68

Marc
Navy
'68-'69
HM1 FMF

I grew up in Brooklyn. I did a couple of years of college after high school, but I mostly screwed around and didn't take it all that seriously. The draft was breathing down my neck, so in March, 1966, I enlisted in the Navy. I scored high on all their standardized tests, and they wanted me to become a radio operator. I thought that would be boring as hell, so I volunteered to be a Corpsman. After Boot Camp, that school was full, so they sent me out to the fleet for a cruise on the *USS Canberra*, an old World War II cruiser. Eventually some slots opened, and they sent me to "Corps" school in San Diego.

After that, I was sent to the Philippines, where the Navy had a huge presence. For the first ten months, I was stationed at the hospital at Sangley Point Naval Air Station at Cavite, across the bay from Manila, flying on medevac casualty flights back and forth to Vietnam. Navy and Marine Corps casualties came to Sangley Point, while Army casualties usually went to Tokyo. Mostly we transported Marines from the EVAC hospital at Danang, where they'd already had emergency treatment and were stabilized. The way the system worked was I'd get a phone call in the late afternoon to be on the flight line at 0700 the next morning. That meant you were going out on an Air Evac flight to pick up wounded. Sometimes we went on a C-41 and sometimes it was a C-130, which was noisy as hell. Those medevac flights weren't all that safe. One time, we got hit with gunfire going in and I got shrapnel in my shoulder. It wasn't cool getting wounded going to pick up wounded.

While we handled a lot of casualties from combat, we also handled a lot from accidents and injuries, especially from the aircraft carrier flight decks. Those were very dangerous places to work. By its nature, the job I performed required me to have a top-secret security clearance, so that I could communicate with the patients and the ships and units they came from.

Toward the end of my tour at Sangley Point, I was sent to the Marine firebase at Khe Sanh where they were running short of medics. The big siege was winding down, but we came under heavy mortar and artillery fire every night. As soon as the first round came in, we'd spend the rest of the night in the bunkers. They were horrible places —dark, damp, filthy, and smelly. However, no matter how bad things got, you could always find something amusing. There was this one Marine who was a total, avowed atheist, but you remember that old line from World War I or World War II that there were never any atheists in a foxhole. Well, one night, the hill was really getting pounded. I look over, and there he is down on his knees, his hands clasped together, praying, "God, if you get me out  of this, I swear I'll never say another bad thing about you!" Sure enough, after that, I saw him going to church.

From the Khe Sanh firebase, they would send us out on medevac helicopter flights to pick up wounded guys in the bush. When you paint a white square with the Red Cross on the side of a Huey, you become a big target. The helicopter I was in got shot down twice. I've got to say, though, it's a great feeling to crash, look up, and see a couple of heavily armed gunships flying cover, and protecting you.

One day, I was told to get on a helicopter and help pick up a downed pilot. We had a torpedo-like thing with a seat called a Jungle Penetrator. They had lowered it down through the jungle on a steel wire, but the pilot was too injured to be able to get in it. I had them haul it back up, I got on, and rode it down. There were enemy all around, so I dragged him into the torpedo, jumped on top, and hung onto the cable for dear life as they hauled us both back.

Unfortunately, Corpsmen aren't supposed to leave the helicopter, and the aircrews file reports on the missions they go out on. Sure enough, somebody snitched. A couple of days later I got called into the XO's office and told I was being put up on charges for doing that. He was a tough Marine Lieutenant Colonel, and he looked at me and asked, "Doc, what the hell were you thinking?" I shrugged and told him, "Colonel, you spent hundreds of thousands of dollars to train that pilot, and my job is to save lives." He stared at me for a minute and looked at his watch. It was 11:45, so he says, "Okay, let's go have lunch," and took me to the Officer's Mess. On the way he asks, "If I let you off, you gonna go do something like that again?" I smiled and said, "Yeah, Colonel, you'll probably be talking to me again. I'm no hero, but it's my job. Besides, sometimes you just react; you don't think." The next week he called me back to his office and they awarded me a Bronze Star.

I spent my last eight months in the Philippines at Clark Air Force Base as the Navy liaison with the Air Force on casualty flights. As part of that assignment, I wrote some of the policies and procedures for the plan on how to handle returning US POWs. That was what they used when the POWs came back from Hanoi four years later, in 1973. I remember watching that on the news, seeing the film coverage, and pointing at the screen, saying, "I wrote that!"

When I was finally discharged in December, 1969, I went back to school and got a degree in Respiratory Therapy. I may have screwed around before I went in the service, but I had a 3.7 grade average when I went back the second time. In physiology, I hate to say that I knew the human body parts cold, but I did. With my combat experience, I had seen most of them up close and personal, as they say. That's why everyone in the class hated me. I set the curve. When the final exam came around, the rest of the class took seats and squeezed in as close as they could get to me. The Professor came in, smiled, and asked if everyone was sitting where they wanted to be. When they all nodded yes, he told me to get up and move over by the window.

I went to work for the New York City Fire Department and stayed with them for the next twenty-two years. After that, I did Respiratory and Inhalation Therapy in a variety of hospitals in New York, and subsequently in Ohio for another eighteen years. Like a lot of guys, I've tested positive for Agent Orange, have Type II Diabetes, and vascular and heart disease. Some of that I probably got out in the jungle around Khe Sanh, but I was also exposed from the residue all over the uniforms of the casualties we treated. I'm retired now, and I like to play golf and participate in a lot of veteran's activities.

JIMMY HILL'S WAR

**US Army, Specialist 4th Class,
MAC-V Advisor Teams 21 and 22,
Kontum Province, Two Tours,
1967–68 and 1970–71**

After I graduated from high school in Columbus, Georgia, in 1965, I knew my number was coming up in the draft; so, I enlisted in the Army. That began my twenty-two-year career as an Infantry NCO, retiring as a Master Sergeant in 1987. I did both Basic and AIT at Fort Polk, Louisiana, the one post everyone in the Army hated. But instead of being sent straight to Vietnam, I was selected to be a member of A company of the 3rd Infantry Regiment, "The Old Guard." That's the precision drill team that performs at the funerals at Arlington National Cemetery, complete with twenty-one-gun salutes. It's a very difficult unit to get into and a great honor to be selected. I spent eighteen months there, but it was not easy duty. We wore formal dress blue uniforms, and drilled and practiced five hours a day, even in the heat of the Washington, DC summers. We also guarded the Tomb of the Unknown Soldier. I applied for a slot on the Tomb detail, but my orders to Vietnam came through first.

I arrived there for my first tour in May, 1967 and was assigned to Military Assistance Command Team 21. We were advisors in the Central Highlands, close to the Laotian border, working with a Special Forces B team and an ARVN battalion. But most of our time was spent up in the mountains working with village militias to protect the rice crop. There was a captain, me, an interpreter, and a few others in the team. I was the Spec-4 radioman and provided security. We had frequent skirmishes with small VC units. Being the radio operator, I heard a lot and knew a lot more about what was going on than an ordinary soldier might.

That area of Kontum Province along the Laotian border was mostly mountains. We would be out in the field for three to ten days at a time, working out of Special Forces

Camps and small firebases. Only rarely did we get to a larger base for a hot meal or a hot shower. What we did get was a lot of leeches and mosquitoes. Dehydration was always a problem, and clean water very hard to come by. We ate with the Vietnamese quite often, especially when meeting with village elders up in the mountains. You ate what they ate, dipping small bowls into their communal pot. The trick was to never look inside and see what was in there, because they ate almost anything. I spoke no Vietnamese when I got over there, but I picked up enough to get by, with the usual pidgin English. One thing the villagers taught me to like was rice wine, which was very powerful stuff. The other thing was to never forget that while we owned the people during the day, the VC owned them at night.

I had been in country for nine months when the Tet Offensive hit at the end of January, 1968. Up until then, we had only been fighting small bands of VC. But during Tet we were up against main force NVA, and we continued to see NVA along with the VC after that. There was a Special Forces A Team on the other side of our compound. One night they were almost overrun, and called in a "Spookie," with its four miniguns to provide close air support. They would circle a target and drop flares while the mini-guns fired, putting out 300 rounds per second, which was enough to put a bullet in every square foot of a football field in ten seconds. Every fifth bullet was a red tracer, and when they cut loose, it looked like four garden hoses spraying red water. Even still, that ended up a seven-day battle. When it was over, there were over six hundred dead NVA lying outside the compound. We searched their packs, looking for documents, and were surprised by how much drugs and narcotics they were carrying. We also accompanied the ARVNs in the big Junction City #1 and #2 battles in the central Highlands, and in the attack on the Plei Mei Special Forces camp nearby.

At one point, I volunteered to be an aerial observer in one of the Bird Dog spotter planes up in the mountains. When the pilot would approach a ridgeline, he would cut off the engine so he could slip quietly over into the next valley. Those planes didn't have any armor. I figured we were most likely to get shot at from underneath, so I brought two flak jackets and sat on them. This pilot was a little bit crazy. He brought a case of grenades along. When we were giving air support to the guys on the ground, if he ran out of rockets, he'd put the stick between his knees, have me pull the pins on the grenades, and hand them to him, so he could drop them out the window on the enemy bunkers.

When my tour was over in May, 1968, I went home, was discharged, and went to the University of Georgia for a year. It didn't take long for me to realize I wasn't cut out for that, so I went back in and reenlisted. I was promoted to Spec-4 and in 1970 I ended up right back in a MAC-V assignment, with Team 22 this time, operating near Pleiku. The work was almost the same as my first tour, except that was the era of "Vietnamization." There were far fewer US troops around, far less air and artillery support, and mostly ARVN troops working in the countryside. Once again, we were working with the local militias and the Montagnards in the mountains. They were a dark-skinned tribal people, and I really liked them. They knew the land and were very loyal. I guess you could compare them to our own Native Americans.

One of the big issues today is Agent Orange. Back then I'd never heard of it, but we knew they were spraying a defoliant. When we were out in the bush we'd get a white, dusty powder all over us, and just brush it off. I've been tested several times, but for some reason, despite all the places I was, I have never tested positive.

My strongest memory of that second tour was a very bad road ambush. A couple of us were in a jeep headed for Pleiku to pick something up, so we joined a truck convoy headed that way. We're about halfway there when a gasoline tanker truck ahead of us carrying JP-4 aviation gas was hit by an RPG and exploded. The convoy was hit in other places too. Interspersed in the convoy were the "hard trucks" that the MPs used for convoy defense. They were Deuce-and-a-Half trucks with half-inch steel plates welded on the sides—do-it-yourself armor. Up top, they would carry a dual or even a quad .50-caliber machine gun, M-60s, and anything else they could get their hands on, because when the shooting started, their job was to roll to the fighting and put down suppressive fire. The hard truck behind us pulled out of line and began shooting. One of their gunners up top was shot and killed, and their sergeant yelled for me to climb up. So, I ended up manning one of their M-60s as the fighting raged on, with a kid lying in the truck bed at my feet, dead. That was rough. The battle continued for almost six hours and I think there were twenty US killed before it was over. That stuff you remember.

Worse still was the first night of Tet. Up the road a few miles from us was a Belgian mission. There were seven missionaries there, three women and four priests. We drove up there in jeeps with no lights on to get them out, but by the time we got in there they had all been murdered. There were a dozen or more NVA bodies nearby, apparently from artillery strikes. Unfortunately, there was nothing we could do there, so we piled back in the jeeps and raced back to our compound. We arrived just as it came under a mortar attack. We heard one coming in and we all jumped out of the jeep. It rolled on and took a direct hit, turning it into burning scrap metal. As someone said, "It isn't the bullet that has your name on it you need to worry about; it's the one that says 'To whom it may concern.'"

After I rotated home from my second tour, I remained in the Army and held a wide variety of assignments, from Drill Sergeant to Mechanized Infantry First Sergeant, to First Sergeant of a training company at Fort Benning. As the years went on, however, I reached a point where my physical ailments caught up with me. My back was bad, and I was coping with PTSD. My next step would've been Sergeant Major, but I could no longer hump a rucksack with the kids anymore. They deserved better, so I knew it was time to hang it up. I had been in the Army for twenty-two years and retired as an E-8 Master Sergeant with a 100% disability.

I took some time off, and was hired as the vice president of operations for a small company that owned a series of paper mills and printing plants. The Army was better than an advanced degree when it comes to organization, personnel management, and leadership, and those skills served me well for the next sixteen years until I retired again. I am 68 years old now. I spend my free time playing golf, traveling, and working with the Band of Brothers veteran's organization.

MIKE DEMAIO'S WAR

**US Marine Corps, Squad Leader, G company,
2nd Battalion, 4th Regiment, 3rd Marine Division,
Quang Tri and Con Thien, I Corps, 1967–68**

I grew up in East Harlem and the Bronx, and enlisted in the Marine Corps when I turned seventeen. That was when I still had hair, and they called me "Red." I came out of Parris Island and Camp Lejeune as an 03-11 Rifleman. After a Caribbean deployment, I reported to G company, 2nd of the 4th in the 3rd Marine Division in Vietnam. Some Marines stayed south or west of Danang, doing sweeps through the NVA "rocket belt," while I spent my whole tour north of Danang, north of Hue, north of Phu Bai, and north of Quang Tri, in Dong Ha and Con Thien, right on the DMZ. From any hill, you could look across into North Vietnam. The NVA had at least two infantry divisions sitting over there looking back at us, and you can't get any further north than that.

For my first six months, we'd go out on two- to six-week long patrols, come in for maybe a week, then go back out and do it again. That meant sleeping on the ground in foxholes and eating C-rations, day after day after day. Once in a while, they'd send us hot chow like spaghetti and meatballs. It didn't matter what it was, anything was better than another meal of Cs. Once, we were sent to provide security at a radio relay site with a team of LRRPs, long-range  recon, who went out in small groups on long patrols in enemy country. They had their own LRRP meals. They were as fed up with them as we were with Cs, so we traded, each group thinking they'd just won the lottery. But it didn't matter. Whatever I ate, I went there at 165 pounds and came home at around 150.

To relieve tension, guys were always joking around. We had a machine gunner we called Boris. One day we were sitting around waiting to go out on night patrol, when he walked up fiddling with a grenade and complaining that he couldn't get the damned pin back in. He stumbled and dropped the grenade in the middle of all of us. Everyone scattered, and he cracked up laughing. It was a dud, of course.

For a while, in September, they rotated us back to Camp Evans north of Hue to provide perimeter defense. That meant we manned the fortified bunkers around the base and went out on patrols and ambushes. At least we got to eat in a mess hall and sleep in tents with wooden floors, although it didn't last very long. In October, we went back to the field and fought a series of bloody battles. Once Tet hit in late January, we hardly ever came back in. When we patrolled around Danang, it was mostly rice paddies—lots of mud and water, thatched huts, and banana trees. When we worked in the upper Highlands, Cambodia, and Laos, it was all hills and triple-canopy jungle. In upper I Corps along the DMZ and the Qua Viet River, it was steeper hills, deserted villages, and tall hedgerows.

The rice paddies down south along the coast were beautiful, with small boys driving big water buffalo. The villages were small, but you noticed right away that the only people there were young children and old women, maybe a few old men. The fighting-age men had either been drafted for the South Vietnamese Army or the Viet Cong.

The heat and smell of Vietnam hits you the moment you step off the airplane. In the jungle, especially at night, your senses come alive. It's an insect paradise, with red ants, leeches, eight-inch centipedes, mosquitoes, snakes, monkeys, and rumors of tigers. Add in the roar of Phantom jets, exploding bombs and artillery, napalm, the thump of helicopters, and a "Spookie" gunship stream of tracer bullets light show, and that was Vietnam.

More than all the others, I remember three specific days. On September 21, we were at Con Thien on a battalion sweep. We were the lead company and we ran right into an NVA regiment, dug in in front of a village. That battle lasted ten to twelve hours. I remember the beginning and the end, but none of the middle. I guess that's how the brain works. Our company lost eighteen men killed and one hundred and eighteen wounded, and the fighting was so bad that we had to leave bodies behind. Shortly after that, Con Thien itself came under attack, and we were in action for over a week. On October 11, two weeks later, we returned to retrieve the bodies from the September 11 battle, and had to fight our way back into that village again. The third day I remember was October 14. We had been guarding a construction site on a bridge when night fell, and we were hit. The NVA got into the wire and blew up one of our machine gun positions. That fighting lasted until morning. I started out as a Rifleman and ended up Squad Leader. We called that promotion by attrition. All three of those days were before Tet and became officially known as "The Fall Fighting at the DMZ."

You can't explain combat to someone who hasn't been there. It's mind numbing. A nurse once told me it was like a car crash, which most people can understand. Think of Vietnam as one big car crash that never stops. You hear the sound as it goes on and on. Sometimes it is a little fender bender, and sometimes it is a big crash, but it goes on and on.

Most of my friends were wounded two or three times, and most of them only lasted six months before they were sent home. I was never hit. I don't know why. I was one of the very few who lasted all twelve months over there until the end of my tour. I received the Combat Action Ribbon, a Presidential Unit Citation, and a Vietnamese Cross of Gallantry, of which I am very proud, and a whole lot of PTSD.

When my tour was over, I still had two years left. That was the time of the King and Kennedy assassinations, the riots, and all the rest; and I couldn't stand it. I volunteered for embassy duty, and spent the next two years in Guatemala. After I was discharged, I went back to college, got a degree in Humanities and Religion, and went to work for the Department of Social Services in the Bronx, in mental health. I got my MSW and moved to Oregon, where I worked in a VA vet center, counseling other veterans.

I never knew about PTSD until I worked in the Bronx Vet Center. The diagnosis had just come out. There was one vet I connected with more than the others, and I could see myself in him—the reactions, the outbursts, the hyper-depression, the moods, nightmares, the bad memories, and even the road rage. It took a long time for me to accept it; but it was impacting my family. They were walking around me on eggshells. This began in the early 1990s and grew worse until I crashed in 2004. That was when I went to the VA, got counseling, and got on the right meds. That was why the Vet Centers were established, so we could go to people like us who understood. I'm now 69 and live in Corvallis, Oregon, with my wife. I am writing my own book on my Vietnam experiences titled *Amends—a Marine's Journey Home*. Be watching for it.

LARRY SUMNER'S WAR

US Navy E-5, 128th Mobile Construction Battalion, "The Sea Bees," Marble Mountain, Danang East, and Quang Tri, 1967–69

I played a lot of sports in high school and was wrestling at Kansas State when the Navy recruited me to wrestle for them in May, 1966. Being a farm kid from western Kansas, I grew up operating heavy equipment. My Granddad and Dad were dirt contractors, and it was my mother who taught me how to run a Cat. So, when the wrestling petered out, I ended up in the Seabees.

I was put in Mobile Construction Battalion 128. A lot of Army titles and acronyms don't make any sense, but ours did. We were a mobile construction battalion, and that's exactly what we did. We moved around a lot and built things. We went to Vietnam as a unit in June, 1967, and came back out again twelve months later. We were based at the Marble Mountain Air Facility, sometimes called East Danang, which was a helicopter base located south and east of the main Danang base on a spit of sand along the ocean near China Beach. About all I remember from the first few months was driving in truck convoys to the Marine bases all over I Corps. After that, I became part of a team they flew in to bulldoze the perimeters of small Marine LZs and Special Forces camps. I would run a small Cat to push the trees and jungle back, and sometimes help drill wells. At other times, we'd fill holes and patch the runways every time a Marine base took rockets, which was almost daily.

Seabees have always been known to be "enterprising." I wasn't there twenty-four hours before I stole a pallet of beer—144 cases—from the main base when we went to pick up our equipment. Later, we needed a road grader, so I stole one from Cam Ranh Bay and we took it up north on a flatbed. It was a Cat, which was much better than the crap equipment the Navy gave us, so we painted it green and no one ever knew. Another time, three of us stole an air conditioner from one of the officer's clubs and traded it to the Special Forces based at Marble Mountain for 1,000 M-1 rifles, a Jeep, and a bunch of Jim Beam whiskey. We didn't really want any of that, but like they did in *McHale's Navy* and *M*A*S*H* on TV, it made great trading material for things we did want, which was the only way you got along over there.

None of our officers knew anything about dirt work or site construction. They had a lot of engineering degrees, but no practical experience running job sites and work crews. The same was true for our NCOs. The Seabees got a reputation from World War II and the John Wayne movie, but they were prohibited by law from doing any construction work within the US. That meant that between wars the only experience they got was the occasional foreign goodwill job. The same was true for their equipment procurement. They caved in to the politicians and overpaid for the wrong stuff, using the wrong specs, which always were over-designed to do too many things, from a company in some Congressman's district.

I was on the Battalion Advance Party when we went in, and part of the final cleanup group when we came out. That last trip back home was fun. A C-47 came in, dropped its ramp, and we piled in with our backpacks, sea bags, and weapons. All that was on that airplane was us and a load of caskets headed home. I had an M-16, my .45, my favorite M-79 grenade launcher, and ammo for all of them. We flew in that cold, noisy C-47 all the way to Houston, where they let us off at the civilian airport. We quickly stuffed the weapons inside our sea bags and walked from the flight line through a service door into the terminal. No customs, no inspections, just the mud of Vietnam all over our fatigues and boots. Then some anti-war jackass decided to throw blood on us and call us baby killers. It was a good thing my M-79 wasn't easy to get to.

I couldn't stand stateside duty and volunteered to go back to Vietnam six months later. This time, I was sent to the Mobile Construction Battalion at Quang Tri. That was a whole lot worse than Danang. Nothing but bamboo, red dirt, mud, rice paddies with water buffalo, and flat scrubland. The airstrip was taking so much fire when we came to land, that the pilot told us to grab our bags and jump off the back ramp, because he wasn't stopping.

I was usually put in charge of road grading. In fact, I graded most of the gravel roadbed from Quang Tri to Hué, and was put in charge because I knew how to get the work done. We had to level the sand, put dirt down, and lay a bed of gravel for the pavers.

When I was finally sent home after nine months, I ended up working hurricane Camille on the Gulf Coast near Biloxi. That was bad. We found a lot of bodies, even up in trees. After that, my grandmother passed away and I was sent home and eventually discharged. I went back to school and got my degree in business and accounting. I have a lot of service-related hearing loss from the heavy equipment and have been diagnosed with several Agent Orange issues. I'm 69 now and enjoy spending my time on motorcycles, fishing, playing golf, working on my Corvette, and playing bridge. I still spend a lot of time out in Western Kansas, checking on the family farm.

DR. ED SCHEIN'S WAR

US Army Doctor, Flight Surgeon, and Captain,
52nd Combat Aviation Battalion,
the "Flying Dragons" Pleiku, 1967–68

I was an Army MD and the Flight Surgeon for the 52nd Combat Aviation Battalion, the "Flying Dragons" at Camp Holloway; and called "That crazy Doctor" by the four Special Forces guys we rescued from the Ho Chi Minh trail in Cambodia. My job was supposed to be to service the unit and evaluate the pilot's condition to fly, not flying around myself as a door gunner on a Huey gunship, but I couldn't help myself. One day we had a Huey door gunner come in to the clinic who had lost thirty pounds in four months. It was obviously stress and PTSD, and the guy needed a break, so I took his missions as door gunner once or twice a week. It gave me a break too, and let me see what the men did and how the unit operated. For the first month or two, I never fired a shot, but I liked going on the missions. Mostly we dropped troops into LZs and picked them up again.

Then came the Battle for Pleiku. They brought in twenty-five to thirty body bags to Graves Registration. These were US troops from the 4th Infantry Division and every one of them had their hands tied behind their backs and had been shot in the head, murdered by the NVA. One of them was a friend of mine from Fort Lewis. That really pissed me off! Screw the Hippocratic Oath, I began flying gunships in earnest, looking for some payback. After that, whenever I had a day off, I started going up in a Huey or in the rear seat of a Bird Dog spotter plane, claiming I was just checking on the pilots, but the real reason was I liked it.

I'd take along an M-16 and a bucket of grenades, just in case. One day, flying northwest of Pleiku I looked down and saw four guys come out of the wood line below wearing black pajamas. I pointed them out to the pilot, who made a big turn and dove down. He fired several white phosphorus spotter rockets at them as I stuck my M-16 out

145

the window and grabbed a couple of grenades. As we came back around, he told me not to bother. You could still see the smoke coming up from the bodies.

It wasn't my idea to be a flight surgeon. I graduated from medical school at the University of Florida and was about to do my internship when I got drafted in May, 1966. Yes, they even drafted doctors. The Medical Corps sent me to be the surgeon with a battalion of the 4th Infantry Division at Fort Lewis, Washington. They were headed for Vietnam, but for some reason, my orders came through first in May, 1967. When I arrived at Camp Holloway, no one knew what to do with me, until another doctor asked me if I wanted to become a Flight Surgeon with the 52nd. I jumped at it. Apparently, they wouldn't let that guy leave until they got a replacement, so he went out and found one. It worked out for both of us.

Vertigo, combat fatigue, and stress were big problems with pilots in Vietnam. My job was to periodically check them out and make sure that they were good to fly. We also had a small clinic. I ran sick call and provided other clinical services for the unit, usually with a second doctor, a couple of physician's assistants, and maybe three or four nurses to help.

It was in January when the legend of "That crazy Doctor" was born. I was on one of my usual flights as a door gunner on a Huey, when we received an Emergency Notification that a four-man Special Forces team was in trouble over by the Ho Chi Minh Trail in Laos. Our bird and another one immediately went "nose over" and headed west. We located the Green Berets in a clearing too small for us to land in, so we had to hover and drop Maguire Rigs from the side doors for them to get into. We didn't have hoists, so they were supposed to sit down in the rig and we'd take off, hopefully pulling them straight up, and not bang them into too many trees on the way.

Anyway, just as they got into the rigs, we began taking incoming fire. You could see the tracer rounds coming at us from the jungle on my side, and the pilot screamed in his mic to me, "Goddamnit Doc, shoot!" I screamed back, "Shoot what? I can't see where they are!" The pilot replied, "They don't know that!" So, I opened up and blazed away at the edge of that jungle clearing, from one side to the other. That was the first time I did that, and holding an M-60 in your hands when it's firing full automatic is an amazing feeling. I have no idea if I hit anything, but the NVA stopped shooting, and we got away.

We flew to Dak To with the four Green Berets dangling under the two helicopters and set them down on the runway. After we landed, they came running over to shake our hands and thank us. One of the Special Forces guys saw me, looked at my uniform, saw the insignias I was wearing, and asked in an astonished voice, "You're a Captain? And a Doctor? Flying as a door gunner? What? Are you crazy?"

To my surprise, it took three to four weeks for our colonel to come storming into my infirmary glaring at me. "Doc, if you ever fly again, I'm gonna put you in jail! We need you here!" I tried to look chastened. "But we have plenty of help," I answered. "I don't care! Don't you ever fly again!" Well, of course I kept flying, once a week, at least; but I told the pilots not to put me on any manifests or put me up for any Air Medals. As it was, I think I got seven or eight.

After I got home and was discharged, I finished my residency in nephrology and became a kidney specialist in Texas and Gainesville, Florida. I had previously studied under Doctor Bob Cade, a world-renowned nephrologist who invented Gatorade at the University of Florida, and I did more work and research with him, published sixteen research papers and created several dialysis centers. When that federal research money died, I went into private practice and even tried law school, which I did for two years until I quit. To me, law school was lie school, and I had had enough.

But the funniest thing that happened to me was in November, 2014, when I was in one of our neighborhood squares in Florida and I saw a guy sitting on a bench with a Special Forces baseball hat on his head. I walked over and said hello, thinking he looked familiar. After we mentioned a few dates and places, his eyes lit up, he jumped up and asked, "Are you that crazy Doctor?" His wife jumped up and began to hug me too. He was the same guy who asked me that same question back in Pleiku all those years before. Even stranger, I met another of those guys a few months later in a restaurant and got the same reaction. And then just last week, in a different town about twenty miles away, I was in a food store and another guy looked at me and asked, "Doc? Tell me that isn't you?" That made three out of four of those guys. Amazing!

I'm now 78 and still live in Central Florida. Other than bad hearing in both ears from all those "unofficial" flights I took, I have no other Vietnam-related illnesses, at least not yet. I still enjoy fishing. I was the 1986 Florida State Bass Champion, thanks to a lure I invented… and it had nothing to do with the bucket of hand grenades I snuck on board.

JOHN McCABE'S WAR

US Army, Spec 4 Track Mechanic,
709th Maintenance Battalion, 9th Infantry Division,
Ben Luc, 1967–68

I came from Providence, Rhode Island, and enlisted in the Army in 1965 instead of waiting to be drafted, because I wanted to be a heavy equipment mechanic. Naturally, the Army sent me to clerk-typist school and tried making me a chaplain's assistant. After I complained enough, they finally sent me to an engineer unit where I operated bull-dozers and backhoes and was trained to operate the big M-88 Track Retriever, which hauled away tanks and APCs if they broke down. They were M-113 Armored Personnel Carriers, a steel box on tracks that could carry a squad of infantry.

I arrived in Vietnam in June, 1967, and was sent to the 709th Maintenance Battalion in Ben Luc, thirty-five miles from Saigon in the Mekong Delta. We supported the 9th infantry division and particularly the 5th Battalion of the 60th Mechanized Infantry. Our compound was about the size of a football field,

small and crowded, surrounded by fences and concertina wire. That whole area was swampy, and the ground was so soft that the M-88 was useless. We had one, but it never left the compound, because it was too heavy for the roads and would sink up to its axles in the rice paddies. One of our guys painted a big red racing stripe on it from the front, across the roof, and down the back.

It was early summer and already extremely hot and humid when I got there. We had about one hundred guys in our unit and we slept in big twenty-four-man tents. There were probably four of those in the compound, plus shops and storerooms. It was so crowded, that we had to park most of the vehicles waiting to be repaired outside the gate along the access road. We scrounged some plywood and built our own hooches, with wooden walls, screens, a roof, and concrete floors. After a while, the place was halfway civilized. We even had a Vietnamese barber who came in and cut hair, and Vietnamese women who washed our clothes and cleaned the hooches.

I spent most of my time repairing APCs and following the 5th of the 60th, when they went on an operation, pulling one of our maintenance trailers, which I did at least a half-dozen times. They rode in M-113 Armored Personnel Carriers. If one of them broke down, we'd have a Chinook helicopter come in and pick it up. By September, I'd made friends with the company clerk. He was rotating home soon. Since I could type a little, I got him to recommend me to the First Sergeant as his replacement. An air-conditioned office beat the hell out of fixing machinery in the heat. I got the job, which also meant driving the CO around in his Jeep, but mostly I kept the company roster as well as scheduled all the duty sheets for KP, guard, and other things. Do that stuff right, the First Sergeant's happy, and you're golden.

Sometimes, I'd have to go up to Ben Cat to pick up an APC after it had major repairs done. To get back, I had to drive through the middle of Saigon, which was always interesting. There was a very tall bridge over the river I had to drive over. At the bottom, the road swung sharply to the left; but if you kept straight, you went right through the gate into the Navy compound. One day, coming down the other side of that steep bridge, the brakes failed, and the damned thing wouldn't stop. All I could do was shout and wave for the Navy guys to open the gate and get out of the way, as I came barreling on through, hoping I could get it stopped before I hit something, or it went off the pier into the water. Fortunately, I got it stopped.

The best time I had during my tour was taking two R&Rs to Sydney, Australia, which I was able to arrange. The Aussies were wonderful to us. I got to know some people and got to know a girl, who invited me to her parents' house to stay, and we had a great time.

When Tet hit at the end of January, we didn't get too much action down our way: some mortars and rockets, but not much worse than usual. A week after it stopped, I had to drive up through Saigon again. I saw a lot of big buildings that had been destroyed, some burnt out, with bullet holes everywhere.

In May I suddenly got very sick. They sent me to the Division doctor at Dong Tam who diagnosed me with hepatitis. Turns out, it came from the water trucks we got our water out of. They were never disinfected right. Fortunately, the Doc wrote it up that way in my records before he sent me to the hospital in Saigon and then up to Cam Ranh Bay where they told me I had contracted not only Hepatitis C, but A, B, and D, too. Six weeks later, I got sent back to my unit just in time to pick up my gear and head for the airport to fly home. My tour was over.

I still had eight months left, so they sent me to Fort Meade, Maryland, training troops on APCs, but the thing that bothered me the most was traveling home in uniform and never having anyone say anything to you. I got a steak dinner in Oakland, but no thanks, no nothing for serving from anyone in any of the airports I passed through.

I was pretty stressed out when I finally got off active duty. I went to a tiny cabin up in the north of Vermont with three other vets. I spent a year there before I came back down and enrolled in the local community college. After that, I went to Providence College nights, and got my BA in Liberal Arts. I worked sales for a while and then drove a tractor trailer, until I got a job with a company selling chemicals and did that for twenty-five years.

In 2005, I was diagnosed with liver failure due to the hepatitis I contracted in Vietnam. Thanks to the detailed notes that 9th Division doctor wrote in my records back at Dong Tam, I ended up in the VA hospital in Pittsburgh for a full transplant. I was also diagnosed with PTSD, and between the two, I ended up with a 100% disability. I am 68 and retired now and spend my free time playing golf and working on our family ancestry.

DAN TRICERI'S WAR

US Army, Sergeant E-5 and
Communication Center Cryptographer,
29th Signal Battalion, 1st Signal Brigade,
Bang Pla, Thailand, 1967–68

I was a "tape ape." I spent eighteen months as a teletype operator and cryptographer with the 29th Signal Brigade at the big AMARS satellite communications center in Bang Pla, Thailand. It was a large building in a flat open area surrounded by dirt, dust, and swamp, which the Thais called a "quon." We were a communications hub and I dealt primarily with coding and decoding and transmitting and retransmitting top-secret communications between Vietnam and anywhere else around the world. Why they had to put the Center in the middle of nowhere, I'll never know.

We operated in three shifts with twenty-one guys on a shift, and used box decoders. The codes changed every day, using dedicated channels that went directly to the Pentagon, the White House, several places in Hawaii, the Philippines, and all the major headquarters in South Vietnam. Many of the reports we sent out were daily casualty reports, bombing reports, and things like that. Each message we sent or received had to be meticulously accounted for. If you ever lost one or screwed up the accounting, you were in big trouble. When the Tet Offensive hit, we worked nonstop. We had four or five guys listening to each radio circuit, all the traffic was "Flash," and I worked twenty-six straight hours in one shift.

We were in a large, locked room inside the Comm Center, with no windows, guards outside the doors, tight access, and we all wore pistols. The good thing was, it was nice and cool inside. We had lots of air conditioning, but it was for the equipment, not us. While I was there, we had no rocket or mortar attacks, just some threats.

In Basic Training, our Platoon Sergeant tried to get me to switch to Green Beret training instead of the crypto class. I was interested; but when I went home on leave and told my father, he said he'd kick my ass if I did anything that stupid. So, I went to the crypto class and I did well in it. When it was over, almost everyone else got orders to Germany. For some reason, my orders never came. I waited around and started going to the swimming pool every day, since I had nothing to do. When the Colonel in charge of the pool found out I had a Red Cross lifeguard certificate, he put me to work and I spent most of that summer working as a lifeguard at the pool. Finally, I went back to my company and the CO wanted to declare me AWOL. I had to bring the Colonel over to get me out of trouble. When my orders did come through, they sent me to the 29th Signal Battalion in Thailand, not to Germany with the others.

For the first six months there was no housing for us at Bang Pla, so we had "civilian status." We lived in an air-conditioned hotel in Bangkok, and had a forty-minute bus ride to the Comm Center. We even ate breakfast and dinner in local restaurants in Bangkok. After eating Thai food for a year, when I got home I couldn't bring myself to eat any more of it. They ate insects and grasshoppers, and the fish came with the heads, all the guts, and the eyes. Like I said, I had enough to last a lifetime.

Bangkok was wide open and dangerous. It was a "Wild West" kind of place, where you could get a guy killed for four packs of cigarettes. Living there, we knew where the good places were to go, where the bad ones were, and we'd try to steer guys in on R&R in the right directions. You could buy almost anything in Bangkok. We got to know a guy who owned a jewelry store, and we would sell him bottles of Jim Beam for $12 that we could buy at the Base Exchange for $3. He made them into decorative glass things. One day, we dropped off some bottles to his shop and I saw his wife pouring the booze out down the sink. I asked him, what she was doing? He told me that all they wanted was the glass bottles. After that, we drank the booze and sold him the empties.

The Air Force had a recreation center on the ocean on the other side of Bangkok, and we'd go there on three-day passes. Usually we could rent a cab in Bangkok for three days and drive it down there ourselves. Two months before I was scheduled to leave, we were coming back very drunk and I was driving. The houses out in the country were built on stilts. I fell asleep, went off the road and drove under one of them, crashing into the stilts, and bringing the house down on top of the cab. We got out, and all we could think of doing was running like hell back to Bangkok, which we did. Two days later I got called in by the Colonel and told that the Thais had filed a complaint and I owed them $2,000 for damages. If I didn't pay up, the Army wasn't going to let me go home. The guys all anted up, and I paid them back when I got my separation money later, but that was a lesson learned.

When my twelve-month tour was coming to an end, my platoon sergeant called me in and gave me the bad news that they were extending me six months. I didn't like it, but they would give me a drop when I got home and let me out of the Army. He told me if I went home after twelve months, I'd have a twelve-month stateside assignment. After spending a year in Thailand and operating without any rules, he knew I'd end up in trouble and get busted. He was probably right. So, that was how my twelve-month tour became eighteen months long. Most of that time, I was a Sergeant, E-5.

When they finally did let me go home, I had to leave the country through Bangkok. I don't know who planned my itinerary, but they sent me from Bangkok to Saigon, then to the Philippines, Japan, Hawaii, Alaska, Seattle, and finally to Oakland.

When I was discharged, I went back to my home-town, Pittsfield, Massachusetts, and became a cop for the next thirty years. I also enlisted in the National Guard and served for twenty-four years. My Army time did do one other thing. When I retired from the police department, it counted as another three years of service time.

GARY BEAULIEU'S WAR

**US Army Major, Helicopter Pilot,
and Maintenance Officer,
188th Assault Helicopter Company,
Dau Tieng and LZ Sally, 1967–68**

In the Army, they always say, "never volunteer;" but somehow, I kept getting volunteered. I didn't think of it that way, though. I thought we were just doing our jobs. When I arrived in country in June, 1967, I was a Major with ten years' flying experience. Most of that was in fixed wing aircraft. I didn't have more than a hundred hours in helicopters, but helicopter pilots were what they needed.

I was sent to the 188th Assault Helicopter Company, at Dau Tieng northwest of Saigon in the Central High-lands to fly and be the Maintenance Officer. We supported the 25th Infantry Division with thirty-one helicopters, mostly Huey "slicks," plus a smaller section of Huey C-model gunships. Pilots being pilots, the 188th called themselves the "Black Widows," and had big spiders painted on their nose bubbles. Those might have been good for troop morale, but they made awfully good targets for the VC, too. As Maintenance Officer, I oversaw the 603rd General Maintenance detachment. I had never taken a maintenance course, I just did a lot of "watch and learn;" but our sixty-three men were responsible for keeping everything in the air. I would also fly combat missions several times a week, usually in one of the slicks.

The countryside we operated in around Dau Tieng was dense jungle, with Nui Ba Den, the Black Virgin Mountain, to the northwest, near Tay Ninh. That was an area of heavy fighting throughout the war. The mountain was honeycombed with NVA caves and tunnels. We held the top and the bottom, and the NVA held the middle. When I arrived, we had just gotten new H-model Hueys, then the VC got inside the wire, got on the water tower with some mortars, and destroyed our new helicopters. After that, they'd only send us older B models.

154

One day I was sent out to pick up a damaged Huey in the "Ho Bo Woods," as it was called. It was an NVA stronghold with rice paddies and big dikes surrounded by dense jungle. It was riddled with NVA bunkers and tunnels, some of which went three and four levels underground. My mechanic and I were supposed to get the Huey and fly it back if we could. No sooner did we land and get inside the machine than the NVA started coming out of tunnels all around us and we began taking fire. I could tell right away that the hydraulics were damaged. I turned to my mechanic and asked, "Will this thing fly?" because there was no going back now. I got it in the air, but one of the rotor blades was missing its tip. It bounced
us up and down and it felt like getting punched in the chin with a fist, over and over again. The best I could do was hop the Huey along from clearing to clearing until we reached a small firebase where we could leave it. But, we saved the machine, and we were both given Bronze Stars.

Another thing we did was fly Special Forces teams into nearby Laos and Cambodia all the time. Supposedly, we weren't there, but we were, and those flights were always hairy. We would take off before dawn and go in low, at treetop height, to drop them off. They would be looking for enemy base camps, snooping along the Ho Chi Minh Trail, or trying to capture some prisoners. We would go back and pick them up around dusk, or earlier if they got in trouble.

Midway through my tour, I went on R&R and met my wife in Hawaii. That was great, but when I came back I found out that my best friend, the guy who took my place that week, had been killed on a mission right after I left. That's bothered me ever since.

As soon as I got back, the unit moved to LZ Sally, in the middle of a Vietnamese graveyard, to support the 101st Airborne. It was a flat, mostly sandy area near the coast way up in I Corps, north of Hue, south of Quang Tri, and east of the A-Shau Valley. There was always a lot of fighting there. The base was new, but it was much smaller than Dau Tieng and our helicopters took up a lot of space. At both Dau Tieng and LZ Sally we lived in tents. We had a mess hall at Dau Tieng and they finally built one at LZ Sally; but like everyone else, I ate a lot of Cs.

One day we got a call that a Marine unit was being overrun. I didn't volunteer or even think about it. We ran to one of the slicks and took off. It was me, a warrant officer in the copilot seat, and my crew chief and a machine gunner on the two M-60s in the rear doors. There was a Marine Corps lieutenant in charge of the unit who directed us in. My two gunners fired nonstop as we dropped into the clearing. We barely touched down when six or seven Marines jumped aboard, and we took off out of there. When we landed, and they piled out, I made a quick check and could see my Huey had been shot full of holes. It looked like Swiss cheese. Fortunately, none of its important mechanical parts had been hit, but that was when I was told that a Marine was still back there, wounded.

Operations asked me if we could go back in and get him. I turned to my copilot and asked, "What you think? Want to go back?" I never got an answer, so I took a closer look and saw he had a bullet hole in his forehead and was dead. I cinched his seatbelt tighter to hold him in place, and looked back at my two door gunners. They nodded, so we took off again. As we came into the clearing we were receiving a lot more gunfire than the first time. I told them to shoot the hell out of everything, and landed. The gunner jumped out, grabbed the Marine, pulled him on board, and we got the hell out of there. I flew him straight to the hospital. I never did find out if he made it or not, but it was the Marines who put me in for my Distinguished Flying Cross. The DFC was special. After I retired, I met one of the Marines we picked up that day. Knowing that I'd done some good for those guys was a nice feeling.

After Vietnam, I remained in the Army for a total of twenty-one years, retiring as a Lieutenant Colonel. After that I spent fifteen years in the nursing home business with a large corporation, until I retired for keeps. I'm 83 now. I used to play a lot of pickle ball and pool. However, they diagnosed me with Agent Orange-related prostate cancer, and I now also have a serious problem with macular degeneration. I'm afraid my vision isn't good enough anymore to follow bouncing balls in pickle ball or lineup pool shots.

LARRY MILOSCIO'S WAR

**US Air Force Sergeant and Electrician,
377th and 366th Civil Engineering Squadrons,
Tan Son Nhut and Danang, 1968–69**

I grew up in the Bronx. After high school, I tried City College for a year, but I wasn't a very good student. My thing was sports. Like a lot of other guys, I went back to college after my time in Vietnam and got straight A's, mostly because I wanted to do well that second time around, and I learned how to follow directions.

The Air Force trained me as an electrician, and I spent my first year and a half at the airfield on the far end of Long Island rewiring the runway and repairing other things, seven days a week. When orders came down and I was sent to Vietnam, I was assigned to the 377th Civil Engineering Squadron at Tan Son Nhut, arriving on December 31, 1968, New Year's Eve. A CE squadron does everything. We repaired runways, runway lights, demolished and reconstructed buildings, poured concrete, erected telephone poles, and ran heavy equipment.

Since Tan Son Nhut was an international airport as well as an Air Force base, and tall structures such as towers were a common sight. Runway approach towers had red blinking lights on the top for the safety of low-flying aircraft and helicopters, and had to be operational at all times. Some of those structures reached heights of 50 to 75 feet; and for some reason, it seemed the highest lights were always the ones that failed on my shift. Repairing or replacing those fixtures was always a challenge at night.

But it wasn't all hard work. One day I was sent to the general's office. He had a doorbell buzzer on his desk and thought it rang too loud. I frowned, and pretended to study the problem up and down. When he wasn't looking, I stuffed some Kleenex inside and put it back together. After that, it rang nice and soft. He thought I was an electrical genius.

The Air Force had a heavy construction unit like the Seabees they called "Red

Horse"—the Rapid Engineer Deployable Heavy Operational Repair Squadron—Engineer. Don't you wonder who comes up with names like that? Anyway, we worked with them quite often, wiring the prefab buildings they would build for small airstrips or mini command centers used elsewhere. They would be hung under a couple of Hueys, and flown to the construction site first thing in the morning. If it weighed too much, we'd split it in half and bolt the unit together once we had it on site. If we got it all put together and wired up with a generator before sunset, we'd be choppered back to base that evening. If not, we spent the night. Not a bad incentive to get your work done on time.

Our unit also did some Civic Action volunteer projects for the villages in the area. One time, a fellow airman and myself went to a nearby village to remove a dead tree limb that was hanging over a village elder's house. We drove a boom truck from our base to the village, only to discover that the boom wasn't long enough. I had to climb out of the bucket and into the tree to hook it up, which was a challenge I did not want to repeat. At the end of the day, the limb was removed without dropping it onto the chief's house. Another civic action project we performed was to go out with a truck and an auger to dig holes for utility poles to support electric or telephone lines.

We got hit with a few rockets every now and then, but we could go into Saigon whenever we had time off, which I did, and met some nice local people. There was a war going on; but all things considered, Tan Son Nhut, was pretty laid-back.

So, after I finished my first tour in the heat and humidity of Vietnam, where does the Air Force send me? To Colorado Springs in January. I froze my butt off, so I volunteered to go back to Vietnam. For my second tour, they sent me to the 366th Civil Engineering Squadron at Danang. It was a very different war up North. Danang Air Force Base was a major target of the NVA throughout the entire war, and we were hit with rockets my second night there.

I was a Sergeant by then, but the work was pretty much the same for an electrician as it had been on my first tour, except that at Danang the workweek was six days long. Once again, we spent a lot of time rewiring the runways and renovating buildings, but there was a lot more battle damage to repair. One of the more exciting things that we did was keeping the control tower and runways operating during a typhoon. We had a big backup generator, but it had to be switched on manually. Doing high-voltage electrical work in 75 to 90 miles per hour wind and heavy rain was not something you look forward to. The 366th received a unit citation for that.

Then there was the "not so bright moments" of my tour, like when some idiot decided to decorate the radar tower with strings of colorful Christmas lights for the holidays. That made a great target for "Charlie". The VC didn't hit the radar tower itself, but it made a great aiming point to hit the fuel dump. I remember sitting on top of our barracks, watching the fuel tanks burn. That was impressive. The fire was so hot that the firemen couldn't get in to turn off the interconnecting valves between the tanks, and they all ended up exploding.

I was discharged when I got home in May, 1971, went back to college, and got my degree. I was hired by the Long Island Lighting Co. as a lineman, powerline specialist, and control technician for the next thirty-nine years. I've had service-related hearing loss, and like so many others am dealing with prostate issues. Also, I'm still working on Agent Orange-related issues. I retired from the utility in 2012, but I stay active with softball, water volleyball, golf, and various clubs and organizations, including the color guard for our local Vietnam Veterans of America chapter.

MIKE EARL'S WAR

US Army, Spec 4 and APC Driver, 3rd Squadron,
5th Cavalry Regiment, 9th Infantry Division,
Camp Bearcat and the DMZ, 1967–69

I'm an Ohio kid, from Columbus, and graduated from North High School, where I played football. I tried Eastern Michigan University for a while, and was drafted into the Army in July 1967. They sent me down to Fort Knox where I was trained as an Armored Personnel Carrier driver. APCs aren't all that hard drive. They steer a little bit like a tank. The driver sits way up in the front, which is not a good place to be if you hit a mine. The biggest problem is, if you try to stay low and just look out the slit, you don't have much visibility from the driver's seat. I usually sat up high, and had my head out of the driver's hatch.

I arrived in-country in December 1967 and was assigned to the 3rd Squadron of the 5th Cavalry, the "Black Knights." They were a mechanized infantry unit assigned to the 9th Infantry Division at Camp Bearcat near Bien Hoa. It had been an old French army base and I think the Japanese before that. Pretty soon though, we were sent up to the DMZ. The area where we operated in was rugged hill country, and a terrible place to try to drive an APC. It was mostly scrub brush, but not like the jungle areas to the south and west. APCs made much more sense in the flatter country down there. With all the hills and ravines up along the DMZ, it was an easy place to get ambushed, which is exactly what happened to us.

On March 30, 1968 my APC was hit in the side by an RPG. It all happened so fast, I never had time to do much of anything. It was maybe 9:00 p.m., but not completely dark. Out of the corner of my eye, I saw the flash of the RPG coming at us and tried to scream, but even that was too late. Everyone else inside the APC was killed, even my Lieutenant and an RVN Captain who was riding along with us. Because I was upfront, that kind of saved me. I crawled out through the top hatch, not realizing how badly I was wounded, and went around to the rear hatch try to pull some guys out, but it was too late. There were more explosions and as I tried to drag one guy away I got shot. The bullet went in one cheek and out the other, taking out most of my teeth in the process. By that time, the Medic track had come up. I managed to get over there, but that was about all I remember.

They medevaced me to Tokyo, where I spent over a month at Camp Zama. When I was able to get up and around, my wife came over for a week. That was nice. We really liked seeing Tokyo. After I was released, they sent me back to my unit. I extended my enlistment by one month, so I would have less than six months left when my tour was over. That way, they'd give me an early out. When I got back to the company the First Sergeant came over to me and said, "What am I going to do with you?"

"Well, you could send me home," I answered.

He shook his head. "Oh, no, we can't do that."

"Oh, yes you can," I smiled, but they didn't. On the other hand, since I'd been badly wounded like that, they weren't going to put me back in a track. I had made Sergeant, E-5, so they gave me a job in the company orderly room as a clerk.

Finally, in January, after fourteen months, I went home and got out. My wife was a schoolteacher, and I went back to school myself. After that, I got a job at the big Ford Hydra plant at Willow Run, outside Detroit. Later, we moved to Pennsylvania and I got a job at Wheeling Corrugated Steel in Harrisburg. They made steel barns and I was mostly out selling them. When we lived in Pennsylvania, one of our favorite things to do was snow skiing. We were part of a big group that went all around the world to the big ski resorts until I retired in 2004 and moved south. No skiing, but I like to play golf, kayak on the lakes, and participate in the veterans' activities with the VVA.

KENNY LOHR'S WAR

US Army, Spec 5 and Marine Engineer,
5th Heavy Boat Company,
159th Transportation Battalion,
Vung Tao, 1968–69

I grew up in Hampton Bays, Long Island, and enlisted in the Army right out of high school. I had always lived around water, and my draft number was coming up, so two of my friends and I decided we'd enlist and get assigned to something having to do with boats. After Basic at Fort Jackson, I was sent to Fort Eustis in Virginia. That's where the Army Transportation School was, and they trained me as a Marine Engineer. Back then, the Army had more floating craft than the Navy and more aircraft than the Air Force. Of course, they were helicopters and small prop planes, and the boats were for harbor work and cargo; but a boat is a boat.

I was assigned to the 5th Heavy Boat Company in the 159th Transportation Battalion, as an engineer on a Landing Craft—Utility, or LCU. We were home ported at Vung Tao, a logistics center where the Mekong and Saigon Rivers meet the South China Sea. We went over as a unit on a troopship and arrived in May, 1968. The only good thing about going over on a boat as opposed to an airplane was that my time in-country started the day I left the US, so I arrived with twenty-one days credit.

An LCU was a good-sized cargo boat: one hundred and fifteen feet long and thirty-five feet wide, with the bridge in the stern. It could carry one-hundred-and-fifty tons of cargo and had a big ramp up front. It only drew two and a half feet of water in the bow, and four and a half feet of water in the stern, so we could run up on a

162

beach, drop the ramp, and load or unload our cargo. Vung Tao was a good-sized port serving the III and IV Corps areas. Our job was to take cargo that came in on the oceangoing ships and deliver it to units up the rivers. Sometimes we'd go down to the 9th Infantry Division at Dong Tam in the Delta, up to Saigon, or even over into Cambodia.

Most of the rivers we ran were narrow, with vegetation and jungle that came right down to the riverbank; and an LCU was slow. Fully loaded, we only did about six knots, maybe two knots going upriver in monsoon season, when a lot of water was coming down the river. We carried two .50-caliber machine guns, one starboard and one port, and could call in the Navy riverine patrol boats, when we needed help. Still, going upriver we were sitting ducks if we came under fire. That happened fairly often, from snipers, RPGs, and mortars.

The LCU had a crew of nine. The captain and chief engineer were warrant officers. The rest of us were enlisted, and we all lived on board, which was good. Our bunks were three high and we had a cook, a galley, a head, showers, generators for electricity, and all the rest. It wasn't luxurious, but it beat a tent in the mud, and it moved with us.

I remember one trip when they sent us way upriver into Cambodia to drop off some cargo. We were hit with mortars going in, and hit again on the beach right after we dropped the cargo. We only had half the cargo we were taking back loaded, but we backed off downriver and called in air support. They told us we should hang around until morning and go back for the rest of the retrograde cargo. Most of it was scrap anyway, so that wasn't going to happen. A little while later they told us the stuff they wanted us to pick up had been destroyed.

One thing I'll never forget had to do with the 1960s rock band the "Young Rascals." They were from the next town over from mine on Long Island, and we used to go listen to them at a local bar all the time. On our LCU, we could pick up AFVN television from Saigon. One day I heard the Rascals were going to be on the Leslie Uggams show. Our LCU and another were scheduled to make a run down to Dong Tien with cargo for the 9th Infantry Division. I talked to the Chief, and we decided that our boat "had a mechanical problem" that would take an hour

or so to fix. So, we got the TV turned on, watched the Rascals, and then motored over to the beach to pick up our cargo. They had already loaded the other LCU with the cargo that was supposed to be ours, so we took theirs. Normally, we don't pay much attention to what our cargo is, but the other boat ended up with a full load of 105 howitzer shells and we got a bunch of containers headed for the PX. Later, as we got near Dong Tam, we took an RPG that hit us in our cargo hold and it exploded. If we had been carrying those 105 howitzer rounds, we'd have been blown to hell and all of us killed. Sometimes, that's how things went over there: a lot of luck.

Forty-three years later, I caught a Rascals show in Florida. I got backstage, and told that story to Felix Cavaliere, the leader of the group, and thanked him. I also ran into Leslie Uggams a few years after that and did the same.

After my year was over in May, 1969, I rotated to the States. The Army stationed me at Fort Story, Virginia, but I was able to get reassigned to Fort Hamilton, New York, closer to home, where I became part of the crew on the general's yacht. We mostly took VIPs out on tour, and on fishing excursions for bluefish. On occasion, we provided security for the water side of Fort Tilden to secure their rifle range when firing was going on. When my three-year enlistment was over, I went back into the family ready-mix concrete and block business on Long Island. Eventually, my son took it over when I retired.

Like many vets, I never talked about the war until a few years ago, after I was diagnosed and treated for Agent Orange-related prostate cancer. You'd think I'd have been safe from exposure to that stuff, because I was in a boat on the river and not out tromping through the jungle; but you'd be wrong. They sprayed Agent Orange all over the river banks to push the vegetation back and make it harder for the VC snipers to hide in the tall grass and jungle. At the time, that seemed like a good idea. Now? Not so much.

I'm completely retired now. I like to play golf, do ballroom dancing, and do intense workouts. On my property in upstate New York I have a five-mile obstacle course with workout stations, and that also keeps me fit.

BRUCE TAYLOR'S WAR

US Air Force E-5 Tech Sergeant
and Airborne Radar Repairman,
Super-Constellation AWACS Planes,
3 Tours, 1967–73

My father was in the US Army Air Corps in Australia, where he met my mother. They moved to the States and I graduated from high school in Baltimore in 1965. I thought about enlisting to avoid the draft, but my father said, "The Air Force—that's where you want to go. The training's better and they'll take better care of you," not that he gave me much choice. So, in November, 1965, I found myself at Lackland Air Force Base for Basic, followed by the fifty-one-week Airborne Radar Repair course, one of the longest they offer, at Keesler Air Force Base in Biloxi, Mississippi.

I was assigned to the EC-121 Airborne Warning and Control System (AWACS) Squadron at McClellan Air Force Base in Sacramento, after which I went on my first thirteen-month deployment to Vietnam. That was late 1967. We spent one month in Korea for an operational shakedown before we were sent to Korat Air Force Base in Thailand. For the next twelve months we flew out of there, and occasionally out of Danang and Tan Son Nhut, flying three days or more each week. Our job was to coordinate all aircraft in-country, whether they were on bombing runs, refueling, search and rescue, or whatever, keeping them advised of what other aircraft near them were doing, ground action, and the weather.

An AWACS is a huge aircraft. They were converted Lockheed Super-Constellations with a horizontal radar bubble underneath and a big antenna dome on top, and they carried a lot of gas. They were heavy and slow, maybe 140 to 150 knots tops, but we could stay up for fourteen to sixteen hours, if needed. The bottom dome was the search radar. It could see out over two hundred miles. The top was a "height finder" for plotting storms, which helped the tactical aircraft we controlled. Because our flights were so long, we had a double crew on board: two pilots, two navigators, two radiomen, two controllers, two repair techs, and four "Scopies," so we rotated and switched off. They gave us bagged lunches for the flight, but I would collect the hard-boiled eggs nobody else wanted, mix them with some mayonnaise, and make my own egg salad sandwiches.

We put in long days in the air, usually being "on station" by 7:30 in the morning and not leaving until 5:00 or 5:30 p.m. The other repair tech and I sat in the center of the plane, over the wings. Our job was to keep the electronics working, and there was always something going wrong. Much of the equipment was "old tech," with scopes and tubes, and they kept adding more onboard, making it even worse. Still, we were sitting in the perfect place to see and hear everything going on inside the airplane and in the war below us.

My second tour was in 1969–70, again based out of Korat, except we spent our pre-month shakedown in Taiwan, not Korea. By then, the major focus of air activity had shifted to Cambodia and Laos, where there was a lot of ground and tactical air action. When aloft, we always flew a large, circular "racetrack" pattern at around 12,000 to 14,000 feet. It happened to cross a big hill that was about 8,000 feet tall. We could see an old man on the top with a bolt-action rifle who would take shots at us every time we came around. We laughed about it, until one time he actually hit us! The bullet came up and broke one of the scopes inside the cabin.

We had a crazy aircraft commander on one of my tours. He was a captain who was being "rifted" out, and he didn't care about much. Rifted is a military term for being downsized and booted out. It happened to a lot of guys in the late 1970s, as the services had to shrink down to peacetime strength levels. Of course, when your employer is the Air Force or the Army, there's no competitor that you can apply to.

On our aircraft commander's last mission, he asked the Korat tower for permission to do a fly-by. The tower refused, but he did it anyway. An AWACS is big, slow, and not very nimble. We came roaring down the runway a few feet off the tarmac before he turned, just missing the tower with our wing tip. The tower ordered him down, but he swung back around and did it again. And then he did it a third time! When he finally landed, the Base Commander and a jeep full of Air Police met us and took him into custody, but he didn't care.

When we flew out of Danang, we always posted a guard on the aircraft at night. When it was my turn, the aircraft was parked not too far from the fuel bladders. They were big rubber gas tanks full of jet fuel. Suddenly, the runway was hit by mortars, and I watched the explosions come marching across the runway toward the fuel bladders, our airplane, and me. As they got close, for some reason, they stopped. The Base Safety Officer, a lieutenant colonel, came out and decided to immediately inspect the runway, forgetting that an old VC trick was to fire, then wait, and fire again to catch anyone who came looking. That's exactly what happened, and the next mortar round came down right on top of him. It blew him apart and knocked me down. I got sick when I found myself covered with his blood. That was my worst day over there.

My third thirteen-month tour was in 1972–73. This time, when I left, so did my first wife. That was the year of Operation Linebacker and Linebacker II, the big Christmas bombing campaigns over North Vietnam, which included B-52s and Navy and Air Force fighter bombers. We were based at Danang and were the big traffic cop in the sky. We circled out to sea beyond Haiphong Island and coordinated the attack routes, ingress and egress, airborne refueling, and the all-too-frequent search and rescue operations when a plane was shot down. The NVA knew what we were doing, because one day they sent MIGs up after us. We might be very slow, but we saw them coming a long way off, dove down to the deck, and called for help. The Navy scrambled some jets, which came to our rescue and chased the MIGs away.

When that tour ended, I stayed in the Air Force, but transferred from AWACS to repairing the "Hound Dog" air-to-ground missiles the B-52s carried. In 1976, I was offered a commission and promoted to captain in the Air Police, where I ran missile convoys and performed anti-terrorism inspections on all the air bases in the Middle East, from Pakistan to Kenya. In 1986, I retired with eleven years enlisted and ten years commissioned service. I went to work for Fairfax County Virginia in traffic control, and worked there for the next twenty-one years until I retired again in 2007. Now, I like to spend my time playing golf, reading, and serving as a paramedic with our local Community Emergency Response Team.

MILTON CENTER'S WAR

US Army Specialist 4th Class,
Company Clerk, Headquarters Company,
86th Signal Battalion, Cu Chi, 1967–68

I grew up in Potsdam, New York, just south of the St. Lawrence River in upper New York State. In May, 1966, after graduating from high school, I worked in the mailroom of a big market research firm in Manhattan until I got drafted. The Army sent me to Fort Jackson, South Carolina, for Basic. For some reason, they always sent the southern guys up north and us northern guys down south. I was pretty big and overweight then. I couldn't pass the PT test, so they put me in the 'Fat Farm,' to slim down. I went from 242 to 180 pounds, which was the best thing that happened to me. In the process, they also turned me into one nasty son-of-a-bitch.

After basic, they sent me to Fort Gordon, Georgia, to learn how to be a clerk typist. I wanted to go to the West Coast, away from New York. Naturally, they sent me to Fort Dix, New Jersey, and then, in September, 1967, to Vietnam. People ask what was it like, going over there? After three long airplane flights and a truck ride, I was dropped off at the 86th Signal Battalion at Cu Chi, about twenty-five miles northwest of Saigon. Right off the bat, the First Sergeant told me not to make any friends. Unfortunately, I did, and most of them went home in body bags.

This building is our commo center. We supported the 25th Infantry Division which was also based at Cu Chi. They were a tough outfit, especially the "Wolfhounds," the 27th Infantry Regiment. All hell broke loose whenever they came back from an operation. Our battalion had a lot of linemen who put up telephone poles and strung wires that the VC kept knocking down. I was a Spec-4 clerk, working in the headquarters, mostly typing reports.

Our battalion had four long, odd-looking hooches that held forty men each. They had con-  crete floors, metal roofs, and wire mesh screens. Outside they'd stacked sandbags around the building, and dug some bunkers for us to jump in if we got attacked. That was fine until the mon- soon hit and the bunkers filled with water. We had homemade showers made from empty napalm bomb casings. They would fill with rainwater and worked great. Our mess hall was a tent, but they'd hired Vietnamese to handle the KP and cleaning work, including burning the 55-gallon drums from the latrines every morning. Better them than me.

 We'd get mortared and rocketed around 6:00 to 7:00 p.m. every day, so we'd always be jumping into the bunkers. One night at the end of January, I was playing cards with the sergeants. We were sitting around in our underwear, when sirens went off and we started hearing gunfire. We didn't know it then, but that was the start of Tet. We all ran to our hooches and grabbed our weapons. I crawled under a truck for a while, until the First Sergeant told us to get up and reinforce the perimeter. There was a real light show going on with the helicopter gunships from the 25th Infantry attacking the enemy outside the perimeter with tracer rounds. It started around 8:00 p.m. and went on all night. In the morning, big patrols went out looking for the VC. That's when I saw that the truck I'd been hiding under was loaded with ammunition. If it'd been hit, there'd be nothing left of it or me but a big hole in the ground.

One good thing our battalion did was to help a Vietnamese school in town as a public service project. We built it, and I think we rebuilt it three times, because the VC kept blowing it up. It was a Catholic school, and I'll never forget the kids that were there. They really got to me. There were also some beautiful Buddhist temples out in the countryside that had been destroyed and reduced to rubble during Tet.

Some of my best memories were of the entertainers that put on shows at Cu Chi. We had Bob Hope, Martha Raye, and Carol Channing. I was in the front section for the Bob Hope show. It was about 130° and we sat there for six to seven hours in the sun waiting for him. Then he came out and made us all move, because he decided to move the cameras around, so they'd have a better shot of him. I never liked him after that. But Carol Channing was very nice. So was Martha Raye. She went out to some very danger- ous firebases, like the top of Black Virgin Mountain, which was surrounded by VC. I got a chance to talk to her and take her picture.

With combat pay, I think I was making $285 per month. That doesn't sound like much now, but I bought a lot of stuff at the PX at really great prices. About halfway through my tour, I got a chance to take R&R in Australia. It was great. Turns out I had some relatives down there that my family got hold of and I went to see them. We flew into Darwin and then down to New South Wales where I stayed for five days and they showed me all around. Australians really liked Americans.

When my tour was over, I almost reenlisted; but the night before, five of our Sergeants were killed when a rocket hit their bunker. Afterward, somebody stuck their rifles in the ground and put their helmets on top of the stocks, right outside the bunker they'd been in. That changed my mind about reenlisting. Even after I got home, whenever I heard a truck backfire, I'd jump in the bushes. That went on for six months. After I was discharged, I went back to that Wall Street marketing firm and ran their mailroom, ending up as supervisor.

I think the thing that bothered me most about having been there was not hearing a good word from anyone after I got back home. No thanks, no nothing, until recently. The other thing that still bothers me is that many veterans don't know what their rights and benefits are. The government does nothing to help, and civilian doctors have no idea how to diagnose Agent Orange disabilities or PTSD. The only way to learn is from other vets. I'm 74 years old now, and I have Agent Orange-related diabetes, neuropathy, and hearing loss, as do so many others. Still, I enjoy playing Gin Rummy, Samba, and partici- pating in veteran's groups. I used to play a lot of golf and had an eight handicap, but had to stop playing because of the neuropathy.

DAVE KRUEGER'S WAR

US Army, Staff Sergeant and Artillery Surveyor, Division Artillery, 1st Cavalry Division, I Corps and II Corps, 1967–69

I'm from Sleepy Eye, Minnesota, in the southwest corner of the state near South Dakota. I was good in math, and got hired by a local surveyor and engineer right out of high school. He taught me himself, his way, and I got pretty good at it. With the draft getting closer, I enlisted in the Army to become a surveyor. My first choice was to be an engineering surveyor. My second choice was to be an artillery surveyor, which was similar, and that's what I got.

I went to Basic in April, 1967, at Fort Campbell, Kentucky, went on to Fort Sill, Oklahoma, for Field Artillery Surveyor AIT, and then went straight to Vietnam. Technically, I was assigned to a unit near the DMZ, but the replacement depot at Cam Ranh Bay changed it to the 1st Cavalry Division in II Corps. They said I had about 3 to 6 months to live, because the Cav lost so many people. I thought, "Damn! What have I gotten into?"

When I reported into the surveying section at LZ Two Bits, they decided I needed some field time; so they assigned me to 1st of the 9th Recon, the "Head Hunters" as an RTO for 3 months. After that, I returned to the survey group and worked directly for Division Artillery at Bon Son, halfway between the coast and Laotian-Cambodian border.

Firing artillery is a geometry exercise. If you want to hit a target, you need to know where you are. To do that, you need two known points of reference. From those, you can traverse with the angle and distance to where your gun battery is to be located, humping all the way on foot, or preferably by helicopter. When you have all that geometry right, you can fire a howitzer with some assurance the shell will go the right direction and distance and hit your target. The trick is to have surveyors go out ahead of time and map all the new firebases and LZs. We would go in as soon as a site was cleared with some infantry protection, before the guns arrived. Sometimes we'd go even earlier than that, and establish the "control points," as they were called. We also had our own snipers, who would be in position near the new LZs two or three days before we were to enter the area.

My MOS, was 82C20, and eventually 82C40, or Section Chief. A division survey section contained forty to fifty surveyors and two in-house snipers. We surveyed not only for the field artillery but also for the aerial rocket helicopters, the Air Force, the Marines, and even the Navy. One time, we had the Battleship *New Jersey* fire on some enemy positions nearby. When a shell from one of those 16-inch naval guns comes over, it sounds like being buzzed by a Phantom jet. I asked one of their Forward Observers, how accurate those big guns were. He smiled and said, "All we have to do is get close."

We mostly operated in the Central Highlands of II Corps. Then, in January 1968, we were sent up to I Corps further north, where Hell began, just south of the DMZ and east of the Laotian border. That was Camp Evans. One evening, a single 122-millimeter rocket from the NVA hit our ammo dump and fuel storage area. Talk about a blind pig finding an acorn! It was like a Fourth of July celebration, except this wasn't July. What a rush. It was the best fireworks show I've ever seen. The next morning, when things finally stopped blowing up, they ask for volunteers to go in and pick up the duds. I said, "No thank you, I have some surveying work to do. Get the EOD guys to do that."

That area of Vietnam was more mountainous than the Central Highlands. It had sharp valleys and steep cliffs, like those that surrounded the A-Shau Valley. To this day, I believe that II Corps was more beautiful than I Corps or III Corps, with flatland and rice paddies along the coast, and then the hills, rubber plantations, and triple-canopy jungle as you moved back toward the Cambodian and Laotian borders.

In the A-Shau Valley, we also set out new devices that could detect ground movement. A grid system was established with coordinates to locate each one. The only problem was how to distinguish between a man and the large animals that roamed the valley. So, when in doubt, we used artillery to stop the movement.

I believe 1968 was the hardest year of the war. We had the Tet Offensive, the Hue counter-offensive, the relief of Khe Sanh, plus the A-Shau Valley Incursion, all within a six-month period. What a way to start a year!

The North Vietnamese used their artillery the same way we did, except they had a big head start, going back to their battles with the Japanese and French. The NVA had some very good Chinese surveying equipment, which was small and very accurate to survey-in their big guns. They used the big Chinese-made 152-millimeter howitzers, and they knew every inch of the countryside. They were very accurate, had well-trained forward observers, and could out-range our 155s. You can ask the Marines in I Corps what that was like. I preferred not to work with the Marines up there, because the NVA just love to shoot at them and anyone else who happened to be with them. They were bullet magnets.

Around September, 1968, we received orders to relocate south to III Corps, northwest of Saigon. Our survey teams usually consisted of six men plus all our gear. When we went out, we were always very heavily armed, because we never knew what we were getting into. We also carried enough C-rations for a week in case resupply became a problem, plus Claymore mines, ammunition, grenades, our surveying gear, C-4 to cook with, 6-volt batteries, and any other type of armament we could find. It was the same basic field gear as the infantry, plus we had to carry our surveying equipment.

I agreed to two plus extensions, and stayed in Vietnam for a total of twenty-five months. I was pretty good at my job, and became the Section Chief as an E-5, despite the fact it was an E-7 slot. That was when the Colonel told me they needed to fix that, and he promoted me to E-6. Unfortunately, I was only twenty years old at the time, and the 1st Cav Division required a guy to be twenty-one to make Staff Sergeant, or to buy hard liquor. The Colonel had to wait a few weeks until my birthday to promote me.

From the time I arrived in country in October, 1967 at LZ Two Bits in II Corps until September, 1969, when we were based at Phuoc Vin in III Corps, we never had an Enlisted Man's Club, or for that matter were we given much beer. Finally, things became a bit more civilized when they built a PX at our base camp. There went my savings.

After you survey a new LZ, there's a lot of down time before they need you for the next one. Because I was good with maps, I would fly as an Aerial Observer in a Loach helicopter or a Bird-Dog single-engine plane. Then, someone came up with the bright idea of putting me with a Hunter-Killer team. That was when a small aircraft would fly at treetop level and at a slow speed to draw enemy fire from the ground. At that point, you were supposed to drop smoke grenades and let the Cobra gunships, which were flying higher up, come in and "light them up." I often wonder if the genius who thought that up ever tried it himself. Only the Army would come up with something like that.

Another job we had was "crater analysis." Whenever a rocket would hit, if we could get to the impact area quick enough, sometimes while other rockets were still coming in, we could use a lensatic compass to shoot a line from where the rocket motor had buried itself, across the crater, to where it had been fired from. Then, we could call in counter-battery fire and hit the launch site. Here again, I'll bet that the guy who thought it up hadn't done it, or never realized that there might be still more rockets fired, as the NVA got away.

Another job we had was to determine the wear and tear on the barrels of the 105-millimeter howitzers, the 155-millimeter howitzers, and the 175-millimeter and 8-inch self-propelled guns. With this information, the Fire Direction Center could adjust the line and elevation of the round for accuracy, and determine when the barrels needed to be replaced.

We also surveyed the location of every building and bunker in our compound, the location of perimeter bunkers, and the wire. That way, if we ever got hit and overrun, they could call in artillery very close to the friendly positions.

In 25 months you see a lot of things, some good and a lot bad. You see new guys come in, and before you know it, he's a short timer going home. Pretty soon, you start to forget them, as more new guys come and go. I toted too many sand bags and ammo boxes, built too many bunkers, laid too much PSP, strung way too much razor wire, dug too many holes, flew too many combat missions, humped through too much jungle, got rained on way too often, sweated way too much, trembled too often from fear, did not drink enough BEER, and did enough stupid things to last a life time or maybe two life times. I don't remember any of this being mentioned when I enlisted. I guess I should have read the fine print in the contract more closely.

With my two extensions, I only had one hundred and forty-nine days left on my enlistment when I rotated home on November 15, 1969. The Army offered me a teaching position at Fort Belvoir, Virginia, if I reenlisted, but I had had enough. I got out, went back home, and enrolled at the University of Minnesota for surveying and engineering classes until I ran out of money in my third year. I then went to work for several civil engineering and surveying firms, and stayed up in Minnesota until 1985. That was when we were doing some surveying on a frozen lake and fell through the ice with all our equipment. I decided to move to Florida, where I continued to do surveying for two firms, until I got stupid, started my own company, and ran it for twenty-five years.

I'm now 69 and retired. I play golf, fish sometimes, and camp other times. I guess I still love the smell of molding, rotting canvas. I also stay active in the Vietnam Veterans of America and a few other groups that will put up with me. It has been a wonder life, except for the side effects of Agent Orange and the other nasty thing they sprayed on us over there.

RAY GODFREY'S WAR

Royal Australian Navy Flight Lieutenant
and Huey Helicopter Pilot,
135th Assault Helicopter Company, the "Emus,"
Vung Tau and Camp Blackhorse, 1967–68

Australia made a big commitment to the Vietnam War. After all, it was in our backyard. We had from one to three infantry battalions there for most of the war, plus Air Force and Navy units. Less well known is the Royal Australian Navy Helicopter Flight Vietnam (RANHFV) attached to the US 135th Assault Helicopter Company, which consisted of about 280 US Army aircrew, maintenance, and administration personnel and 48 RAN aircrew, maintenance, and administration personnel. It was called an Experimental Military Unit, or EMU, which we Aussies had a good laugh over, because that was the name of one of our indigenous birds. The fact that an emu can't fly was completely ignored, but the name stuck. The 135 AHC's motto was "Get the Bloody Job Done," which we did to a high degree.

The unit was fully integrated. The CO was American, but the XO was Australian, and so on, all the way down the ranks. I was a Navy Lieutenant when I arrived in country in October, 1967, and made Section OIC. In all, some two hundred Australian personnel served there during our almost four years in country. The Australians tended to have much more flight experience than our American counterparts, because of our military system, and how we were trained. In my case, I enlisted in the Navy in 1960, when I was only seventeen years old, and rose through the ranks until I qualified for flight school. By 1967, when I arrived in Vietnam, I had over fifteen hundred hours as a pilot, with some seven hundred hours in a helicopter, while many US aircraft commanders only had three hundred and fresh US warrant officer pilots might have only one hundred or two hundred. Still, we lived in the same tents with the same wooden floors, slept on the same

175

cots, put up with the same monsoon mud and summer heat and dust, and we were equally daring in the air.

We operated out of Vung Tau at the mouth of the Mekong River, before moving to Camp Blackhorse about 60 miles north. Later, we moved to Bearcat east of Binh Hoa and to Dong Tam in the Delta. There were several Australian Army battalions at Nui Dat, which was why we had been sent there originally. They didn't have sufficient tasking for us, however, so our helicopter company operated throughout III and IV Corps, supporting the 11th Armored Cav, the 191st Light Infantry Brigade, the 1st Infantry Division, the 9th Infantry Division, and many ARVN units. We had two "slick" or "troop lift" platoons, with eleven Huey-D models each, and a gunship platoon with eight heavily-armed Huey-Cs. Despite our different services and backgrounds, we strove for seamless integration with the Yanks.

As a Navy pilot, I had flown the Wessex antisubmarine warfare helicopter, similar to a Sikorsky H34, and had also flown Hueys. In Vietnam, I flew Huey "slicks," which carried a pilot, co-pilot, a crew chief who doubled as a second door gunner, two M-60 machine guns, at least four thousand rounds of ammunition. When we were doing combat assaults we'd also carry six to eight troops plus all their gear.

Australian pilots had extensive training in night and instrument flying. That came in useful in December when we had to do a night extraction of a unit of the 199th Light Infantry Brigade that had come under heavy attack north of Binh Hoa. To make matters worse, we couldn't use lights or fire back at the enemy for fear of hitting the American troops. So, it was a slow process, spending up to thirty minutes on the ground, to ensure we got them all out. We had to go in five Hueys at a time, and fly out beneath heavy artillery fire. Frankly, we were more concerned about colliding with each other or a stray 105 round, than we were about the enemy. In the end, we got all the 199th guys out without losing a ship.

The TV series M*A*S*H might've been a lot of nonsense, but one thing they had right was all the swapping, trading, and outright theft that took place between units. We could trade a case of our Australian beer for a case of steaks anywhere. One of our guys even traded a case for a Jeep. Somehow, we even ended up with several extra helicopters. We got tired of living in tents at Vung Tau, so some of our guys went up to Binh Hoa with forged papers and drove back with a truckload of plywood, ignoring the MPs, and driving right out the main gate. I even heard that when the airfield at Vung Tau needed a new fire truck, some enterprising souls went all the way up to I Corps, stole one, and drove it back.

During Tet, everything got very serious. In one of the more interesting developments in the war, the 135th ran critically short of helicopter door gunners. One of our Australian platoon leaders got with the CO of B Company of the 2nd Royal Australian Infantry Regiment, and asked for volunteer machine gunners. Nine Australian infantrymen were then "seconded" to the 135th Assault Helicopter Company to fill that need. The troops were enthusiastic about getting out of the jungle and riding in a Huey, only to later discover that they got shot at ten times more often. Since this was done without approval from our stuffy and bureaucratic headquarters, it was a professionally daring move by both officers. Fortunately, the Aussie gunners showed their mettle and there were no casualties among the nine soldiers who rotated through the 135th between November 1967 and February 1968.

When we flew back to Blackhorse after dark, we would often follow the highway in, not wanting to turn on our lights for fear of drawing enemy fire. However, after dark in the wet season, visibility would drop to zero and we couldn't see a bloody thing. One night, I was Section Leader for a flight of ten aircraft, and it was one of those times when my night flying and instrument experience paid off.

The clouds had dropped to treetop level, and I could tell from the voices from the other ships that there were a lot of twitchy pilots behind me. Seeing no choice, I told them to turn on their lights and tighten up the formation, so they could at least see each other. There might be VC out there, but at our speed, all they'd see was a big, glowing white cloud quickly passing over them in the fog. Besides, the VC weren't our problem, finding our base was. In a few minutes, I found the highway and we followed it in without losing anyone. As we always said, "If you get back alive, you should be happy."

We put in a lot of flying time over there. The Americans had a rule that their units couldn't fly more than twenty-five hundred hours per month, but the 135th AHC routinely flew up to thirty-five hundred hours, which we felt we owed to the troops we were supporting.

One serious problem we had, far worse than the Americans, were the atrophied brains at our headquarters, particularly in our Air Force. They were still working on peacetime regulations and didn't understand there was a war going on. I had a senior Royal Australian Air Force (RAAF) officer fly with me one night, when we went into a hot firebase to resupply the unit and pick up some bodies. There was a C-47 "Smokey" circling the area putting down suppressing fire and dropping flares. When it was my turn to go in, his last flare had gone out, and everything turned black. I quickly told my "second seat" Air Force pilot to "Turn on the bloody lights!" He bristled and answered, "We... we can't do that, it's against regulations!" I reached over and turned them on myself, muttering, "Bloody fool!"

As if that wasn't enough, we lifted out of there with nine bodies and headed for the mortuary barge anchored off Vung Tau. When I went to land, the controller down there didn't want to let me in, because I didn't have the "proper clearance." I wasn't known for tact, and asked him, "Okay, what do you want me to do with them? Take them back?" He let us land.

By the end of the war, our Royal Australian Navy Helicopter Flight was the most highly decorated unit in the Australian Navy. We usually had forty-eight Australians attached to the 135th. While I was there, we lost three aircrew killed and several wounded. During four detachments in Vietnam the HFV lost 5 KIA and twenty-five wounded, a 15% casualty rate.

A major controversy since the war has been the awarding of medals and decorations. While both American Generals, Westmoreland and Abrams, wanted to award us US decorations on the same basis as they did their own troops, our generals would not accept them. Two Australians were awarded American Silver Stars, but they only received the medals long after the war. In 2012, I was finally awarded the twenty US Air Medals which I earned. What we did receive, and in the same proportion as your own troops, were Agent Orange-related illnesses and PTSD, the latter of which affected me to some extent.

After my service in Vietnam, I remained in the Australian Navy and returned to antisubmarine warfare flying the Grumman S2E Tracker on the aircraft carrier *HMAS Melbourne*. In 1980 I assumed command of VS 816 before eventually retiring as a Lieutenant Commander. I'm now 75-years old and live in Queensland, Australia, where I like to fish, play lawn bowling, and garden.

The following poignant poem was written by Leo Petrie, a Leading Seaman Weapons Sailor in the RAN Helicopter Flight Vietnam. It deals with the tragic, fiery crash of one of our helicopters, which cost the lives of two of our men on March 28, 1970. The poem was Leo's way of coming to grips with his horrific memories of that crash, and of a terrible war.

"DISJECTA MEMBRA"
(Scattered Remains)

Two men down
but who's to know
Their lives burnt out, cut short
What does this war achieve
But pain and hurtful fear
the mental taunt, with
Bitter memories left to haunt
Help is what we need
our lives now twisted
hard to straighten out.

Two men down
But who's to know
That on that fateful day
Machine in pieces, scattered 'er the ground
But what is left, ne'er enough to tell
of two young men no more to live
The world is poorer now
for life's a gift to treasure
This memory hurts
and aches my body so.

Two men down
but who's to know
"Bearcat" hard grown bare rock
Devoid of foliage, trees now gone
A piece of cloth its colour green
with half a boot is all I see
This horrid space a grave
to mark their resting place
Among the mines and scattered scrap
The once proud flying ship.

Two men down
but who's to know
Their duty's what they did

Our war's now wrong
and we're no good
So, people in our faces spit
But first we honour Flag
We'll be here, till we're sent home
No hero's welcome
Marching in the street.

Two men down
but who's to know
Everlasting, now but peaceful
with their blackened wreck
No spit for them
Their force now spent they'll know
that on the altar
Their blackened boots and helmets
Moved hardened men to tears.

Two men down
but who's to know
The pain they knew beyond
In peace, they dwell
Sweet Mothers' sons,
who now live on
In God's radiant light
Shine out across the World
That wars might cease
and men will live in peace.

BOB VAN NUISE'S WAR

US Army, Lieutenant and Bird Dog pilot,
184th Reconnaissance Aircraft Company,
Phu Loi, 1967 to 68

My father was in the insurance business, so I grew up in a lot of places from Syracuse to Indianapolis, and Mount Lebanon and Harrisburg, Pennsylvania. I began college at Duke in 1961, and then transferred to Tennessee, where I joined the Army ROTC program. After I graduated in 1966 and was commissioned, the Army sent me to Fort Sill, Oklahoma, where I became a Field Artillery officer. I stayed at Fort Sill for four months until my slot in flight school opened up and I became a Bird Dog pilot.

I arrived in Vietnam in November, 1967, as a first lieutenant assigned to the 184th Reconnaissance Aircraft Company at Phu Loi, north of Saigon and west of Bien Hoa. We had twenty-four airplanes and covered the entire II Corps area, supporting the 1st Infantry Division. Their Division Artillery and staff were very good, and their Aerial Observers were located at Phu Loi with us. They would almost always send one of their guys up with us when we covered one of their operations.

Being a trained artillery officer, it was easy for me to communicate with them, but it was useful to have a second guy in the aircraft. Supposedly, we couldn't fly more than one hundred and forty hours in any thirty-day period, but there were many days we blew right through that average. We usually flew low, at eight hundred feet circling the target area, and I had to be constantly aware of where we were, where our troops were, the enemy positions, any other aircraft in the air, where our artillery was, where rounds would be coming from, and whether it would be artillery or mortar fire. That mattered, if you didn't want to get your aircraft ventilated.

Our base camp at Phu Loi was always busy with a lot of different kinds of aircraft. One of our persistent problems was from the rotor wash from the helicopters that used the same runways we did. A Bird Dog doesn't weigh much. Early in my tour, three of us

181

came in to land at the same time. We could land on a very short strip, so we came in one long, one middle, and one short. I was the short guy and didn't notice a Huey coming in to land at their hangar alongside the runway. I was hit with a fifteen mile-per-hour crosswind that almost blew me off the runway. That's bad enough during the day; but when we came in to land at night, and they were making repairs and suddenly started one up, things could get very interesting.

In addition to support for the 1st Infantry Division, we supported the Special Forces who ran stealth operations into Cambodia with squads of ARVN infantry. They would be dropped off somewhere and disappear in the jungle. Since their radios weren't powerful enough to reach their base, we would fly loosely over their positions three times a day to relay any radio messages. We were their lifeline and we had to listen carefully because they usually whispered. On one such mission, they were looking for "the mailman," a messenger on a bicycle known to use certain trails to carry messages between NVA units. They spent several days waiting for him, until I finally heard their CO whisper, "Send in the slicks." They had stashed the courier's body in the bush and hightailed it out of there, bringing his bicycle and saddlebags to the helicopter. We later learned that one of the things they found was a report from an NVA commander describing a B-52 strike on his camp. He said 50% to 60% of his men were killed outright, most of the rest were wounded and would soon die, and the handful of survivors were useless.

In December, I was providing cover to a night truck convoy near Long Tien. I had been up since maybe 5:00 a.m. that day doing other things, so I began the day bone-tired. A Bird Dog held six hours of fuel, so we would come in and refuel every two and one-half hours. I had an artillery observer in the back seat, and we did that all night long, with no food and no water. By 6:00 a.m., it was taking all I had to stay awake. I noticed an Air Force Bird Dog some distance away, but didn't give it much thought. We circled around again, and the next thing I knew I heard a loud bang and the observer in back nearly jumped out of the airplane. Obviously, we had hit something, but what? I looked up and saw the Air Force Bird Dog pilot looking back at me, just as surprised. With only two little planes up there, somehow, we had hit. It wasn't until we got back to base that I saw he had clipped the antenna on my wing. It was that close.

I rotated back to the States in November, 1968, and was stationed at Fort Meade near DC until June 30, 1969, when I got out of the Army. I started as a pilot with United Airlines the next day, although I remained in the Army Reserves. I spent thirty-four years flying for United, mostly based out of their Western hub at Denver. In 2015, I attended the Army's Bird Dog reunion at Fort Rucker, which brought together the pilots and crews from the eleven Bird Dog companies that served in Vietnam. We had a great time.

JOHN THOMSTATTER'S WAR

US Army, Specialist 5th Class,
Radio Repairman and Company Clerk,
709th Maintenance Battalion,
Ben Luc, 1967–68

I had an Associate's Degree in electronics and instrument systems, a Secret security clearance, and was working at McDonnell-Douglas Aircraft in St. Louis, writing tech manuals for the new F-4 Phantom Jet. If I close my eyes, I think I can still draw the layout of its cockpit. Anyway, after eight months, my Draft Notice arrived. I could have gotten a tech job with the Air Force. That was a "no-brainer," but I didn't want to make a four-year commitment. So, I enlisted in the Army for their Nuclear Electronics Technician course. The classes were at Redstone Arsenal in Huntsville, Alabama, and then at Albuquerque, New Mexico. It was fifty-one weeks long, one of the Army's longest, hardest, and most expensive schools. What they taught us was how to test and repair the automatic diagnostic equipment that monitors the nuclear warheads on tactical missiles like the Honest John, which were designed to stop the Russian tanks if they attacked West Germany. It was a tough class, and I was one of the very few who passed it the first time through!

Nuclear warheads, Honest John Missiles, Germany, and all that Top-Secret stuff? When the course ended and I got my orders, where did the Army send me? Vietnam, of course; where they had no nuclear warheads, no test equipment, and no missiles. The Navy probably had nukes on the aircraft carriers in the South China Sea. The Air Force probably had them in Guam, the Philippines, and Japan. The Army never had nukes in Vietnam, but it had me.

When I arrived there in November, 1967, they didn't have a clue what to do with me; and when the Army doesn't know what to do with someone, the easiest solution was to put them on KP. That's how I spent Thanksgiving at the replacement depot at Long Binh —doing KP. Wonderful. With my security clearances and MOS, they couldn't put me on perimeter guard duty. I was scheduled to go to an artillery unit at Chu Lai, but that wasn't going to work, either. So, they kept me there at Long Binh for two months, mostly supervising Vietnamese laborers who were filling sandbags. Finally, in late January I was ordered to report to the 9th Infantry Division headquarters at Camp Bear Cat, but it was late in the day and there was no transportation available. A guy with a jeep offered me a ride through Saigon. We had just arrived there before dark, when the Tet Offensive began, and all hell broke loose.

When I arrived at Bear Cat, the 9th Infantry Division didn't know what to do with me either. When things finally calmed down, they changed my MOS to radio repairman —there went a whole bunch of expensive training down the drain—and assigned me to the 709th Maintenance Battalion in Ben Luc south of Saigon. We supported the 3rd Brigade, and I repaired the RT-524 radios that were carried on the back of jeeps. The good news was that the new MOS got me promoted to Spec 4. Repairing big radios was no problem for me. By and large, the Army replaces modules and components as opposed to repairing them; so, with my Associates degree and the Army course I had taken, it was work I could easily handle.

We would frequently take our repair vans to the field with the infantry units when they went on sweeps. When there was nothing else to do I'd pull guard duty, KP, or make courier runs up to Bear Cat. We would usually wait to leave until the local traffic began moving on the roads, figuring it would be safe by then—we called it Vietnamese mine sweeping.

Halfway through my tour, our company clerk rotated out. With two years of college and being able to type a little, I got the job. The most important thing was to keep the Morning Report and the duty rosters correct. If you do that, the CO and the First Sergeant are happy, so that's what I did. It kept me out of the field and got me promoted to Spec 5.

There were maybe a hundred guys at our compound, and a half-dozen of us were from Pennsylvania. We got our local Congressman to send us a state flag which we proudly flew for parties. On the bright side, I had a great R&R in Sydney and never lost any of my close friends during my tour.

When I finally rotated out, I was assigned to the Army airfield at Fort Benning as a personnel clerk to take care of the flight records of all the pilots. I got an early out in

December 1969 to go to Penn State, where I got my degree in Personnel Management. I got a job with HUD for the Hurricane Agnes clean up, ended up managing a large mobile home park for HUD, and then went to Boeing to write the Tech Manuals and Service Bulletins for a high-tech rail car project, for new helicopters, and for the CH-46, eventually moving on to Fairchild-Dornier, writing more tech manuals.

I've been diagnosed with Agent Orange-induced Type-2 Diabetes; but so far, I've not experienced any of the other diseases many others have. I'm 71, I am the Secretary of our local Vietnam Veterans of America chapter, and I like to play golf.

WILL BODIE'S WAR

US Air Force Sergeant, Security Police,
Da Nang and Dong Ha, 1967–68

I'm a New York City kid from Harlem. I did a year of college and enlisted in the Air Force in November, 1965, to get into the Air Police or Security Police, or whatever they're calling it now. Being from New York, naturally, my first assignment was out in Seattle Washington, guarding a BOMARC missile battery. This was the height of the Cold War, and they protected the Pacific Northwest from Russian bombers.

Two years later, in December, 1967, I arrived in Da-nang and the 366th Security Police Squadron. I was an E-5 buck sergeant and squad leader. Along with the Marines, we provided perimeter defense for the Air Force base, patrolled inside and outside along the runways, and man-ned observation and listening posts on the perimeter.

After fifty years, people ask me what I remember about Vietnam. My problem is I remember EVERYTHING, particularly the little things. I remember the 120° heat and the monsoon rains, which left you cold and wet in the winter. We would buy wetsuits from the local Vietnamese and wear them under our ponchos. They were good, but there was always one icy drop of water that would get inside, run down your back, and drive you nuts.

I was there for twelve months, except for occasional assignments at Dong Ha, up north, eleven miles from the DMZ, and except for two trips to the hospital because of a bad knee. We were out on patrol and received some fire, when one of my troopers accidentally fired his 40-mm grenade launcher and hit me in the knee with a round. Fortunately for me, it didn't go far enough to be "live," but it felt like getting hit with a hammer. Fortunately for him, he didn't come over to see how I was, or he'd have found out. I ended up in the hospital in Japan for a month with that one. Later, I got my leg twisted in some barbed wire. That started the knee up again and they sent me to the

Philippines for surgery. Today, it would all be done with quick microsurgery, but back then it was a whole lot more difficult. I had to learn how to walk all over again.

Dong Ha was a new base, but much more dangerous than Danang. It was small. Only helicopters and small airplanes flew out of there, but it was an important radar base. The 3rd Marine Division worked that area hard, but we heard there were over 40,000 NVA troops along the DMZ and it remained an NVA stronghold. Dong Ha had a mess hall, but we never had enough water, especially after the NVA blew up our water tank. A lot of our food was from powder, even the milk and the maple syrup. With no water tank, the cooks had to use river water. Even purified, everything tasted so bad that we got permission to brush our teeth with Budweiser—only one can a day—but it was better than that river water.

We had bunkers around the perimeter at Danang. They were mostly set below ground, with thick lumber, sandbags, and firing slits. I was posting the guard one night and sent a trooper into one of the bunkers. He came running back out terrified. I asked him what was wrong, and he said, "Sarge, the walls in there are moving." I took his flashlight, looked inside, and he was right. There were a million cockroaches all over the walls. I grabbed a couple of our flares and tossed them in. It set the bunker on fire, but I didn't care. The Platoon Sergeant came running over screaming, "What did you do?" About then, some of the Vietnamese who lived nearby in their little village came running over with cups and bowls. They went inside, started scooping up the dead cockroaches, and came back out grinning. "Numba One Chop Chop!" one of them said, which was Vietnamese pidgin English for "G.I., you just made us lunch!"

Speaking of Vietnamese cuisine, I was in the barracks when a humongously fat rat waddled into the room. I grabbed my pistol and turned to shoot it, when one of the Vietnamese workers stopped me. He grabbed the rat by the tail, ran him outside to where they were burning some trash in a barrel, and tossed him in. Five minutes later he pulled the rat out and held it up. Again, I heard, "Numba One Chop Chop!" Obviously, another local delicacy. Even today, if I so much as see a mouse, I go ballistic. And I never let my kids take food in bed with them, because I was so hyper about the rats getting all over us at night over there.

Danang City was off limits. One night, some of us decided to go into town and hit one of the local restaurants anyway, but we had to be careful not to get caught. We ordered some food, and it was really pretty good. I motioned for the Mama San in the kitchen to come over, pointed at the plate and said, "Numba One!" I tried to find out what it was, but she kept saying "Dok, Dok." I smiled at her and asked, "Duck? Like Quack, Quack?" but one of the waiters corrected me. "No, no duck. Dok, Dok, like Bark, Bark."

After that, I stuck to Air Force food, and never "went native" again.

The beginning of the Tet Offensive on January 30, 1968, was scary. We had radar and spotters on Monkey Mountain to the east of us. The code for incoming rockets was "10-100." We thought the Vietnamese were celebrating the holiday, until we heard the radio calls "10-100 Dong Ha," then "10-100 Quang Tri," "10-100 Phu Bai," and "10-100 Hue." That was when we knew it was big. And when we heard "10-100 Danang," the gasoline tanks went up. There was a huge explosion and the smoke and flames went on and on.

We stayed at our posts on the perimeter for three days. When the fighting finally ended, and we were relieved, we were walking back to our barracks when I saw our reflections in a window—filthy, unshaven, with sunken eyes, and covered with mud. It was that "1,000-yard stare." Man, I wondered. Who are those guys? Even today, my wife finds me doing that. It's classic PTSD, but some things you can't ever forget. Still, the whole time I was there as squad leader, I never lost a man. We had a few wounded, but no one killed.

When my tour was over, just before Christmas, 1968, I still had a year left, so they sent me to the Air Force Base near Niagara Falls, in the winter. After the heat and humidity of Vietnam, that was cruel. At the end of that tour, I was discharged. In 1980 I joined the Air National Guard, remained a member for twenty-five years, and retired as a Master Sergeant.

I did contract malaria in Vietnam, but it really didn't hit me until I was back home riding on a bus. One day, everything turned orange on me, as if I were looking through a film. I got sweats and chills and became all wobbly. I managed to get off the bus and sit with my back against a wall until it went away. The same thing happened a year later. That was when I went in and had it diagnosed. It was malaria.

I also get flashbacks. One year, we took the kids to a botanical garden. I was pushing one of them in a stroller. As we stepped inside one of the big greenhouses, there were big green leafy plants all around me, when the heat and humidity hit. I froze, and whispered to them, "Be quiet!" as if I were out on patrol in the jungle. The malaria, flashbacks, and the knee—you can leave Vietnam, but it never leaves you.

RICK KEENEY'S WAR

US Army, Spec 5 and Combat Medic,
Alpha Company, 26th Regiment, 1st Infantry Division,
Di-An and Lai Khe, 1968–69

I'm from Wilkinsburg, Pennsylvania, a small town eight miles from Pittsburgh. I finished two years of college, but had to cut back and get a job at Penney's to support my mother. I was drafted toward the end of 1967. After Basic at Fort Jackson, the Army sent me to Fort Sam Houston in Texas to become a combat medic.

They didn't waste much time. In March, 1968, I was in Vietnam at Camp Alpha, assigned to Bravo Company, 26th Regiment of the 1st Infantry Division, and spent the whole next year in the bush. Typically, they assigned a medic to each of the company's three platoons, plus one is the CP medic at the company command post. The medics went out on all patrols and ambushes, like everyone else. Night ambushes were scary things over there. All you see is green and red tracer rounds flashing past you. We were green, and they were red, or the other way around. Sometimes you never knew who was shooting at who in the dark.

We never got any news, and never knew what was going on in the States or in other parts of Vietnam. I was never much good with maps, but I know we were at Di-An, Lai Khe, Vung Tau, An Lac, Black Virgin Mountain, the Michelin rubber plantation, and all over I Corps… hell, we were even in Cambodia, although no one admitted it back then. Jungle was jungle, and it was always thick. We slept on the ground and ate C-rations most of the time. I thought that was how everyone in the Army lived until I got med-evaced to Vung Tau, the place they called China Beach in the TV show, to get some wounds treated. That was when I saw the big wooden hooches with metal roofs and screens, mess halls, enlisted and NCO clubs, PXs, and all the other stuff they had in the rear. I couldn't believe it.

The worst thing I went through was at Landing Zone Rita, where our company was overrun by the NVA on October 31, Halloween Night, 1968. It was in the mountains. Most of the area was jungle, except for the area right around Rita. That was clear. One of my best friends was another medic named Jimmy Ciupinski from Chicago. He had more time in country than I did, but they made me the CP Medic. I felt bad, so I put him with the mortar platoon, so he wouldn't go out on patrol. That was a little bit safer. Unfortunately, one of our other medics got hit, so I had to switch Jimmy from the mortar platoon to one of the rifle platoons. Sure enough, that part of the perimeter was right where the NVA attacked that night. They knew what was going on, because they hit us with 133 mm rockets, sappers, and then infantry about 10:00 or 11:00 p.m. They got through the wire and were everywhere. We fought them all night. The ARVN, the South Vietnamese units that were on Rita with us, were useless. They were for whichever side was winning. It was so bad, that our artillery depressed their barrels and the 105s and were firing "beehive" rounds "direct fire" into the tree lines to break up the attack. That's like a shotgun round with 5,000 little darts in each shell

The next morning, I went around with some guys treating the wounded and picking up the dead bodies in a deuce-and-a-half truck. I don't know how many bodies we picked up. It was a lot, a real mess. That's when I found Jimmy's body. A machine gun got him. That really hit me hard. Later, I found out that our night defensive position at LZ Rita was bait. There were a bunch of NVA regiments all around us and the Army was trying to suck them in. They sure did.

I blamed myself for Jimmy's death for decades; but back then, nobody talked about the war or got counseling. A few years ago, I started going to Vietnam Veterans of America meetings and ran into a fellow vet who was a psychologist and a counselor. That helped. People asked what it was like over there, but you can't describe it. If you weren't there, you won't understand. Anyway, that guy finally convinced me that Jimmy could've just as easily been killed in one of the other platoons or the mortar platoon. It was just his bad luck.

I was wounded twice with shrapnel—once from a grenade and once from a mortar round. I was awarded the Combat Medic Badge, two Air Medals, two Bronze Stars, and two Purple Hearts. I never knew I was given that stuff until one of the VA guys got them for me. You see these pictures where they pin metals on guys and hang stuff around their necks, but that wasn't how it happened. You just got a box in the mail. Maybe.

I spent a year out in the bush, and never knew about the protests or what was going on back in the States, "the World," as we called it. When I arrived back in the US at Travis Air Force Base near San Francisco, as we got off the plane, some crazy lady came running at us with a wooden knife painted red, screaming and calling us baby killers. When I got to Pittsburgh, I couldn't even get a ride home from the airport, so I walked down the road with my bag. Finally, a guy in a red pickup truck stopped and gave me a ride to Squirrel Hill, where I called my uncle.

To me, the only good thing I got out of the Army or Vietnam was the G.I. Bill. Nobody in my family had ever graduated from college, but with the G.I. Bill I was able to go back to California State Teacher's College in Pennsylvania and get my degree. I spent the next thirty-five years as a Special Ed teacher, and then four years as a school principal.

Now, I spend my time playing softball three days a week, playing some golf with my wife, fishing over in the Crystal River, hunting turkey every now and then, and as a member of the VVA Color Guard. I also like to write what I call "rhymes," about 'Nam.' I don't think of it as poetry, but my daughter likes them. This is one of her favorites:

"Faces Not on the Wall

Forty-six years have gone and passed, and yet my mind remembers all.

Faces and names of soldiers, who answered their government's call.

Yes, faces and names of heroic young men and women, many thousands, not on the wall.

T'was in a land far away, where leeches filled rivers, and blood red mountains; and dark canopied jungles gave shelter to an enemy skilled in warfare, and ready to fight.

Yes, an enemy whose only thought was to kill American soldiers, and continue to do so, every day and every night."

I was operated on for kidney cancer in 2012, and had one kidney removed. Later that year I was also diagnosed with stomach cancer, and had one-third of my stomach removed. No one in my family had ever had cancer and I was in areas where Agent Orange was used the whole year; but they weren't on the "politically correct" list of thirteen VA-approved Agent Orange diseases, so my claim was denied. I'm appealing, so maybe I'll be covered when the list changes. But by then, I'll probably be dead and buried.

AL MARTINEZ'S WAR

US Army, Sergeant E-5, 3rd Battalion,
the 22nd Infantry Regiment, 25th Infantry Division,
Cu Chi, Tay Ninh, and Cambodia, 1968–69

I've never seen the Oliver Stone movie, *Platoon*, or at least not all of it. I don't have to. He was in the same unit I was in in Vietnam: the 3rd Battalion of the 22nd Regiment of the 25th Infantry Division, just a different company. What he filmed—humping through the jungle, the elephant grass, the night ambushes, and the quick firefights when you couldn't see anybody, that's exactly what I did, same place, same time, which is why the movie strikes too close to home.

I am a Puerto Rican-American and I had a great childhood in Spanish Harlem in New York City. We were poor, but so was everybody else. I graduated from Benjamin Franklin High School in 1966. After kicking around for a year, I enlisted in the Army. I was eighteen and went on active duty in October, 1967. The Army didn't waste any time. After Basic at Fort Gordon, Georgia, and AIT at Fort Jackson, South Carolina, I arrived in Vietnam the next April.

The 25th Infantry Division was "air mobile." The Regiment's base camp was at Dau Tieng, Northwest of Saigon. We weren't too far from Tay Ninh and Black Virgin Mountain, which we went up and down several times on sweeps and for recon. We ran operations in and out of Cu Chi and went across the border and into Cambodia all the time, although no one ever admitted that was where we were.

When we went out on operations, they made us leave our cameras behind, as if that mattered. We would be dropped into a small LZ by "slicks" or Huey helicopters, and then hack our way back through the elephant grass for about two miles. It was eight to ten feet high, and the triple-canopy jungle was even worse. The point man had to chop his way through it with a machete, so we kept putting different guys up there. We also ran a lot of night ambushes, usually with the whole platoon or at least a squad. Just like they showed in the movie, it was brutal. We would be out in the field from four to six weeks, and then come back in to Dau Tieng for two to three days to the company area, where we had "hooches" and kept what little belongings we had. When we were there, we'd eat, barbecue steaks, get drunk, or get high. A few days later, we'd turn around and go right back out to the field again on another operation. That's what we did for twelve straight months.

People ask me what I remember from back then. I usually answer being scared every day. The only days I wasn't scared was when I got a five-day R and R to Bangkok. And I was one of five guys who got chosen to go to Cu Chi in December, 1968 to see the Bob Hope show. That was cool. They gave us all new uniforms and new boots to wear, and then when we got back they took them all away. I respected Hope for coming over and doing all those shows. Same for Joey Bishop. He would go out to the very dangerous firebases by helicopter and put on a show. I never forgot that.

When we were out in the field, which was most of the time, all we had to eat was C-rations and the packages we got sent from home. One arrived for me one day, and by the time I got to it, all that was left was an empty cardboard box. My buddies had eaten everything. I think they were high. Whenever we got back into base camp, there was a lot of marijuana smoked, not any hard drugs, and a lot of booze and Colt-45 drunk. A few guys would even get high out in the field on sweeps, not me. We had one guy named Dutch who had the point one day, and he was walking so slowly you could tell something was wrong. You could see it in his eyes. He was stoned so we sent him back and had somebody else take point.

After a few months, I got made squad leader. The best thing about that was that I got first pick in the food boxes when we got resupplied. Some of the C-rations weren't too bad, like the pound cake, chicken noodle soup, peaches, and Spam. We ate a lot of Spam —hot, cold, or right out of the can. It didn't matter. We all lost weight, because you just couldn't consume enough calories with what we were doing all day long.

One funny thing I remember, was me and one of my friends playing chicken with a bayonet, throwing it in the ground near the other guy's foot. You know how guys are, crazy sometimes. Well, I threw the knife and got him in the foot. He was bleeding all over the place, so he got sent back to the hospital. Thirty days later, he came back smiling and thanking me. He had hot food, showers, female nurses, and clean sheets, so he didn't complain. He thought it was worth it.

Another time, my squad got told to go get a sniper who was hiding out in the bush. As we got near to where he was, all of a sudden, we heard gunfire and we all jumped back and hit the ground. One of my guys starts moaning and grabbing his leg. I figured he got shot, so I turned around and asked him what's wrong? That's when he told me to get off his foot. When I jumped backwards, I had stomped right down on his ankle.

In the first week of September, 1968, we got involved with a big battle around Fire

Base Buell. It went on for most of a week. When it started, we were out on an operation, ended up getting surrounded, and had to run back to the firebase. We were getting shot at from both sides. The VC and NVA kept attacking, but in addition to all the wire and bunkers, we had tanks and APCs on the firebase as well as big artillery and airstrikes that were called in. It didn't matter. They kept attacking. When it was finally over, we counted something like six hundred enemy bodies around our positions. There was no quit in them, I'll give them that.

I got "scratched" twice, once by "friendly fire" when a dumb Lieutenant fired an M-79 grenade launcher and hit a tree near me. I got pieces of wood and shrapnel in my back. The other was by not-so-friendly fire.

When my tour in Vietnam ended in April, 1969, I was a Sergeant E-5 with a Bronze Star and a Purple Heart; but I still had over a year left on my enlistment. I got sent to Fort Meade near Washington DC. That didn't work out too well for me. I was already having PTSD "issues," so I volunteered to be a Body Escort, to accompany the remains of servicemen coming home. I did that for seven months, until I got orders to Germany, to the 8th Infantry Division in Baumholder. That wasn't a fun place either, and my drinking and PTSD problems only got worse.

When I was discharged and came home, I got a job in New York City with Bankers Trust, went on to get my bachelors in business administration, and worked my way up through that bank and several others as a portfolio analyst, retiring at fifty-five. But I couldn't take New York anymore, either. I found myself drinking more and more heavily every weekend, not on the weekdays, but I ended up getting diagnosed with PTSD and a 100% disability. Now, I play a lot of stickball and softball, and I like pickleball so much, I teach it. I'm sixty-eight, and I like participating in various veteran's activities, like our local Band of Brothers.

DALE BRAY'S WAR

US Army Spec 5, 805th Truck Company,
Vung Tau, 1968–69

I'm from Chesterland, a small town of 2,000 in Geauga County, Ohio. It's farm country in northeast Ohio, about thirty miles east of Cleveland. After high school, I spent "an academically indifferent" year at Ohio State, until I was "invited" by the university to take up other pursuits. After that, I kicked around at some odd jobs until I was drafted in January, 1968. After Basic at Fort Knox I was sent to Fort Leonard Wood where they trained me to be a truck driver, a 64-A-10.

I arrived "in country" on June 3, 1968, and left on June 3, 1969, one year later to the day. They sent me to a truck group in Vung Tau down on the coast. It was a port city southeast of Saigon at the mouth of the Mekong River on the South China Sea. It used to be an old French resort, but by the time I got there it was a large logistics center where stuff was offloaded from the oceangoing ships and put on barges and trucks to go inland.

They assigned me to the 805th Truck Company. During my first two months, I drove in several truck convoys to Saigon, but most of the time we transported ammunition from the ammo dump to the barges headed up river. The area to the south and east of Saigon had a lot of small villages, flat, scrubby countryside, rice paddies, and stuff like that. It wasn't jungle, like they had to the north, or all swamp and wetlands, like down in the Delta. It was hot, boring work, but our truck convoys never got hit. The VC fired rockets at Vung Tau every now and then, and one night they hit the fuel tanks. That was pretty spectacular. It burned for days, but the rockets didn't come close to where I was.

Our company had about a hundred guys in it. One morning at formation, the Captain asked how many of us had been to college. Truck drivers aren't the brightest guys in the Army, but three of us raised our hands. The Captain pulled us aside and asked us how much college. One guy had four years, so he became mail clerk. The second guy had two years, so they made him a clerk in the company orderly room. I had one year, so the Captain asked me, "Bray, do you know what a typewriter looks like?" Fortunately, I had had a one-semester typing class back in high school, so of course I said I did. The next thing I knew, I was assigned to the Legal Office up at the 53rd General Support Group, the Headquarters we reported to. I knew nothing about military forms or styles, but they asked me to type some stuff. I could type fifteen words per minute without any mistakes, and that's all they wanted. One thing this taught me was the priority ranking of mail clerk, company clerk, and then legal clerk.

After a month or two I was typing forty words per minute and quickly taught myself everything I needed about the forms. In the Legal Office, I took statements and depositions on minor proceedings. I didn't work on General Courts-Martial, just Article 15s, drug cases, Summary Courts, and things like that; but I was working in an air-conditioned office, got to travel around to other bases in the area, like Can Tho, and was ED, or exempt from guard duty and patrols, which was really great. Eventually, the First Sergeant realized I wasn't on any of the duty rosters, so I was put back on Company Duty for the last four months. It was good while it lasted, though. And I'll never forget the Thanksgiving I spent in LBJ, Long Binh Jail, the Army's big maximum-security stockade, taking testimony. Some Thanksgiving that was.

I was lucky during my whole tour, and never got hurt. But it's funny how the little things that you didn't think were very important when you were younger, like taking that one-semester typing class in high school, can have a dramatic effect on the rest of your life.

When my tour was over, I was sent to Fort Dix, New Jersey. They sent me to the legal office, but it was already full up with legal clerks, ones with real training, while all I had was on-the-job experience in Vietnam. Since I still had my truck driver MOS, I was assigned to be the colonel's driver, which wasn't bad duty either. I learned I could get an early out if I was accepted to college; so, I applied to Ohio State again, was accepted, and was discharged from the Army.

I had pretty much flunked out the first time there, and I was surprised they even took me. Funny thing though, I had a 1.9 grade average that first year, and got a 3.6 and a 4.0 the first two quarters after I came back. I think that proved how being older, growing up, and serving in the Army and in Vietnam had a big effect on my motivation. I went on to graduate from Ohio State and then moved to Newport News, Virginia, where I started a commercial landscaping company, which I owned and operated for thirty-eight years. In 2003 I was diagnosed with Agent Orange-induced diabetes and am being treated by the VA.

DAVE NELSON'S WAR

US Army, Specialist 4th Class Vehicle Mechanic,
B Troop, 3rd Squadron, 4th Cavalry,
25th Infantry Division,
Cu Chi, 1968–69

After I graduated from high school near West Lafayette, Indiana, where Purdue is, I worked building houses; but I didn't like that much. Other than the parties at Purdue, I didn't like the thought of going to college either. I knew I'd be drafted soon, so I enlisted in the Army for three years to be a mechanic. I thought that was something I might be able use later, and I'd avoid all that reserve time.

I went in in January, 1968. After Basic at Fort Campbell, Kentucky, they sent me to Fort Ord, California for Wheeled Vehicle Mechanic School. They didn't waste any time. Less than six months after I went in, on July 2, 1968, I was in Vietnam. I was a farm kid. My home town had only two hundred people. I had a tough enough time adjusting to a 150-man barracks in Basic, but the "Repo Depo" at Long Binh was in a huge aircraft hangar full of bunk beds and what looked like thousands of guys, and I was expected to go to sleep. I didn't think much of that. After a couple of days, I was assigned to a squadron in the 4th Cav of the 25th Infantry Division at Cu Chi and flown up there in a helicopter. I didn't think much of helicopters, either. The 4th Cav was called "Mac-kenzie's Raiders," which dated back to the Indian wars out West. Whatever, we didn't have any horses. It was a mechanized infantry unit, which meant tanks and APCs on tracks. I'd been trained to fix wheeled vehicles like trucks, not "tracks," but no one there seemed to care.

In the beginning, we lived in tents with dirt floors. Slowly, those were replaced by rough wooden "hooches" with canvas tops, screens, sandbagged walls, and bunkers outside. In the summer, it was so hot that I always woke up soaking wet. We did have a wooden mess hall with hot food when we were in camp. Since I was a mechanic, I learned how to repair a track. We didn't really fix broken things so much as replace them. That included engines, transmissions, or whatever. I figure I spent 60% of my time out on the road with the maintenance track, and maybe 40% back at camp doing mechanical repairs; because swapping out an engine or transmission took a lot of time.

Our unit's main job was to keep the roads open west of Saigon, between Long Bin, Cu Chi, and Tay Ninh. This was the wet season, and you couldn't take a tank or an APC off the road. I was in B Troop. We had nine tanks and twenty-two APCs, one of which had a big 4.2-inch mortar inside. We would alternate with A and C Troops running the roads, and providing defense for the truck convoys. D Troop was a helicopter unit, and E Troop was long-range recon, or the "LERPs," as they were called. During Tet that January, the VC got through the wire at other places, but they left us alone, except for lobbing in a few mortars. With thirty tanks inside the wire in our squadron's compound, they didn't mess much with us.

The M48-A3 tanks we had were too heavy to go off road without sinking in the mud, so they stuck to paved roads or sat in base camp as pocket artillery. In May, we finally got the new, lighter, Sheridan tanks. An M48-A3 weighed fifty tons, while a Sheridan only weighed twenty tons. The good thing was it could go off road. The bad thing was it had thinner armor and a mine could blow it to pieces.

We would run the road out to the Michelin rubber plantation, Bien Kat, and the Plain of Reeds on the Cambodian border, and our maintenance track would go with them. The distances weren't great, but it would take us a full day to go out and a full day to come back. We always got harassing fire from snipers and an occasional mortar, and sometimes that escalated into a full-blown ambush. So, we spent a lot of time watching for snipers, land mines, RPGs, and things like that. That's pretty much what I did my whole tour, and we would do it three weeks at a time, when I wasn't back working in the shop.

In July, we were on a night convoy from Cu Chi to Tay Ninh. It was quiet, and I was riding on top of the Maintenance Track. One of my daily dilemmas was whether to ride on top or down inside. On top, you ran the risk of snipers, but inside, a mine always killed the driver. So could an RPG. It might blow you off the top, but at least you'd survive. As we rolled along. I was sitting up in the hatch, half asleep, when the big 4.2-inch mortar in the track right behind us "hung one," or fired off a big flare round and I about pissed my pants.

One convoy I'll never forget was on August 26. It was a long one and it was hotter than hell out. We'd always been told not to get out of our vehicles or draw attention to ourselves. I was so new that my fatigues still had creases, and I listened to what I was told. For some reason, our CO didn't. He dismounted from his APC and stood on the side of the road waving and motioning for the vehicles to get moving, when a sniper shot him and two other guys. When something like that happened, the tanks would "herring bone": pull forward, aim their main guns to alternate sides of the road, ready to open fire. I was sitting up on top of our APC with my M-16, swinging it around, and looking for a target, when one of our sergeants asked whether I had the safety on. I looked down, saw I didn't, and he told me I should; because if it accidently went off, I'd probably shoot our driver. That lesson stuck.

When my tour was finally over, I was assigned to Fort Ord in California. When I went over to Vietnam, I weighed 190 pounds. When I came back, I weighed 175 pounds. I was twenty-one years old and that was the "Summer of Love" in San Francisco, so we spent a lot of time up in Haight-Asbury and Carmel. The hippies took one look at our hair and could tell we were Army, but nobody cared. I really liked Fort Ord, but I still had a year left on my enlistment. In January, they sent me to Germany, to the 8th Infantry Division in Mannheim. After being in Vietnam and then California, I froze. In September, my father was diagnosed with leukemia and was in the Mayo Clinic, so I got a compassionate reassignment to Minnesota for my last few months until I was discharged in January, 1971.

After trying a few jobs, I got on at the Eli Lilly plant, right back in Lafayette, Indiana, where I stayed for twenty-nine years making pills until I retired in 2001. Since then, I've been diagnosed with Agent Orange-induced diabetes and I have substantial hearing loss due to all the gunfire that went off around me.

In 2003, I went back to Vietnam on a tour to some of the same spots where I had served and fought. I was surprised at how healthy the rubber plantations looked, until someone told me that they'd all been replanted. We also visited a Vietnamese military cemetery and learned that after the war the Communists disinterred the ARVN bodies and replaced them with VC and NVA. That's what they said, anyway. I'm sixty-eight now, and when I'm not playing golf I enjoy line dancing and attending veteran's meetings.

OTIS LANE'S WAR

**US Army, Spec 5 Medical Specialist,
C Company, 7th Support Battalion,
199th Light Infantry Brigade,
Long Binh, 1969–70**

I grew up a sharecropper's son in rural Georgia, near Valdosta. My father grew cotton and tobacco, and my brothers and I worked on the farm. It was a hard life. I attended a little, seven-room county school, and went on to graduate from Morris Brown College in Atlanta in Pre-Med. A week and a half later, I got a letter from the draft board saying that since I graduated, my college deferment was over, and I was now 1-A. The next week, I got another letter with a bus ticket to Jacksonville telling me to report for my physical. I didn't get too worried. I had always been a sickly child. I was held back in school because of asthma, so I figured they'd never take me.

In my family, you tell the truth. When the doctor asked me when I had my last asthma attack, I said it was when I was fifteen. The next thing I knew, I was following the green line to a room where everyone had their right hand raised and a captain was about to read them something. I quickly said, "Pardon me, Sir, but I think I'm in the wrong place." He wasn't upset. He came down the aisle, looked at my papers and said, "No, son, you're in the right place. Raise your right hand." And like that, I was in the Army.

They put us on a bus and drove us up I-75 to Fort Benning for Basic Training. We passed Valdosta and I waved, but I never even had a chance to call my Mother and tell her I wasn't coming home. In Basic, they rode college graduates pretty hard; but I had a strict upbringing, and was used to doing what I was told. I

200

maxed all their physical and mental tests. When they asked me what work I wanted to do, I said I had a degree in pre-med and I would like to do something in the medical area. So, they said that's where they would put me.

When Basic ended, I was put on a bus to Fort McClellan, Alabama, for Advanced Infantry Training. I knew that every GI has the right to see two people: his CO and the chaplain; so, I asked to see the CO. I explained to him that I was pre-med, I was supposed to go to medical training, and that I didn't want to be in the infantry. That didn't go over very well. After he cussed me out, he told me that for damn sure I was staying in the infantry. So, I went to see the chaplain. He thought I had a good point, and sent my appeal up the chain of command.

A few days later, I was pulled out of class and put on permanent KP. I knew something had happened. After a week, the First Sergeant came to see me. He needed a supply clerk, so that's what I did for the next eighteen weeks, until he came to see me again and told me to pack my bag. A jeep was waiting to take me to the bus station, and I was headed for Fort Sam Houston in Texas for medical training. Another Jeep met me in Houston, and I had a personal interview with the CO there. He told me I was being put in the twenty-one-week Medical Specialist class, not the shorter Combat Medic course, if that was okay with me. Medical Specialists were trained to provide limited nursing services and assist doctors, like an LPN. I was stunned. I had no idea what was happening, or why... until months later.

In May, 1969, I arrived in Vietnam, assigned to C Company of the 7th Support Battalion at Long Binh. We provided medical dispensary services to the 199th Light Infantry Brigade, forty miles northeast of Saigon. Our job in the dispensary was to deal with illnesses and minor injuries, usually non-surgical, like a clinic, where we could get the patient back to his unit in ten days or less. Out in the field, the combat medics treated battlefield wounds. Anything serious was sent directly to an EVAC Hospital and then to a Field Hospital.

Our unit had five buildings, two for clinics and patient wards, and the other three for the staff. We had five doctors, all Majors, and twenty-one Medical Specialists like me. We lived in two-story barracks, two men to a room, worked twelve-hour shifts, and had a mess hall with hot food, latrines, and showers, so it wasn't bad, except for the artillery unit that would fire over us every night.

I heard Long Binh got rocketed every so often, so I asked my roommate how I'd know whether it was incoming or outgoing? He laughed at me and said, "You'll know." He was right. When we got the first ones, I knew; and I ran all the way to the shelter. We got hit every few weeks after that, usually between 5:00 and 7:30 a.m. and 6:00 to 9:00 p.m.

One day, they brought in a bunch of Vietnamese civilians whose bus had hit a land mine. Two children were hurt bad. One died on the way in, and one died later. That was when I realized how much the ordinary people suffered in the war. That really bothered me. Later, I volunteered for a civic action mission where two Doctors and a few of us Medical Specialists went to a Vietnamese village about five miles away for two weeks to provide some basic clinical services to the local people. That was rewarding. On the last day, the colonel came out to congratulate us. On the way back, his vehicle hit a mine and he got a piece of shrapnel in his leg. I treated him, and he was so pleased that I got an early promotion to Spec-5.

A few weeks later, we were told the 199th Light Infantry Brigade had a critical need for combat medics. Of the twenty-one Medical Specialists in my unit, eighteen were white and three, including me, were African-American. The Staff Sergeant in charge picked us three to go to the field the next morning. That wasn't right, particularly since two of us outranked most of the white guys staying behind. So, I went to see the First Sergeant. The next morning, we were in formation with our field gear, ready to go, when the First Sergeant showed up. He asked the Staff Sergeant if he had looked at any of our records. The Staff said no. The First Sergeant told him that if he had, he'd realize he couldn't send me to the field as a Combat Medic; and that the CO had decided that he, the Staff Sergeant, would take my place. He also told him he could find two white guys to replace the other two African-Americans he had chosen.

After that drama was over, the First Sergeant called me over and asked me if I'd ever seen what was in my personnel file. I said I hadn't, and he handed me a copy of a letter from the Secretary of the Army to the school commander back at Fort McClellan. Apparently, during those eighteen weeks, my appeal had worked its way all the way up to the Secretary of the Army. He pointed out a 1942 Army Regulation which said that when a draftee came into the Army with a skill, the Army is obligated to give him a job as close as possible to that field, and that he could refuse any assignment not consistent with it. The Secretary then reprimanded all those in the chain of command who didn't know that. The First Sergeant gave me a copy of the letter and told me I should hang onto it.

They offered to send me to OCS, but I politely declined. I was engaged to be married and I wanted to get home and get on with my life. My wife was a schoolteacher in Valdosta, and I applied. With my Pre-med degree, they grabbed me up, got me certified, and made me a science teacher. I loved it and spent seven years in the classroom and another thirty-five years in administration before I retired. I'm now seventy-two. While I'm presently healthy, I'm being tested for early signs of Agent Orange-induced prostate cancer.

BOB SULLIVAN'S WAR

**US Army Platoon Sergeant, Mobile Riverine Force
in the 47th and 39th Infantry Regiments,
9th Infantry Division,
Mekong Delta, Two Tours, 1968–70**

I am a career Drill Sergeant and proud to say it. Having spent thirty-five years in the US Army, rising from Private Soldier to Command Sergeant Major and Commandant of all Drill Sergeant Schools, FM-22-5 sat on my bedside table next to the Bible. Once you become a Drill Sergeant, you're a marked man, literally. They put an "X" next to your name on your 201 File. After that, regardless of where your orders say you're going, the receiving Personnel Officer is honor-bound to rat you out, remind the Pentagon, and off you go to another Training Center, because Drill Sergeants are the Army's most prized commodity.

One of the few times I wasn't assigned as a Drill Sergeant was the one time I'd rather I was. No marching or close order drill—I ended up slogging through the muddy hell of the Mekong Delta during two tours with the Mobile Riverine Force of the 9th Infantry Division. People ask me what was the Delta like? Simple. It was the s**t hole of Vietnam. We pushed through mud up to our waists, and through vegetation so thick and tall you couldn't see ten feet. When we took fire, we couldn't tell whether it was one sniper, a VC squad, or an NVA regimental base camp we'd just stumbled into.

Every day, we went out in "Tango Boats," small LSTs that held a rifle platoon of thirty to forty men, and head upriver looking for a fight. It wouldn't take long to find one, and we'd be hit with B-40 rockets and Chinese machine guns. Tango Boats had thin skins. Bullets would go in one side and right out the other. They'd run the boat up on shore, the front ramp would drop like on Omaha Beach, and we'd go charging ashore into the mud and thick jungle to see how many bad guys we could kill. Not a real smart thing to do, but those were the tactics someone dreamed up. We were in fire fights three to four times a day, which was one reason the 9th Infantry had the highest casualty rate of any American Division in the war. Would it have made more sense to do some recon and probe by helicopter before we went charging in? Of course, but that wasn't what we did.

We carried everything we needed for the day on our backs—rifles, bandoliers, machine guns, hand grenades, food, and canteens of water. You could never carry enough water; but it all weighed a ton and you'd sink up to your butt in mud. It was so thick that sometimes it would rip your boot off. And insects were everywhere. So were red ants, which I particularly hated, and so many snakes that you just ignored them. Still, they weren't bad broiled over a slice of C-4.

When we finally returned to the Tango Boat, we'd be so covered with mud that the Navy wouldn't let us back on. They'd hook up a firehose to one of their pumps and hose us down with river water, like they did in movies with prisoners. That really pissed everyone off. The Navy crews on the boats were afraid of us. They thought we were all nuts to be doing what we were doing, and they were right. It was the worst job in the whole war.

Day after day we went up against large numbers of hardcore, regular NVA troops, and they didn't withdraw on contact like the VC did in other parts of the country. They kept fighting, because the Delta was their rice bowl, the one place they couldn't afford to lose. They were dug in and bunkered with tunnel complexes everywhere. Their goal was to kill as many of us as they could. We were trying to do the same thing, but frankly, we were overwhelmed.

When I arrived in country, my battalion had been in heavy fighting for weeks. There was only one platoon sergeant left in the entire rifle company, which usually had four or five E-7s. I was only an E-6, but immediately became a platoon sergeant. We were in contact every day. The heavy casualties continued, and we received new "fills" of riflemen right out of Basic every four to five days. But you can't replace experienced troops or NCOs like that without destroying unit cohesion, morale, and competency. To clear the enemy out of the Delta, the 9th Division needed to be pulled out, rebuilt, and replaced by at least two American divisions, but that wasn't going to happen. So, the young men in the 9th were left down there to bleed and die. It was truly tragic.

Day after day, our company would try to muster two hundred men for an operation and come back with 170. The troops knew that. You could see it in their eyes and hear them crying at night, scared silly to go back out again, and who could blame them. We even had trouble getting resupplied with food, water, and ammo, because of the hits the helicopters took from ground fire. That was why I checked what each of my men was carrying every day. Water and ammo were essential; but if you didn't watch them, they'd try to lighten their loads by cutting back on those, and that was dangerous. That, and feet. We were in the water and mud every day, and immersion foot was a serious problem. So were the guys who sprayed their feet with bug spray. They'd swell up and get the guy out of the field, at least for a while.

After nine months, I was wounded by shrapnel in my knee and back from an RPG and sent to the rear area. They wanted to reassign me to a mechanized unit, but I wouldn't have that. I wanted to go back to the Riverine Force. Someone else had my job by then, so they put me in a different regiment, but still leg infantry. While all that was going on, they lost my paperwork. Rather than sending me home after my last three months, my new regiment thought I was new in country, and I ended up staying there for another ten months. I didn't say anything, because I hated to leave those kids out there on their own with no leadership.

I finally rotated out of Vietnam in September, 1970, and was assigned to Scofield Barracks on the beautiful island of Oahu in Hawaii. Thirty days later, the battalion commander called me in, all apologetic, and pointed to the dreaded "X" next to my name on my 201 File and told me he couldn't keep me. The Pentagon was desperate for drill sergeants and they were sending me back to Fort Dix, where I'd spent four years before Vietnam. I really liked Schofield Barracks, too. But let's see, Hawaii in December, or New Jersey in December, for a guy who had just spent almost two years in the heat of Vietnam? Wonderful!

Most of my career was spent at Fort Dix, Fort Leonard Wood, Fort Riley, Fort Lewis, and even Fort Polk, the Army's large infantry training centers. As I rose through the ranks I graduated from running individual training companies to supervising classes, supervising the training brigades, and eventually as the Command Sergeant Major supervising the entire system, for both active duty and reserve soldiers. I take great pride in that and my thirty-five-year career. While I don't wear it much anymore, my dress uniform has six rows of ribbons, including a Silver Star, Bronze Stars, Purple Hearts, and many others. What isn't on the uniform is the Agent Orange-related Type II Diabetes and the PTSD that I also carry.

GARY ROSENHOUSE'S WAR

US Navy Seaman, Harbor Protection Unit,
Nha Trang, 1968–69

Gary

After I graduated from high school in New Brunswick, New Jersey, I got a job in the printshop at the Johnson & Johnson plant there. The draft was getting close, so I enlisted in the Navy. They sent me to Great Lakes, where the Navy sent most guys for Boot Camp. I was supposed to be a radioman and was in the middle of that school when I got into some arguments with the staff. They were going to drop me from the school and recycle me into some other job I didn't want, so I volunteered for Vietnam.

I was twenty years old when I arrived at Nha Trang in December, 1968, which was a port on the coast about thirty miles north of the big port at Cam Ranh Bay, where I flew in. Nha Trang was all Navy. They assigned me to the 120-man "Southeast Asia Harbor Protection Unit," as they called it. We guarded the water and the ships that were docked there, watching for swimmers and boats trying to sneak in. We rode around in small gunboats with heavy machine guns, patrolling the coast and the Bay. If we saw anything suspicious in the water, we would drop in concussion grenades. The fishermen always liked that, because it would bring up a lot of dead fish, which made their day easy. But we had to be careful with the guns, particularly the .50-caliber machine guns, not to shoot in the direction of any ships or the port buildings. The bullets could skip off the water and cause big problems.

All things considered, it wasn't a bad duty station. We lived in wooden barracks, with two men to a room, not in the big open bays like we had in Boot Camp. We had showers and toilets, but everything there had been built from scratch when the Navy moved in. That included a regular mess hall and an enlisted club, and other things. It was very hot there, particularly since I'd come from Great Lakes in the winter. The water was undrinkable; so, to stay hydrated, they let us drink as much beer as we wanted, as long as we didn't get drunk. I think they turned the port over to the South Vietnamese in 1970, a year or so after I left.

Outside the Navy Base, to the west, we had the South Korean Army, the ROKs, guarding us. We used to socialize with them a little bit when they came in, although I didn't speak any Korean and they didn't speak much English, but they were nice guys. As soldiers, though, they were professional killers, no nonsense, and they took no prisoners.

One of the things I remember most about my tour was riding shotgun on garbage trucks. That was one of the duties I got stuck with every now and then. We would be hauling a lot of food from the mess hall that was being thrown away, and haul it outside the base to the dump. As soon as we got close, Vietnamese civilians—a lot of women and children—would surround the truck and try to grab anything they could. But our orders were to burn the garbage. We would pour diesel fuel on it, light it, and leave. That didn't matter, the Vietnamese would keep picking through the burning trash. I hated that, and refused to do it anymore; because I thought it was a hell of a way to make people live. I guess they were the same as us. You do what you gotta do.

Another day I'll never forget was when they used trucks with sprayers to spray the whole base with Agent Orange to kill all the vegetation, as if it was Roundup or Weed-Be-Gone, or something. As it turned out, they were killing a lot of us too.

In March, four months after I arrived, I had a phone call that my father had died, and my mother and my younger brothers were having a difficult time, so I got a Compassionate Leave to go back home to New Jersey for a while. When I reported in at the end of the leave, the Navy decided to just discharge me and not to send me back.

Johnson & Johnson gave me my old job back in the printshop and I worked for them for the next twenty-two years. Finally, I moved to Florida and had a couple of different jobs there. Mostly, I worked for a Toyota distributor, ran their printshop, and then ended up doing all their purchasing for printing when they outsourced the work.

I'm 69 years old now. Eight years ago, I developed diabetes and neuropathy in both legs and one of my arms. Basically, they are numb. It's all been diagnosed as Agent Orange-related, and I've been given a 100% disability.

I used to play a lot of golf, but I can't do that anymore. I used to make a lot of things in the community woodshop, but I can't do that anymore either. I don't want to do anything that might get myself or anyone else hurt because of the numbness from the neuropathy.

DAVE KRAEMER'S WAR

US Army, Warrant Officer and 1st Lieutenant
Helicopter Pilot, 101st Airborne Division,
Camp Eagle, Two Tours 1968–71

I'm from Summerdale, New Jersey, a small farming community halfway between Philadelphia and Atlantic City. In 1964, I enlisted in the Air Force, which I quickly decided I didn't like. When that enlistment was over, I enlisted in the Army for their Warrant Officer helicopter pilot training. In December, 1968, I arrived in Vietnam and was assigned to C Company, 2nd of the 17th Cav assigned to the 101st Airborne as an OH-6 pilot. That's a light observation helicopter, which everyone called the "Loach." It had a round Plexiglas nose bubble and looked like a pregnant guppy. It was armed with a mini gun and sometimes with rockets, so it had some real punch, but it had no armor and its main function was to snoop around and find the enemy. Sometimes we went out by ourselves, but usually we operated with Cobras and slicks full of infantry in what were called Hunter-Killer teams. We were the bait, trying to get shot at, so the Cobras could swoop down and blow them away. Being the bait was not a good thing.

We operated out of Camp Eagle, a flat, dusty, basecamp between Hue and Phu Bai in the Central Highlands, but we would also fly over the Ho Chi Minh Trail, in the A-Shau Valley, and all over I Corps. They would also send us out to do Bomb Damage Assessments after an "Arc Light" mission. That was when B-52s would bomb an NVA target and cut a swath through the jungle. I was flabbergasted at the damage.

I extended after my first year, and had been there fifteen months when I was wounded for the first time. I was flying with another Loach, two Cobras, a command helicopter, and some slicks loaded with infantry when we were called in to help some ground troops. It was an area of low mountains, like the Poconos. The infantry was on a sweep through a large boulder field when one of their guys got shot and they couldn't find him. I went in low, trying to see behind the rocks and in the crevices. For some reason, I felt a lot of compassion for the guy, and I didn't want him to be left behind. I had a spotter with me, and we kept going lower and slower, which was inviting trouble.

The only protection we had in a Loach is the seat. It's ceramic fiberglass and wraps around, covering your back, your bottom, and your side, but you have absolutely no protection from a bullet that comes right in the bubble in front of you. I heard the gunfire, but I never saw the shooter. The lower left section of the bubble exploded inward at me, and everything slowed down. Even now, I can close my eyes and see it in slow motion, frame by frame, as the pieces of plastic came floating up at me. I didn't feel anything, but I saw something pluck at my flight suit on both sides of my knee, and knew I was hit. I immediately pulled up on the stick, got us out of there, and radioed in. We were far from base, and I knew I needed to quickly assess the damage to me and the helicopter. I could fly, but I was in sensory overload and almost passed out.

Whenever I took an Observer up with me in the second seat, I always told him the basics of how to fly the machine, enough for him to keep it level, but not how to land or anything like that. I flew the helicopter up a streambed to get away from the gunfire. My depth perception wasn't very good at that moment, so I told the Observer to fly it. He grabbed the stick from me, and that was when he locked up. He was flying it straight and level, but he wasn't listening to anything I said. I tried to get the controls back; but he was a big guy, much bigger than I was. I pulled back on the stick, but he kept pushing it down. I was afraid it was going to snap off, in which case we'd crash for sure; so the best thing I could do was to try to control the impact.

We came down in the sandy streambed at about 35 mph. The skids hit something, and we flipped three times. That broke off the rotor blades and the tail boom, leaving us looking like a big plastic egg rolling and flipping over and over. When the helicopter finally came to rest, it was lying on its side, with me on the bottom and him on the top. I reached up, turned the power off and yelled at him as calmly as I could, "Undo your seatbelt, we gotta get out of here before it catches on fire!" Finally, he understood and climbed out the top. I managed to do the same, while the infantry troops, who were in the boulder field, came up and gave us some covering fire. They were still a hundred yards away, but we managed to run to them. As I did, I looked down. I was bleeding heavily, but surprised to see that my knee was still holding together.

One of our Hueys came down, picked us up, and got me to a field hospital. I had several shattered bones and a severed artery. The doctor wanted to take my leg off, but I told him, "I did my job. It's time for you to do yours, and do what you can to save it," and he did. After I was stabilized, they shipped me to Camp Zama in Japan, then to Valley Forge hospital in Pennsylvania, and finally to Fort Dix hospital for physical therapy. When you're young, you recover fast, but the big thing was regaining my "range of motion," which happened surprisingly fast. The Army wanted to send me to Fort Rucker to be a flight instructor, but I wasn't having any of that. In truth, I was already having serious problems dealing with the war; but I was way too caught up in combat flying to stop. So, I volunteered for another tour in Vietnam, under the condition that they'd send me to Cobra school first.

Once you are an experienced pilot, the transition course to another model is only four to six weeks long, when you learn the systems and flight characteristics of the new machine and qualify on night flying and night attacks. While I was in rehab I was given a Direct Commission to First Lieutenant. The rank didn't matter to me. All I wanted was to be back with the guys. I was young and dumb, and I really missed that camaraderie.

While the Loach was like a sports car—quick and very nimble—the Cobra was like a Ferrari. It was fast too, and it carried rocket pods, grenade launchers, miniguns, and 20-mm cannon in various configurations. The problem with a Cobra was to carry all that gasoline and armaments in the heat and humidity of the central Highlands and still get the bird off the ground. It's called Density Altitude. Sometimes I had to slide it along on the skids, until I could get enough forward motion to reach "transitional lift," and get it into the air. That was called a running take off.

I was assigned back to Camp Eagle, to C company of the 7th of the 17th, a sister battalion of the one I was with before. I flew support for the 101st, but also the 173rd Light Infantry Brigade from time to time. One of the things they monitored very closely was "Combat Flying Time," which wasn't the same as just flying around. After sixty hours we were grounded and had to see the Flight Surgeon, to get checked out physically and emotionally. For us pilots, there was always that love-hate relationship with the Flight Surgeon.

This was now 1970 and 1971. I was flying the same type of missions as I did during my first tour, except I was in a Cobra, not a Loach. I was there nine months when I got my second wound. We were on the ground and I had just brought the helicopter in for maintenance. The doors were wide open. I was standing on the "wing," when a fire started. Apparently one of the fuel lines had a leak, and it went up quick. I had taken off my flight suit and was only wearing a T-shirt and shorts, so I was burned badly on my face, ears, and arms. They got me back to the field hospital and then back to Camp Zama and Valley Forge again. I was married at that time, so they assigned me back to Fort Dix, working as the executive officer of the Replacement Depot. I was drinking more and more, which had started years before, continued to have pain in my leg, and was having marital problems, all at the same time. Eventually it all caught up with me. I loved the Army and loved flying, but I knew I had to get out. After that, I took on several private flying jobs in the US and overseas, and eventually went to work for the Post Office.

Someone said that when you go to war you become a prisoner and can never get away from your experience. I was raised in a Christian family. When you're involved in the fighting and killing, it's something you can never fully adapt to. You are a human being, and it changes you in many ways. As time passed, I became more and more troubled about it. Flying was a big high. It's like an adrenaline rush, and it's addictive until you come down.

When I flew a Cobra, it was more of a high-altitude gun run. Sometimes you see the enemy, but always at a distance. In a Loach, on the other hand, your target is right there in front of you, up close, especially when you fire the mini gun. As they say, you end up having two targets, you and the enemy. When you go into combat like that you either become fearful, or you become a predator, seeking revenge for the people you ate breakfast with, who didn't come back. Some guys can back away from it, and some become more aggressive. You killed my friend, and now it's your turn. I remember getting so caught up in it one time, shooting at a guy who was shooting at us, that I flew back over him a second time, and tried to drop a grenade in his trench.

I spent twenty-four months in Vietnam, fifteen months the first time, and nine months the second time. Combat flying like that can become a sickness, and that's not something I'm proud of. I was drinking heavily every night, but we were doing what our country asked us to do. Still, it isn't something you have to do, not like that. Decades later, those are the things that bother me the most now. It's the human side versus the aggressive side, the testosterone, the fighting side. I learned the tender side from my mother, but I learned the other side from the military. Unfortunately, as I said, it changes you forever.

I tried to get some help in 1974–75, but without much success. The war was still too much of an open wound then. Fortunately, I went back to the VA in 2002 and got the help I needed.

DAVE DASINGER'S WAR

US Marine Corps Master Gunnery Sergeant,
F Company, 2nd Battalion, 1st Regiment,
1st Marine Division, Da Nang, 1968–70

I was born and raised in Montgomery, Alabama. After high school, I kicked around for a while and then enlisted in the Marine Corps in June, 1968 instead of waiting to be drafted. I stayed in the Marines for the next twenty-five years, eventually rising to the rank of E-9, Master Gunnery Sergeant, one of the highest enlisted ranks in the Corps. After twelve weeks of Boot Camp at Parris Island and eight weeks of Infantry Training Regiment, or ITR, at Camp Lejeune, I was an 03-11 Infantryman, a Grunt. That December I was sent to Vietnam and assigned to Fox Company, 2nd Battalion, 1st Marine Regiment, 1st Marine Division. Our basecamp was five miles south of Danang. Our other regiments, the 5th and the 7th were in the same area, in a line all the way down to Chu Lai, but we worked all over the place.

I spent eighteen months there, extending to two tours. Most of my time was in the bush, but when we were back at Base Camp, which wasn't very often, it was a typical Marine Corps battalion rear area, with wood-wall hooches, canvas tops, screens, sandbags, bunkers, berms, a gate, guard posts, lots of barbed wire, artillery gun emplace-ments, tanks, and heavy mortars. After an operation, we would come back in for a few days and then go right back out on another one. If we did stay in camp for a while, we would run patrols out of there.

When we went out on operations, it was always to the same general area. They were called Pipestone Peak, Meade River, Hill 55, and a lot of other names. We ran sweeps through Go Noi Island, ten miles south of Danang, and "Dodge City," a thirty-six square-mile area that was ten miles further out. It had been a long-time NVA strong point and R and R center, chock-full of tunnels, bunkers, weapons caches, and NVA regulars. Marines went on many different operations with many different names into that same area; but in the end, it was one long, bloody battle the whole time I was there.

I arrived in-country just as Operation Meade River was going on. That was a big sweep through Dodge City by the 1st Regiment, with seven battalions, APCs, tanks, and fire support from the battleship *USS New Jersey*. The NVA's main objective in our area was to shut down the Danang air base. This was the "rocket belt" south of the runways, and it couldn't be ignored. The central part of Dodge City was five miles by three miles of low ground, crisscrossed by rivers, streams, caves, tunnels, hedges, ditches, and bunker complex after bunker complex. The only way it could be cleared was by infantry, so we would cordon off an area, search it, and clear it under miserable conditions in a steady, cold rain.

Apparently, the attack came as a surprise to the NVA. We used 7,000 troops and the entire First Marine Air Wing to pound them. We trapped huge numbers of them inside the cordon and captured large stockpiles of weapons and supplies. Still, they knew the ground, had operated there for years, and a lot of them managed to sneak out. By the time the operation was over we had 108 Marines killed and 510 wounded. By late December, after we pulled back, the NVA had already crept back in; and it remained a hotspot until the end of the war.

In May, 1969, the 1st and 5th Marine Regiments made a big push through Go Noi Island with 2,000 ARVNs and some ROKs. When we went out on operations, sometimes we'd sweep, and sometimes we'd be the blocking force. In the end, we drove the NVA out, but it wasn't very long before they infiltrated right back in. Pipestone Canyon was another big operation that summer in the same general area.

One night, when we were hunkered down in our foxholes on the perimeter during Pipestone, I had gotten my hands on a three-legged milking stool. When we were on guard, it was a lot better than sitting in the mud. I was all comfortable, when a mongoose ran right across me and scared the hell out of me. It took off down the hill and I threw a grenade at it. Another guy in the next hole crawled over and asked me if I saw that explosion and if I knew what it was. I smiled and said "No, I've got no idea."

Hill 55 was another prolonged battle, ten miles south of Danang. Two French battalions had been wiped out there during their war, so it had "history." We also made pushes into the Que Son Mountains. They towered over the valleys and the jungle and had steep ravines. This was where the NVA had withdrawn after we pushed them out of Dodge City and Go Noi Island, and was one of the major infiltration routes from the Ho Chi Minh Trail to the coast.

But my strongest memories of that time were the difficulties of simply getting through the day in the heat of the summer, during the heavy monsoon rains, being cold and wet in the mountains, and plodding through knee-deep mud in the rice paddies. I began as a Rifleman and was soon promoted to Fire Team Leader and then Squad

Leader, and finally Platoon Sergeant as casualties took their toll. In the Marines, it was the next man up, and you took your turn.

Another thing I remember was one day in base camp, when we put some new guys on the detail to burn the sawed-off fifty-five-gallon oil drums that were underneath the latrine. What you were supposed to do, was pull the drums out, pour in some diesel fuel, and let them burn for a while. Somehow, when someone told the new guys to, "Go burn the shitter," they didn't quite understand, and burned down the whole latrine.

In May, 1969, our base camp got hit hard, and we had NVA coming through the wire. The position to the right of mine was taken out, and they finally had to call in "Spookie," a DC-3 weapons platform with four miniguns sticking out the side, to push the NVA back. It was quite a sight watching those miniguns with their streams of tracer rounds go to work. Meanwhile, we kept taking mortars and rockets. In addition to the normal outhouse latrines, there were a few urinal tubes placed around, usually hidden behind an L-shaped wooden screen. That night, the NVA managed to drop a rocket right on top of one of our urinal tubes. I was in a bunker with a couple of our brighter lightbulbs, one of whom looked out and said, "Lookie that, Sarge, they done blowed up our piss tube!" Marines! What could you say?

In June, 1970, I rotated out after eighteen months. During the next four years, it seemed like I was always deployed, going on six-month cruises six times, working as a recruiter in Tupelo, Mississippi, and serving in the headquarters of the 9th Marine Regiment on Okinawa.

When you make E-8, the Marine Corps gives NCOs two career track choices. You can either become a First Sergeant or a Gunnery Sergeant. The First Sergeant oversees unit administration, while the Gunnery Sergeant is in charge of everything in the field. I chose the latter and was promoted to E-9, or Master Gunnery Sergeant, or "Master Guns." in sixteen years, a very short time. During Vietnam, it was very common for NCOs to accept a "Limited Duty" promotion to Captain or even Major for the duration of the war, and then revert to their enlisted ranks when the war was over. I chose not to do that, remained an NCO, and never regretted it.

In June, 1992, I retired and went home to Montgomery, Alabama. I sold BMWs, and ran a security company for a while but remain very proud of my service in the Marine Corps. While I have not had any physical Vietnam-related disabilities, I have suffered from PTSD, which did not rear its ugly head until after I retired. Perhaps the day-to-day life in the Marine Corps helped keep me busy enough to ignore it. However, as the years passed I found myself more irritable and more depressed.

Finally, I went to several VA therapy group meetings. I sat and listened, but finally stood up and told them I thought it was all a bunch of bullshit. "There's no such thing as PTSD!" I said. After all, I was a Marine Master Gunnery Sergeant, and that just didn't happen to guys like me. I was in total denial, but after enough therapy, the denial finally stopped. I had PTSD, and so do a lot of other guys, whether they want to admit it or not.

I have taken up golf, saltwater fishing, and am active in veteran's groups like The Band of Brothers. And Roll Tide.

I continue to have strong feelings about the Vietnam War. I felt we fought it the wrong way from the very beginning. We won all the battles and had the NVA and Vietcong defeated on the battlefield, but you should never try to win a war of attrition in Asia. You also cannot fight an undeclared war, where you can't make up your mind whether or not you want to really win it. If it was worth fighting, war should have been declared and turned over to the generals to win. We didn't do that, and a lot of good people died there as a result. That was criminal on the part of some.

JOE FINCH'S WAR

US Army, Lieutenant and Helicopter Pilot, 25th Aviation Battalion, 25th Infantry Division, Cu Chi, Dau Tieng, Tay Ninh, and Thailand, 1969–71

Early in my tour, I did a lot of Combat Assaults and gun runs supporting our infantry units in the field. Other times, I was stuck flying incredibly stupid battalion commanders around, while I watched our infantry companies get chopped to pieces on the ground below. After that, I made medevac flights my personal top priority. No matter what mission I was sent out on, if I heard a call on the radio that some unit somewhere needed a medevac pickup, I broke off and answered the call, no matter what. That's what I did, because I thought it was the most important and useful thing I could do.

During that year, I picked up 826 wounded men, whom I airlifted to a hospital and got them there alive. That was an entire battalion of men! I only know of two times when the guy didn't make it and died in my helicopter, and I still remember both of their names. Many of the men I picked up had very bad wounds. I'd love to know how they came out, but that was impossible. Usually the calls came in the heat of a battle, and we were under fire when we went in. The credit goes to my co-pilot, crew chief, and door gunner, who were crazy enough to keep flying with me. One morning, I picked up twenty-five men, for which I was awarded my first Silver Star. That is more casualties than some Medevac choppers picked up in an entire tour.

I flew slicks, unarmed courier ships, and gunships, not an official Medevac helicopter. Those were unarmed and had no protective armor, just a big white square with red crosses painted on the sides. The NVA loved to lure them in and then open up, adding to the chaos and wreckage on the ground. When I went in, however, I went in with guns blazing.

Our CO decided that I had good night vision, and assigned me to one of the

Nighthawk ships. It was a Huey to which they'd added a Mini Gun with 5,000 rounds of ammunition, a powerful Xenon searchlight with 1 million candlepower, and an infrared light. We also had our normal M-60 door guns, so it carried a lot of firepower. We would fly low over suspected enemy positions at night, almost begging them to shoot at us, so we could light them up.

Later, my helicopter was selected for a special attack on an almost impregnable bunker complex on the side of Nui Ba Din, Black Virgin Mountain. Through most of the war, we held the top and the bottom of the mountain, and the NVA held the middle, due to an elaborate tunnel complex they had. One of their cave entrances, about the size of a double door, was on a steep part of the slope. Many attempts had been made to take it out, but none worked. So, someone came up with a clever idea of having a helicopter carry three 55-gallon drums of "Foo Gas," a mix of napalm and explosives, slung below the helicopter, and drop them into that entrance.

After looking over photos of the target, I decided the only way it could be done was to make a run straight at the hillside, get as close as I could, pull up, release the drums as they swung forward, and sling them in the cave opening. When I did that, the helicopter's nose would be too high. I wouldn't be able to see the entrance, but I still had to get enough elevation to climb over the ridge. Despite all that, somehow, I managed to drop the three drums right into that cave entrance; but as I pulled up and tried to climb over the ridge, we came under ground fire. An RPG round hit one of the skids and punched a hole in our gas tank. I got the helicopter back under control and "auto rotated" it back to the ground, almost out of fuel. I was awarded my second Silver Star for that.

A lot of American lives were lost on and around Nui Ba Din during the war. I haven't been back, but I understand that you can now ride a funicular cable car up to the top of the mountain, where the Vietnamese now operate a small amusement park.

I was assigned to the 25th Aviation Battalion of the 25th Infantry Division at Cu Chi. It was a large base. One night we were hit with VC inside the wire, and no one could figure out how they had gotten in. That was when we learned that our base was sitting on top of an old tunnel complex, and they had just walked in.

Another memory I have of Vietnam was when they put a 200-gallon tank and two Chemical Corp officers in the rear cargo area of my Huey, hung sprayers underneath, and we sprayed the countryside. Later I figured out it was Agent Orange. Once we began spraying, every time we turned or the wind shifted, all that chemical blew inside and got all over us.

No doubt the funniest exploit I was involved in was dropping leaflets on the Bob Hope Christmas show at Cu Chi in 1969. Our company was assigned to provide perimeter security and air cover for the show, so none of our guys would get to see it. The night before, some enlisted men came to me with boxes of small white leaflets upon which they had written messages welcoming Bob Hope to Cu Chi. Three platoons had stayed up all night making these things, and they begged me to drop them on the show, since they knew I'd be up there. I told them it was closed airspace and you can't do that without getting in big trouble, but in a weak moment I let them talk me into it.

Sure enough, in the middle of the show, I took a sharp turn, ignored the controller in my earphones, who wanted to know what I thought I was doing, and we dropped the leaflets. If you watch the videotape of that show, you can see Hope looking up as the leaflets came down. Finally, he says, "What's this? Snow in Vietnam?" The next day, I was called in front of the CO, but he let me off when I explained why I had done it.

In 1975, I was finishing my college degree at Saint Martin's in Olympia, Washington. Nobody could figure out who to get for a graduation speaker, so I suggested Bob Hope. Everyone said, "Great, you go get him." It took some time, working through his assistants, but I finally got him on the phone and explained that I was the guy who dropped the snow on his show at Cu Chi. "Why'd you do that?" he immediately asked. When I explained how I couldn't turn the troops down, he said, "Okay, I'll speak at your graduation." And he did. I was his escort the whole day, and he continued to pepper me with questions.

When my first one-year tour was up, I asked for a second one and was shifted to Thailand as part of the U.S. Army Support Mission there. We flew out of Ubon, Korat, and Udorn on combat missions into Laos, to the Plain of Jars, and even into North Vietnam in support of Special Forces and intelligence operations. I remained in the Army for twenty-three years, retiring as a Lieutenant Colonel.

During my career, I received a Distinguished Flying Cross, two Silver Stars, thirty-eight Air Medals, several Bronze Stars, the Vietnamese Cross of Gallantry with silver stars, a Meritorious Service Medal, and many others. Unfortunately, in 1989, I had a massive stroke while on active duty. I lost my math skills and couldn't solve even the simplest problem. I went down to the basement every day and did math problems for hours, until it started coming back; unfortunately, not fast enough, and I had to retire. In addition to the stroke, I have had substantial hearing loss, bladder cancer, and other Agent Orange-related issues.

While recuperating in DC from the stroke, my wife and I began sponsoring a dinner each month at Walter Reed, Bethesda, or the VA hospital in Richmond, bringing in various celebrities and entertainers. In the process, we met thousands of patients. It took some time, but I was finally able to obtain a good job in the defense industry, where I worked for the next twenty-three years until I retired again and moved to Florida. At seventy-two, I'm active in my church and its choir, I participate in Honor Flights, and I'm active in the Distinguished Flying Cross Society.

I have also been busy writing. One of my most popular books, *Angel's Wing,* can be found on Amazon and on Kindle. And I have recently released *Faces of the Distinguished Flying Cross, Central Florida,* individual stories of DFC recipients, also available on Kindle, and am working on *The Erawon Wars,* about my time in Thailand.

MARC TUMAS' WAR

US Army, West Point Graduate and Captain,
S-1 Adjutant and PIO, 17th Combat Aviation Group,
1st Aviation Brigade Nha Trang, 1969–70

I grew up in Lowell Massachusetts and graduated from the US Military Academy at West Point in 1966, intending to make the Army my career. When it came time to choose a branch, I wanted a technical field, where I could do R&D in strategic defense. That's why I chose Air Defense Artillery. After completing the Air Defense Artillery Officer Basic Course at Fort Bliss Texas, and the Prefix 5 Course in Nuclear Weapons Deployment, also at Fort Bliss, I was assigned and subsequently became Commanding Officer of a Nike Hercules air defense missile base in Sausalito, California.

While the Bay Area wasn't exactly a hardship tour, it was ground zero of an increasingly vocal and nasty anti-war movement that lashed out at anyone in uniform, and left its share of scars. After that assignment, I went to White Sands, New Mexico as a technical project manager and worked on the Sentinel Anti-Ballistic Missile System with Raytheon, Bell Labs, Martin Marietta, and McDonnell Douglas. That was precisely the type of work I thought I could contribute to.

My Vietnam tour started in February 1969. Since there weren't any slots for ADA missile officers there, my year with the 17th Combat Aviation Group in Nha Trang was split between serving as the S-1 Adjutant and the Public Information Officer. I then went as the Air Liaison Officer to the 5th Special Forces Group.

When I arrived, Vietnamization was supposedly under-way, and the US was beginning its withdrawal; but we were at the highest troop levels of the entire war, and the fighting was even more intense. My Aviation Group was 8000 personnel strong! As PIO, I spent a lot of time collecting information from our air crews at places like Pleiku and Kontum, only to learn how bad it was getting out in the field. It was easy to see how capable the North Vietnamese were, and how green and inexperienced our air crews were, whose job it was to stop them. It was hard to put a smiley face on that to the press. The Army reporters, many of whom were draftees, had good training, and were out in the field all the time. They knew what was going on.

When I finally got out of those staff jobs and into the field, most days I was planning air support for the Special Forces, primarily inserting Army Ranger and Navy Seal Teams into Laos and Cambodia, where we weren't even supposed to be. Our pilots would take off before dawn and insert them into some tiny clearing where they would disappear into the jungle to blow up bridges and disrupt traffic on the Ho Chi Minh Trail. We would pick them up that afternoon or a few days later. The bridges were mostly made of bamboo, and by the time our teams were back to Nha Trang, the bridge would be back up. While our teams were doing that interdiction work, they were also gathering intelligence for the invasion of Cambodia, which came two months after I left. The American people may not have known what was going on, but the NVA did.

More disconcerting were the meetings I attended with the 5th Special Forces Group and the CIA. Together, they ran the cross-border Special Ops war, but there were no West Point-trained officers in the meetings, except me, and the CIA guys had no military experience at all. They were Ivy Leaguers from CIA Headquarters at Langley, Virginia, Princeton grads; and I could only ask, "Who's running this war?"

For the aviators, Vietnam was an emotional roller coaster. Many would spend hours flying combat missions in the worst of battles, only to be in the bar of the Officer's Club an hour later, drinking heavily, gambling, and carousing. By the time I arrived in country, both the experience level and the motivation of the pilots were in sharp decline. Most were green W-1 Warrant Officers, right out of flight school, and that created an occasional, but serious problem with "fragging." Once thought unique to the infantry out in the jungle, it even affected our Army aviators. They did very dangerous work. If a flight crew thought their new pilot was unqualified and could get them killed, he could find a hand grenade rolling into his hooch some night, or a stray bullet while they were at a hot LZ. We lost nine pilots due to "non-hostile" action.

One of my jobs was to assign new pilot officers to aviation companies within the Group. Many of them were afraid of what was going on and didn't want to be the last pilot killed over there. I was repeatedly offered not-so-subtle bribes, which I did not take, to assign them to places other than Pleiku, Kontum, or the other "hot" areas.

The My Lai Massacre happened a year before I arrived in country, but the story only came out that November. Because I was on the staff and spoke French, I was invited to dinner with Vietnamese officials from time to time. After a few drinks, when the conversation turned candid, most of them no longer understood why we were there. It was obvious to everyone except our own military bureaucrats, that we were fighting a war that no longer made any sense, and we'd lose because we weren't there to win. Like most American officers I knew, I had become enormously conflicted over the US administration's policies by then.

By the time I rotated out of Vietnam in February 1970, I had received a Bronze Star with an Oak leaf cluster, and the other usual medals. After the ADA Officer Advanced Course, I remained at Fort Bliss, but I knew it was time to put in my papers and get out. My five-year West Point commitment was over, and I could no longer balance duty with morality and politics. One thing they taught us early as cadets was that an officer is only as good as the morale and motivation of the troops under his command. Only by treating and respecting people properly can you earn their acceptance and respect. Obviously, those lessons had not filtered up through the chain of command to Washington.

After I got out of the Army, I attended Harvard Business School, where I earned an MBA. I then went to work for Hewlett-Packard in the medical information technology field, leading strategy and corporate development functions. I spent over thirty years with them and their successors, Agilent Technologies and Philips Healthcare, to include an interim position as the COO of a startup company in local area networks.

I have been treated for Agent Orange-induced Prostate Cancer, as have many of my West Point classmates from the "war years." I'm now 73, live in Massachusetts, and spend about one third of my time consulting with medical technology company startups, one third traveling, and one third on staying fit, home improvements, military history, and classical music.

JOE WILSON'S WAR

**US Army, Captain and Huey Gun Ship Pilot,
189th Assault Helicopter Co.,
52nd Combat Aviation Battalion,
Pleiku, 2 tours, 1969–71**

I was born in Texas, but graduated from an American high school in the Canal Zone in Panama. It was very tough academically. With all the US military there, it had one of the best high school ROTC programs in the world. They were very Gung Ho, as was the ROTC program at Auburn, where I went. After college, I was commissioned and went right on active duty to Signal Corps Officer's Basic, although I never spent a day in a signal unit. Instead, I went to Ranger School, Jump School, and Flight School where I was first trained to fly Hueys, and then trained as a Cobra gunship pilot.

With my aviator wings, Ranger tabs, and airborne wings, I was assigned to the 5th Special Forces Group in Nha Trang in February, 1969, and spent most of my tours supporting the Special Forces. At first, the 5th had its own internal aviation unit, but in March or April of 1969 it was moved to the 1st Aviation Brigade and I was assigned to the 189th Assault Helicopter Company at Camp Holloway in Pleiku. It was much closer to the Tri-Border area of Cambodia, Laos, and Vietnam, where the Special Forces were particularly active.

While I was trained on Cobras, the company to which I was assigned flew the older Huey C-model gunships. We were supposed to be upgraded to Cobras, but they never arrived. The C-model Huey was smaller, and not designed to carry troops like the D and H models, which were called "Slicks." We carried a crew of four—the pilot, co-pilot, crew chief, and door gunner, plus fourteen rockets, modified M-60s hanging on bungee cords in the doors, two very nasty electric-powered 7.65-caliber mini-guns, and 12,000 to 15,000 rounds of ammunition for them. Some of the gunships were configured with a 40-mm grenade launcher, which could fire up to 300 grenades per minute, instead of the mini gun and the two pods of rockets. We called those "hogs." Whichever, we carried a lot of firepower, and a lot of weight.

On my first tour, we operated out of Kontum, Dak To, and Ban Me Thuot, escorting Special Forces operations in Laos and Cambodia. They were gathering intelligence on enemy troop concentrations, taking out enemy leadership, and capturing prisoners. Those missions were run by the secretive "Studies and Operations Group" in MAC-V, largely a CIA operation, until the Army's Special Forces took over. The work was highly classified, not that the flight crew knew much about what the SF guys were doing. Our job was to take them in, pick them up, and provide firepower if needed.

This type of insertion mission was new, and as we flew them, we developed new tactics as we went. Unlike a "Combat Assault," we would sneak in, usually with a slick carrying the troops, two gunships, and a Forward Air Controller. We would fly low and fast, hugging the trees and valleys—contour flying, as it was called. Our navigation system wasn't designed for that, so the FAC up above would direct us through the turns. We were covering the slick as it would make fake landings at several possible LZs, until it finally reached the one they wanted. Then they would make a quick insertion and we would disappear.

Pleiku was a big base with a variety of Army units. The 52nd Combat Aviation Battalion, which we were part of, was the largest aviation battalion in the Army with five assault helicopter companies, one aerial escort company, two Chinook companies, one heavy lift company, Bird Dogs, and security, medical, pathfinder, and truck detachments. Living conditions were about average. Our company took over former French Army huts, which were basic wooden buildings with low outer walls, screens, a metal roof, sidewalks, drainage ditches, and a mess hall.

On my first tour, I was a First Lieutenant. One day, we were on the flight line at Pleiku waiting to go out on a mission, when the base was hit by a mortar attack. They were exploding all around us, so I dove into a bunker just as one hit near me. I didn't know it at the time, but I caught shrapnel on the bottom of my feet. We went ahead and flew the mission; and when I came back, I was so tired I fell into my bunk and didn't take my boots off. The next morning, when I did, I found my socks were covered with dry blood, and they were stuck to my feet. And without the adrenaline rush of the day before, they hurt. I went to the flight surgeon, who sent me to the 79th EVAC Hospital to remove the shrapnel. The damage wasn't serious; but for years afterward, little pieces of metal would work their way to the surface, and feel as if I had a pebble in my shoe.

I returned to my unit and completed that tour in February, 1970. They then sent me to the 8th Special Forces Group in Panama, until the 206th Aviation Company was activated shortly afterwards. My mother is Panamanian, and I speak Spanish like a native, so that was exactly where I wanted to go.

In October, I was sent back to Vietnam for my second tour. Because of my experience with highly-classified Special Ops missions, I was sent back to the 189th in Pleiku to do exactly the same thing I had done during my first tour. This time, I had been promoted to Captain, and eventually was made Platoon Leader of a gunship platoon with 8 gunships and 20 officers.

One day I'll never forget, but still have trouble remembering, was when I was shot down forty miles inside Cambodia, and fractured some vertebrae in my back. We went in there to pick up a Special Forces Team that had been spotted by the NVA and were on the run. As pilot, I usually sat in the right seat; but I was the tactics instructor pilot, and I was in the left seat, where the copilot usually sat. We had three helicopters in the formation, two gunships and the slick that would do the pickup, plus a Forward Air Controller overhead. We came in low through rough country, twisting and turning as we approached the small LZ, when my gunship was suddenly hit by a burst from an enemy .50-caliber machine gun. That was a Chinese copy of the old—and very effective—WWII-era Russian "Dashka." My door gunner was instantly killed, and my copilot suffered wounds that he eventually died from, although I didn't know it at the time.

There was a lot of blood splattered around the cockpit and the warning lights on the instrument panel began to flash. I immediately told the copilot, "I've got it!" and took control as we lost transmission fluid. The engine and transmission pressures began to drop, and we lost RPM quickly. I dropped the rocket pods, which were hanging below the aircraft, knowing I had to find a place to put the helicopter down quickly. Once the blades stopped rotating, the Huey would drop like a rock. I saw a clearing off to the left, turned in that direction, and got on the radio. I told the other aircraft that we were going down, and would appreciate someone picking us up. Our FAC answered that he had already called it in and was getting us some backup. Unfortunately, we were forty miles inside Cambodia at the time, and our help was back on the other side of the Vietnamese border.

We came down hard in the clearing. The pilot and copilot seats were armored and designed to absorb some impact, but not that much. I was very busy, with a lot of adrenaline flowing, and didn't realize until afterward that I had fractured three vertebrae in the crash. Our crew chief jumped out and began firing into the wood line around us and the copilot joined him, while I began destroying all the top-secret stuff like the codes and the radio frequencies. Not satisfied that I had completely cleared everything, I ran

around front, opened the cowling and began firing my .45 into the KY-28, the communications encoder unit.

This was not a good place to hang around, so I went back for the door gunner, who I knew was seriously injured with a bad head wound. I cut him out of his shoulder harness, grabbed him, and threw him over my shoulder. At that point I weighed about 135 pounds, the door gunner was a big guy, and I had three fractured vertebrae. However, an adrenaline rush is a marvelous thing. The slick tried to come in and pick us up, but we were receiving more fire and I waved him off, for some really dumb reason. The other three guys looked at me and I shouted, "Let's go!" My crew chief answered, "Where?" I shrugged and told him, "East, to Vietnam," and took off running with this big guy across my shoulders, not particularly remembering that it was going to be forty miles through the jungle to get there. No sweat, I thought, excited.

I had my Special Forces "Carb-15," the cut-down M-16 rifle they used, and began spraying the wood line as we ran. When we started out, the other two were ahead of me. By the time we'd gone a half mile, I was in the lead. My copilot fell a couple of times and I could see he was having problems, but we kept on pushing until we reached another clearing and the slick was able to get in and pick us up. One of the Special Forces guys jumped out and said he was going back to burn the gunship with a thermite grenade. I didn't think he knew how to do that, so I decided to go back with him. We ran the whole distance, and then ran back.

They flew us directly to the 79th EVAC hospital in Pleiku. On the way, I told the others not to say anything to anyone, since it was a top-secret mission. We couldn't even tell our names to the doctors who treated us. A few minutes after we arrived, our company and battalion commanders showed up and took over. By that time, I knew the door gunner I had carried was dead and that really hit me hard. He was just a kid, and I hadn't realized how badly hurt he was. I was covered with blood, and it took the doctors a while to figure out it wasn't mine.

Even today, I remember being in that emergency room, and small flashes of the events surrounding the crash and its aftermath, but not much else. For years, I couldn't even remember the door gunner's name. I thought he had only flown with me that one time. Later, I found out he had flown with me a lot, but I had blocked all that out. Sometimes, the mind knows best.

After a crash, you are required to see the Flight Surgeon. He kept asking me, "Are you okay?" and I kept saying, "Yeah, yeah!" Then he asked, "And you want to go back flying?" and I'd say, "Yeah, yeah!" So they sent me back to the unit and I continued flying, but I had more and more back pain as the weeks passed. Finally, I went to the hospital. They x-rayed, saw I had three fractured vertebrae, and sent me to Japan to see some of the orthopedic and neurology guys. After a while, it was decided that they were just going to send me home. The unit was beginning to stand down, and I was assigned back to Panama.

By 1972, the Army wasn't going in a direction I wanted to go, so I decided to get out. Despite my Special Ops work and all my medals, my lack of any assignments in the Signal Corps, my branch, would have hurt my advancement anyway. I ended up getting a job with the U.S. Customs Service as a Special Agent in South Florida and South and Central America, spending a lot of time chasing drug runners in high-speed boats, as well as investigating drug smuggling by the Colombian cartels. I got a law degree part-time and worked for the Customs Service until 2001 when I retired.

For many years afterward, I didn't want to go to the VA. I thought they sucked, and I refused to go; but I found myself getting angrier and angrier. In Miami, my doctor finally pushed me into going. That's when they diagnosed me with severe PTSD. I didn't want to go see a shrink either; but I finally did, and we got into my memory issues. I still couldn't remember the door gunner's name and ended up bringing a photograph to show him and tell the shrink his name. At that point, the doctor asked me how I felt about him. I exploded at him, and walked out for about three months. When I returned to apologize, it seemed to help, and I went back for more and more therapy. Since then, I've also been diagnosed with Agent Orange-related neuropathy, diabetes, and other things.

During my tours, I was awarded a Distinguished Flying Cross for valor, several Air Medals with V, a Bronze Star with Oak Leaf Cluster, Vietnamese Cross of Gallantry with silver palm, and other medals. I never gave those much thought, but my kids must have. In 2016 I went on a veteran tour to Vietnam and took three of them with me. We visited Pleiku, Dak To, Nha Trang, An Khe Pass, Saigon, and a lot of other places. The old air-fields I flew in and out of were mostly still there. One of them was grassed over, one had houses on it, and one was being used to dry coffee beans.

To me, Dak To was the most interesting. There had been constant fighting there for years. There was a ditch and a big drainage pipe underneath the taxiway from the runway to the parking area that we used to jump into it and use as a makeshift shelter. One of my sons found the silted-up entrance to that old pipe, and thought it was amazingly cool. Now, I am 69, retired from the U.S. Customs Service, and finished last year with those post-retirement jobs. Now, I enjoy my kids, traveling and participating in veterans' activities.

BOB REILLY'S WAR

US Army Sergeant, Truck Driver, and Supply Clerk, Bravo Company, 19th Combat Engineering Battalion, Bong Song, II Corps, 1969

I'm a city boy, born and raised in New York. I graduated from St. Helena's High School in the Castle Hill section of the Bronx, enlisted in the Army, and went on active duty in October 1966. After Basic at Fort Gordon, Georgia, I was sent for AIT to Fort Huachuca Arizona, on the Mexican border near Nogales, and trained as a supply clerk. To my surprise, I was sent to Germany, to an artillery unit near Munich armed with Honest John nuclear rockets to stop the Russians. I was a nineteen-year-old kid and I loved Munich. We would go into town, or down into the Alps to Berchtesgaden. It was great, and it wasn't Vietnam, which I thought I'd missed.

In Germany, I was assigned to drive a gasoline tanker truck. Being from the city, I'd never driven anything, much less a truck, but nobody asked. I'd have 1200 gallons of gasoline in the big tank, plus another 600 gallons of diesel in a trailer, so that was interesting. After a couple of months, I was put in the supply room. Then, when I only had ten months left, I came down on orders for Vietnam to the 19th Combat Engineers at Bong Song in II Corps.

I arrived in March, 1969. As soon as I got off the plane, I couldn't believe the heat, especially after spending all that time in Bavaria, and this wasn't even summer. The 19th Engineers built roads and cleared land mines. The highway ran along the base of the mountains, and we had rice paddies and the ocean on the other side. The VC would plant mines in the road at night, and our guys would go out and find them and dig them up in the morning, do construction work and repairs, and return to base camp at night.

When the road crews went out, it was in a convoy, and we would always have plenty of riflemen and fire support. We had several armored trucks with Quad .50-caliber machine guns up top, and there was plenty of air support that could be called in. I was an

E-5 and I started off driving an equipment truck which went along with the mine-sweepers. I remember we had M-14s back then, not M-16s. One of my friends, a farm boy named Howie from Newark, Ohio, was killed when he went forward to help after the convoy took fire. It was sad, because he only had six days left in-country and he already had his orders to go home. Howie and a new guy were the only two in the unit who got killed while I was there. Funny how you never remember a new guy's name. There was another guy who was trying to light an old barbecue grill we had. He got impatient, spilled a #10 tin can of gasoline on the fire, and ended up in Houston with burns over 80% of his body. You really hated to see dumb stuff like that happen.

After a couple of months, I was made B Company Supply Sergeant when that guy rotated out. I still spent a lot of time out on the road in a truck delivering stuff, but it wasn't as bad as doing it every day. I was small back then, short and thin, with a 30-inch waist. When the fat guys would go through the mess line, the First Sergeant would be watching, and you could hear him tell the cooks, "No mashed potatoes for them," or "No dessert." When I came through, he'd tell the cooks to give me a double portion. I have a picture of myself with no shirt on, just shorts and combat boots, I still can't believe how skinny I was.

While I was there, they moved our unit from II Corps down to III Corps and flew us and our equipment in C-130s. It gave us a chance to see the Air Force bases. They were unbelievable. You'd think you were in New Jersey. We went in the Air Force NCO club. They had a big buffet, air-conditioning, cold beer, and we watched Neil Armstrong walk on the moon on television.

When my tour was over, I flew out of Cam Ranh Bay and got to watch one of the World Series games. The Mets won. That was the year the Jets also won their champion-ship. It was a big year for New York sports. I was out-processed through Fort Lewis, Washington, and flew from Seattle through Chicago to New York. There were three of us sitting together in uniform. When the stewardess found out we'd got out of Vietnam, she announced it on the PA. Everyone cheered and applauded. That's not the kind of reception most vets got, especially if they flew back through California. I figured ours must have been a business flight.

When I got home, I hung my uniform in the back of the closet, and tried to forget about it. I joined the New York City Police Department and did that for fifteen years in Midtown Manhattan and East Harlem. Police work was very hard on family life. They had a great program for cops to go to college. I did that, got a teaching degree, and became a Special Ed teacher. I spent the next twenty-two years teaching social studies to the most troubled kids. I retired from teaching in 2010. Like a lot of vets, I was tested for Agent Orange, and came up negative. However, one of my sons is deaf in one ear and my daughter had brain cancer at the age of seven. New studies are showing that Agent Orange is passing down to the next generation, so who knows? I'm sixty-eight now, and retired. I like to play golf, stay active in police officer and veteran's groups, and give presentations to the local schools about Vietnam.

J. R. WILSON'S WAR

US Air Force Staff Sergeant E-5,
Air Intelligence Specialist,
6th Special Operations Squadron,
Pleiku, 1969–70

I was a forestry major at Iowa State until I flunked out. I figured I'd join the Air Force, where my father served, but I had broken some vertebrae in my back fighting a forest fire in New Mexico, and the Air Force turned me down. That was 1967, and a Draft Notice quickly followed. To my surprise, I passed the Army physical. Apparently, they didn't care what I broke. My father used some pull, and the Air Force changed their mind and let me in. After Basic, they sent me to a photo interpretation and intelligence school in Denver, Colorado. After a year at Offutt AFB in Omaha going cross-eyed staring at photos of Russian ICBM silos, I was the happiest guy in the room when I got orders to Vietnam.

In March, 1969, I joined the 6th Special Operations Squadron at Pleiku in the Central Highlands, the "Spads." We had about thirty pilots and twenty airplanes, old, propeller-driven Douglas A-1 Skyraiders. They'd been around since the late 1940s, and there was nothing sleek or aerodynamic about them. They were old work horses that carried big bomb loads and could take a lot of hits. And being slow was an advantage in close air support and rescue operations, where they could check things out up close. As for weapons, they were versatile. They could carry miniguns, napalm, and a variety of bombs.

When I arrived in country, I was a twenty-one-year-old Sergeant E-4. Right off, I noticed that everyone was wearing flak jackets, carrying M-16s, and looking a bit jumpy. I learned the base had been pounded with 122-mm rockets a few hours before I got there, and for the previous thirty days. I asked guys what that was like, but all I got was, "You'll know it when it happens."

We lived in two-story barracks with electricity, running water, and Vietnamese women to clean and do our laundry, unlike our Army friends across the road. I asked a few more guys about the rockets, and again I got, "You'll know it when it happens." A month later, on the 31st, we got hit, and you bet your ass I knew what it was. There was a stampede down to the bunker outside, where we sat in the dark on a hard bench in our underwear for an hour. It was damp, smelled, and God only knew how many spiders and snakes were down there. After that, when the sirens went off, I pulled the blanket over my head and went back to sleep.

I worked in the map room in the Squadron's Intelligence Section. We had floor-to-ceiling map panels that rolled back and forth on tracks and displayed the Central Highlands of II Corps. I worked at night notating the maps with symbols showing all reports of enemy activity and ground fire that had come in from our pilots, the Army, Forward Air Controllers, or field units. In the morning, our Intel officers briefed our pilots on any threats before they went out. I also wrote up activity summaries that went on to the CIA and even the White House.

The problem with working nights was having nothing to do in the day, so I got a part-time job as a "go-fer" at the Air Force Officer's Club. Imagine having a part-time, paying job in a war zone! Our Air Force base was small, and surrounded by the much larger Army units of the 4th Infantry Division, from whom our O Club requisitioned its food and supplies. Three times a week I'd take a truck over to the Army Quartermaster and bring stuff back. It was a great opportunity to do some trading, and the Army guys weren't good at counting. If I was supposed to pick up three cases of beer, they'd give me six. Same for steaks, hot dogs, and the rest. They didn't care. It held down the food costs at the O Club, and I made some money on the side. Even our colonel got in the act. When he wanted to throw a unit party, he came to me and I got him everything, making me even more popular.

One day, our CO, Colonel Hadder, asked me if I wanted to go on a bombing run with him and one of the lieutenants. Of course! The A-1 is either a single seater or a two-seater, side-by-side, so I suited up in all the flight gear and climbed in next to Lt. Roberts, the Colonel's wing man. It was a gorgeous day. We flew out forty-five minutes and dropped our bombs on some caves. On the way back, the two pilots decided to have some fun. They took turns chasing each other in a simulated dog fight, with twists, turns, barrel rolls, and all the rest. After a while, I must have looked pretty pale, so before I decorated the cockpit with my breakfast, they called it off and we flew nice and level back to base.

After eight and one-half years, I got out of the Air Force, returned to Waterloo, Iowa, where I grew up, and got a job at John Deere, where everyone in town worked. I stayed with Deere for thirty years as a Field Rep and Territory Manager. Eventually, I took early retirement and moved to Puerto Vallarta, Mexico, where I live in a large ex-pat American community. I'm 70 now, and spend my time chilling on the beach, making jewelry, and serving as the Commander of the local American Legion Post, which has over one hundred members.

IRENE VAUGHN GREEN'S WAR

US Army 1st Lieutenant and Nurse Anesthetist,
91st EVAC Hospital, Chu Lai, 1969–70

I was an RN and Board-Certified Nurse Anesthetist at Boston City Hospital, one of the best in the country, making $67.50 per week working in the Neurosurgical Operating Room, but I wanted to do more. I'd seen one too many news reports with Dan Rather hiding behind a wall in Hue complaining about how the Marines were outnumbered and out of ammunition. Well, I thought, maybe they'd have had room for more bullets on that helicopter if they didn't have to fly your fat ass around! Okay, so what was I going to do about it? There was a war going on over there, young kids were wounded and dying, and I decided to help.

First, I went to the Navy recruiters, but they wanted to give me stateside duty for two years before they'd send me to Vietnam. Same for the Air Force. The Army, on the other hand, asked how soon could I leave? One week later, I was a First Lieutenant at the Medical Center in Fort Sam Houston. Six weeks after that, on July 4, 1969, Independence Day, I arrived at Long Binh with five other nurses, waiting to be assigned.

I had several friends at Danang, and asked if I could go there. No, they said they had a critical need for a nurse anesthetist at Chu Lai, but it was only forty miles south of Danang. Just around the corner, I thought. What they didn't tell me was that those forty miles were through enemy country. Besides, Chu Lai was on the ocean, and being from Boston, that sounded cool. Then I found out a nurse had been killed at Chu Lai, when a rocket struck one of the hospital wards a couple of weeks before I arrived.

I was assigned to the 91st EVAC, which was replacing

the 312th EVAC, a reserve unit heading home to North Carolina. The net result was a lot of staff who hadn't worked with each other, or worked in wartime triage medicine. The casualties came to us direct from the battlefield in medevac helicopters. Our job was to sort them out and decide who went to the operating room first, based on who we could save, stabilize them, and send them on to the big hospital in Japan.

I worked in the OR my whole tour. We were staffed with all the major surgical specialties from neurosurgical to orthopedic, thoracic, and the rest, and we had six nurse anesthetists. Two were regular army, two were from the 312th, and two of us were new. We worked twelve-hour shifts from 7:00 a.m. to 7:00 p.m., but one more nurse was always on call. At the beginning, the on-call shift was thirty-six hours. That proved too intense, and was cut back to twenty-four hours. But when the fighting picked up and helicopters kept coming, it was all-hands-on-deck for as long as it took.

In addition to the doctors and nurses, we had Medical Specialists, or "scrub techs," who had more training than a combat medic, and got the patients stripped, cleaned, and prepped, and then helped the doctors and nurses in surgery. They were amazing.

The Operating Rooms were in two Quonset huts, open on the ends, so you could look from one into the other and see what was going on. Periodically, we came under fire from rockets at night. After a while, you got used to it, superficially, anyway. If we were in the OR, or on duty, we'd put on helmets and flak jackets and keep working. When there was incoming, you could hear it, and our orders were to get under the tables. The first time it happened, I remained on my feet, looking after the patient. Afterward, the CO told me that next time, I would get under the table with everyone else. It was our duty. If the medical staff gets wounded, a lot of patients would suffer.

The doctors and nurses lived in wooden barracks-like buildings. I was given a single room, because I was on call so often. At first, we didn't have a bunker. Finally, they built one, a concrete half-pipe. At night, rockets or not, no one wanted to be the first one to go in. Between some really big spiders, rats, snakes, and the smell, we stopped going.

The only thing most people know about Army medicine is from the TV show *M*A*S*H*, and I'm often asked how accurate I think it is. As everyone knows, it was Vietnam stories and characters, set in Korea, because no one wanted to see a comedy about Vietnam. All things considered, *M*A*S*H* was fairly accurate. Our surgeons were excellent, like theirs. The nurses were busy. The CO was a joke. And the head nurse was pukey. We even had a Catholic priest, but he wasn't like theirs. And, there was a lot of drinking. It was a necessary relief, and saved my sanity. One night, we got off at midnight, grabbed a case of beer, went to the top of a sand dune looking out on the South China Sea, and drank the whole thing.

In November, I got a call that they had an emergency need for a nurse anesthetist at the 18th Surgical Hospital up at Camp Evans, near the DMZ. I was the newbie, so off I went. The "hospital" was a new concept—a portable Quonset hut they rolled out the back of a C-130, hooked up to a jet engine, and inflated. Living and working there was horrible. I stayed three weeks and came back with a huge new appreciation for the comforts we had at Chu Lai.

In December, the Bob Hope Christmas Show came to Chu Lai. In addition to his entertainers and singers, he brought Neil Armstrong, the astronaut, whom I got to meet.

Like "Radar O'Reilly," I developed an ear for incoming choppers. One day there were a group of them coming in and I immediately ran to the OR. There were two big MPs standing in front of the door, blocking my way. I tried to get in and they wouldn't let me. "You don't want to go in there, Ma'am," they kept telling me, but I managed to push my way inside anyway. On the gurneys were open body bags with six dead Marines. They had been a Civil Action Team, working in one of the villages, and the VC had captured them. Their hands were tied, and they had all been beheaded. It was the worst thing I saw over there. That was bad enough, but in the center of the room, two of our doctors were fighting. One had a camera and was trying to take photographs of the bodies, probably for some anti-war newspaper, but our senior doctor wouldn't let him. He pulled the camera away and smashed it on the floor.

When my tour was over, I still had nine months left to serve in the Army and was sent to Fort Dix New Jersey. When I was discharged, I went back to my old job at Boston City. I found myself doing the same stuff I did before; but after Vietnam, I felt I was wasting my time and my skills trying to save scumbags and gangbangers. Eventually, I couldn't take it anymore and quit. I tried a string of other things, even taking aircraft maintenance classes at Embry Riddle Aeronautical University in Daytona. Unfortunately, the airlines weren't hiring when I got out, so I took what I thought would be a short time position at the Boston VA Hospital. Turned out I loved it, or at least I loved working with the soldiers; but after twenty-five years, I retired, fed up with how political the VA had become. However, I had stayed in the Reserves and retired as a Lieutenant Colonel in 1996.

Like so many of the men who served in Vietnam, I developed Agent Orange-related Diabetes, no doubt from all the spraying that was done around Chu Lai, and from the residue that was all over the uniforms and bodies of the boys we treated in the OR.

Later, when I worked for the VA, I once asked one of their top people, "If you diagnose and treat prostate cancer, what is the incidence of breast cancer among the female vets?" Not only didn't they know the answer to that question, but they had no firm number on how many women served in Vietnam to begin with. It was roughly 8,000, but there have been no studies.

After I retired from the VA, my husband and I moved to South Carolina where we live on the water, raise chickens and dogs, and just "enjoy the good life."

MIKE JOHNSON'S WAR

US Army, Spec 5, Personal Property Detachment,
US Army Mortuary, Tan Son Nhut Air Force Base,
1969–70

I grew up in Miami, Florida, in Hialeah. After two years of junior college, I enlisted for three years in the Army in September 1967 to go to their photojournalism school, which was at Fort Ben Harrison in Indianapolis. I wanted to be a photographer. Naturally, after Basic they sent me to Fort Lee, Virginia, to Supply School, and I never saw Fort Ben Harrison or a camera. After Fort Lee, I was sent to Germany, to be a supply clerk in a truck company in Mannheim. We were near Heidelberg, a nice area, but that wasn't what I had enlisted for.

Eleven months later, in March, 1969 I found myself standing on the runway at Ton Son Nhut waiting for orders. I was hot, tired, and confused, like everyone the first day they arrived in country. Pretty soon, a truck pulled up next to me and handed me orders, which said I was going to the "USA Mort." I figured that must be a mortar unit, which scared me even worse. Instead, I was driven across the airbase to a small building with a sign that said, "US Army Mortuary." Now I really am confused, and scared. However, I remembered from Fort Lee that mortuary services, oddly enough, fell under the Quartermaster Corps.

That's right, I was assigned to the Personal Property Detachment, which was part of the Morgue, but we had nothing to do with processing bodies. Our job was to examine, document, and screen all of the deceased's papers and personal effects, so that nothing inappropriate, embarrassing, or hurtful would be sent home. Those things were destroyed. Basically, we were the Army censors, but for good reason. Unfortunately, 1969 was the peak of US troop strength; and with "Hamburger Hill" and other big battles, it was the peak year for casualties, too. The mortuary was processing roughly 25 a day. The way the entire Morgue operated, there were no favorites. Regardless of the rank of the deceased, each was processed first-come, first-served.

There were four of us handling personal property, so we were very busy with each of us doing six or seven screenings a day. Very often, the deceased's personal effects would have previously been screened at the company level, but not always. When I was done, the personal effects were boxed up and sent home to the family. I read all their letters and saw a lot of photographs. I also had the individual's records and knew where they had served and what had happened to them. Soldiers died for a lot of reasons, but they became real people to me. After a while, the guys working next door processing the bodies inevitably became numb to it, but I did not. I did the best job I could. Very often I would even write a letter or a note and send it home to the family with the deceased's personal effects, to try to console them in their loss.

In midyear, I got sick and ended up with a burst appendix. I spent a month in the hospital before I was sent back to my unit. Technically, I could have lost my job and been reassigned anywhere, so I bypassed the First Sergeant and went right to the Major in charge, which was a big "no-no," and told him I wanted my old job back. The First Sergeant chewed me out for going around him, but I didn't care. There weren't very many people who wanted to do this work, and I did it well, so the Major let me stay.

The one thing I will always remember, is that I was dealing with death every day for thirteen months, but I took the job seriously and made sure that every family was treated properly. After all, the men who died were our brothers.

I know some guys have gone back to Vietnam to see the country, but I have no interest in doing that. We were less than five miles from Saigon, and I would go down there all the time with my camera and take pictures. A lot of times I would go places I probably shouldn't have gone, but I was careful. The Vietnamese could smile at you one day and try to kill you the next.

I had extended a month to get an early out in April, 1970. When I got home, the protests at the airports were reaching a peak. They flew me into Fort Dix to out-process, and then to Newark Airport to fly home. I slipped into the first bathroom I could find and changed out of my uniform. And after I got home, for the next 46 years I never talked about what I did, not even to my wife or children. I never went to any veterans group meetings, either. I never thought I was as qualified as the others. Finally, I went to some VVA meetings and realized I was wrong. We didn't pick our jobs, the Army did, and they were all different. Mine was as valid and necessary as anyone else's, and I did it the very best that I could.

When I got home, I got a job with Florida Power & Light as an underground cable splicer and equipment repairman. I did that until I retired a few years ago. It was a dangerous job. I was dealing with very high-voltage electricity every day, and I was very lucky to have gotten by for all those years without getting hurt. One thing I continue to do is photography. I'm 69 now. My wife and I like to take camping trips in our RV, and I always bring my camera.

FRED SCHADLER'S WAR

US Air Force Sergeant, E-4,
Communications Repair Specialist, 7th Air Force,
U-Tapao Thailand, 1969–70

I grew up in in Keyser, West Virginia, near the Maryland state line. I was seventeen when I graduated from high school. I wanted to enlist in the Air Force, but had to wait until my eighteenth birthday. I went on active duty in November, 1966 on a four-year enlistment. After Basic at Lackland, I went to Sheppard Air Force Base in Texas and was trained as a telephone equipment repairman on the big inside switch gear. After a year and a half at Hill Air Force Base in Ogden Utah, a Material Air Command logistics center, I was sent to the Strategic Air Command base at U-Tapao, Thailand, arriving in April, 1969.

U-Tapao was ninety miles from Bangkok in flat, wide-open country on the Gulf of Siam, as far south and away from North Vietnam as you could get in Thailand. It was built three years before I got there, and had the longest runways in Southeast Asia. That's why they based some of the B-52s there, relocating them from Guam, because they could hit any target in South or North Vietnam from U-Tapao without refueling. When a line of them would power up, and begin lumbering up the runway, it was a sight to see.

SAC bases are very different from ordinary Air Force Bases. SAC's watchword, going back to General Curtis LeMay, was readiness, readiness, readiness. Everything was redundant, and there was no such thing as failure. Every unit had to assign one repair guy to work in the Trouble Center. It was open 24/7 and we jumped if a single radio, radar, or piece of communication gear went down. If it was in the chain that supported the bombers or fighters, the mission was scrubbed, so our work was very serious. I volunteered for it, because it was a good way to stay busy. In the Trouble Center, we worked sixteen hours on and eight off.

In early 1968, the year before I got there, the B-52s broke the NVA siege of the Marine firebase at Khe San. The B-52s attacked in groups of six every thirty minutes, crisscrossing the NVA staging areas and bunker complexes, again and again. Fully loaded, they carried eighty 500-pound bombs. The NVA were hoping to repeat their big victory over the French at Dien Bien Phu, but the French didn't have the firepower from flight after flight of B-52s. They turned the tide of battle. That was what they were used for, to bomb targets in South Vietnam and Cambodia and bomb along the Ho Chi Minh Trail. The big raids over North Vietnam, when we lost a lot of planes, did not begin until 1970, long after I was gone.

Enlisted men at U-Tapao lived in two-story wooden barracks. They were air-conditioned, with forty-eight men to a floor in four-man cubicles with bunk beds. We even had hot showers, flush toilets, a big gymnasium, an outdoor theater, and a mess hall, which operated 24/7. The life there wasn't bad at all, which would probably drive the Army and Marine guys over in Vietnam crazy if they knew, but the war wasn't my idea any more than it was theirs. Let's face it, we all just got by.

We could go off base. There was a little honky-tonk area just outside the gate, and a small town a few miles down the road. I did not eat much of the local Thai food, except I did come to like water buffalo and the Kung Pao. I had gotten married when I was in Utah, so I didn't mess around or drink very much. There was a lovely beach on the Gulf of Siam, but the water was so polluted I didn't dare go in. Every now and then, some Air Force guy would get robbed and there were even a couple of murders off base. When something like that happened, they would immediately shut down the gates.

I didn't drink very much, and I wasn't very good at it when I did. One night we went out and hit the local bars. When we got back, we were all pretty drunk, but realized one of the guys was missing. We went back and found him lying in a disgustingly filthy drainage ditch. We got him back, and threw him in his bunk. The next morning, our "hooch maid" took one look at him, shook her head and held her nose as she said in pidgin Thai, "Oh, you stink!"

While I was there, they widened the base perimeter and security zone and found a large tunnel coming in, which almost reached the B-52 flight line. Another day I remember was when one of our B-52s came back from a bombing mission fully loaded. Its bomb bay doors had stuck half open, which was why they scrubbed the mission. A bump might dislodge the bombs, but it landed gently and slowly decelerated without a problem.

In March, 1970, I went home and was discharged. I attended Potomac State College and then the University of West Virginia, thanks to the G.I. Bill, and got my BA in accounting. After working for several national and international businesses, I received my MBA from UNC Charlotte and my PhD from the University of South Carolina, and have been on the faculty of the Business School at East Carolina University in Greenville for the past thirty-one years. I am now sixty-eight years old and have cut my teaching load to half time, but I'm not yet fully retired.

ROSS LISCUM'S WAR

**US Marine Corps, Corporal,
G Company, 2nd Battalion,
1st Marines, 1st Marine Division,
South of Danang, 1969–70**

When I was eighteen and fresh out of high school in California, I thought I could outrun a cop on a motorcycle. Not a good idea. The judge asked me, "Well, have you thought about the military? Or would you like me to give you a sentence to cool your heels for a while?" Shortly thereafter, in October, 1968, I found myself in Boot Camp in San Diego, down the coast, where, at eighteen years of age, the Marine Corps miraculously transformed me into an 03-11 Infantryman.

Six months later, in April, 1969, I landed in Danang. Eight of us were told to throw our gear in the back of a deuce-and-a-half truck, and we were driven to the 1st Marine Division's rear area, about five miles south of Danang. It was very scientific. The three guys at the back of the truck were dropped off at Echo Company, the next three were dropped off at Foxtrot Company, and the two of us who were left went to Golf Company. No transition. The next day I was told to gear up and we went out on a patrol for a month and a half. Other than a few short breaks, I stayed in the field my entire year.

I was a town kid who grew up in Santa Rosa, north of San Francisco. For those like me, who didn't grow up in the country or have a lot of camping experience, when you spend a solid year out in the bush, in the open, trying to sleep on the ground, we never could figure out how those guys from Tennessee and Kentucky did it. They slept in the rain like I did, but it didn't seem to bother them, while we were drowning in it. Raining or not, we went on patrols, set up new perimeters, dug holes, ate, filled sandbags, and tried to sleep.

We operated south of Danang doing sweep after sweep around Hill 55, Dodge City, Marble Mountain, Go Noi Island, and from the ocean to the mountains. Most of it was

flat, sandy, dusty, scrub land. Talking to older guys, it was the same area they'd gone through, again and again ever since 1965. It was a major NVA strong point, full of tunnels, bunkers, booby traps, and hardcore regiments. We moved around a lot, usually by helicopter lifts to a new base, where we would set up and start patrolling again. It was the same routine every day as we tried to clean them out and shut down the "rocket belt" around the air bases at Danang.

There was a lot of Black Power stuff going on back home, and I know some Army units had serious racial problems, but the Marine Corps was different. I think we all tried to help each other. Maybe it was because we were in a lot of combat, but it was the Black troops who said that we were all brothers. If we piss each other off, who's going to watch our backs?

We got a lot of Second Lieutenants straight out of OCS with their manuals, new gold bars, and John Wayne attitude. Sooner or later, a platoon sergeant would pull them aside and tell them to pick out some guys with five o'clock shadow and learn from them. If they didn't, they wouldn't be around very long.

We had a First Lieutenant over 2nd Platoon who was an Annapolis grad named Jack Klimp. He was the best officer I ever served with. I was his radioman in the platoon, and then at company level when he took over as our CO. He really knew his stuff, and ended up as a Marine Corps Lieutenant General. In the 1970s, our former CO, Captain Al Selleck, started a company reunion that grew into what is today the 2nd Battalion 1st Marines (Ghost Battalion) Association with 1500 Vietnam era Marines and Corpsman. At a reunion a few years ago, the General gave me the best compliment I've ever gotten. He said, "I had this jackass radio operator south of Danang, who taught me to keep my head down and shut up. He was a Corporal, and he'd tell me, 'Sir, shut up and do this, or Sir, do that.' He trained me quite well!"

I remember a lot of our operations quite vividly. Pipestone Canyon, one of the biggest, lasted for five or six weeks. We went on to Go Noi Island, a major NVA enclave, with our regiments on line, and tanks, and artillery, working our way from one end of the island to the other. It was amusing how one lone NVA would pop up out of a tunnel in front of this line of hundreds of Marines and start shooting at us. We captured tons of weapons and supplies, and killed a lot of them, but as soon as we left, they came right back in. Other operations followed, one after another.

When my year was over, I got out of the Marine Corps and went back home to Santa

Rosa. I went over at 135 pounds and came home at 125. Like a lot of other guys, I lost my appetite. I ended up with nine ribbons, no wounds, and no Purple Hearts, which was amazing given all the bullets that were flying at me.

Once home, I received my Associate of Science Degree from the Santa Rosa Junior College, and experienced the disrespect the college crowd showed to us Vietnam veterans. I got my real estate license and spent thirty-nine years as a broker and owner of up to three Prudential California Realty offices during 28 of those years. I joined the Marine reserves in 1971 and served until 1985, becoming the senior enlisted Marine Reservist on the West Coast. Now, when not working, I am involved with our Sonoma County Fair Board and its Foundation, community business groups, nonprofits helping veterans, and playing golf. And my wife, Jane, and I are enjoying our new granddaughter, Avery, who was born in March 2016. Semper Fi!

JACK COURTNEY'S WAR

**US Army, Sergeant and Military Policeman,
A and B Companies, 720th MP Battalion,
Long Binh, 1969–70**

I played in a rock-and-roll band in Pawtucket, Rhode Island for two years after I got out of high school and took some classes at the Berkeley School of music in Boston, but the draft was closing in and I didn't want to end up in the infantry. Tet and the fighting were all over the TV and I needed to do something; so, in June 1968, I enlisted in the Regular Army for three years as an MP.

After Basic and AIT at Fort Gordon, I was stationed at Fort Monmouth, New Jersey, doing normal MP stuff until my orders came for Vietnam. When I got there, I was assigned to B Company of the 720th MP Battalion in Long Binh. Like most new guys, I filled sandbags, dug holes, and burned the cut down oil drums under the latrines every day. "What the f**k!" I thought, is this what an MP does?

Fortunately, that didn't last long. Pretty soon, I was sent out on recon patrols every day into the jungle, and was doing night ambushes, decked out like an infantry grunt, patrolling way out beyond the perimeter, along the Dong Nai River. The other guys I was with really were infantry, with shoulder patches from all sorts of different Infantry Divisions. We'd go out for a couple of weeks, sleep on the ground, eat Cs, return to base for a couple of days, then go back out and do it all over again. Those guys loved it. Not me. I was supposed to be an MP!

One night I got stung by a scorpion, got all delusional and passed out. The next thing I knew, I was in the hospital. When I got out, I'd had enough. I went in to see the CO. "What the f**k! I'm an MP and Regular Army. That's what I enlisted for." That was when I learned somebody'd changed my MOS to 11-B, Infantryman, so I went to the IG and filed a complaint. Okay, I said, if the Army doesn't want me as an MP, give me my year back! "Oh, no, we can't do that," he said. Then I'm writing my Congressman, I told him. I ended up getting an Article 15 for mouthing off at the CO, but they moved me to A Company and into a real MP unit. Finally!

For the next ten months, I had a different job every day, whatever they needed. The one I really hated was setting up speed traps on the roads around Long Binh. This was the Provost Marshall's idea, and I had quotas on the number of tickets I was supposed to give out, just like some suburban speed trap. All the roads led to infantry units, like the one that went south to Blackhawk. We'd hide back in the jungle with two "mirror boxes" and a stop watch to determine a passing vehicle's speed. That meant we got to stop drunken infantry guys with loaded rifles driving deuce-and-a-half trucks, shooting up the countryside and taking shots at water buffalo. Finally, I went to the First Sergeant and said, "What the f**k! I ain't doing that anymore. Those guys are gonna kill us."

That was probably what got me assigned to a "Combined Forces" unit—American MPs and ARVN MPs, who we called "White Mice." We'd go into Vietnamese villages, they'd throw their weight around and beat up people. I wanted no part of that and stayed in the jeep.

As bad as that had been, the next fun job they gave me was to go out and arrest American deserters who were living in the Vietnamese villages, wearing black pajamas, as if nobody would know they were Americans trying to go "native." There were more of them than you'd think. Some of them even had families, but even the Vietnamese thought they looked stupid. White or Black, there was no way they were going to blend in. Sometimes we even had to send in helicopters to haul them out. When we caught them, they would fight and cuss, wanting us to let them go. But like I told them, "Sorry, but I'm not doing your time for you."

I also worked at LBJ, Long Binh Jail, the military stockade for all of Vietnam. It was a nasty place, like being in a dog kennel. A lot of those guys were in there for refusing orders, like refusing to go back up on Hamburger Hill or to fight in other battles. "What are they going to do?" the joke went, "send me to Vietnam?" No, they're going to send you to LBJ. Every now and then I'd have to take prisoners like that out on work details, cleaning up things and doing hard labor. It was no fun.

Another time they told me to take a jeep and two MPs and go "clear the road" down to the base at Bearcat. Our infantry would leave VC bodies lying along the side of the road to make a point to the locals. Picking them up is what he meant by "clear the road." "What the f**k!" I thought. The three of us? On that road, with roadside bombs and snipers? Some job. There was a girl who ran a grapefruit stand down there, who would always smile at us when we drove by. One day she didn't, and wouldn't look at me, so we stopped and checked out the area. "What the f**k!" Sure enough, there was a booby trap up ahead with a B-40 RPG round buried in the road that would have blown up our jeep. She knew it, but the civilians were caught in the middle.

One nice thing about the Bearcat run was the Australian Army unit based at Nui Dat. They had an NCO Club with Australian beer. Whenever you went there, the rounds always started with a salute to the Queen. "What the f**k!" I smiled, and raised my glass.

Probably the grossest thing I saw during my time there was on a trip up to Chu Lai. We passed an MP standing on the side of the road directing traffic, holding his nose. There had just been a big battle there and I saw at least a hundred VC bodies stacked on the road shoulder all around the MP. Man! I thought I had some bad jobs.

When my tour was over, I got out, but then reenlisted, which you can do within ninety days without losing rank. They sent me to the MP unit at Fort Dix, New Jersey, where I was an investigator, patrol sergeant, and desk sergeant. After that enlistment, I had enough of the Army, got out for keeps, and got a job at the Fram Oil Filter factory in in Providence. I worked there for twenty years until they closed the plant and moved it to Mexico.

My wife worked there too, and that caused a lot of stress. I suddenly got the sweats and pains in my chest, but it passed. They brought in an out-placement company to help us. I got to know those guys and they offered me a job, so I grabbed it. We went on the road for a job in Chicago, and I had another attack. "What the f**k!" I thought.

One of my friends told me I should go to the VA and get checked out. It didn't take long before they diagnosed me as having Agent Orange-related Hodgkin's Disease, a cancer in the lymph glands which hits your immune system. They gave me 100% disability. Later, I also had a stroke. Goddamned Vietnam! Since then, I took up the guitar again, but I couldn't find a garage band. I also spend time with veteran's groups.

CHRIS POLLOCK'S WAR

US Army Spec 4, 330th Radio Research Company,
509th Radio Research Group,
Pleiku and Nha Trang, 1969–70

I grew up in western Illinois, across the river from St. Louis. I kicked around for a year or two after high school and finally enlisted in the Army in 1968 to avoid getting drafted and stuck in the infantry. After taking the usual tests, they told me I had an aptitude for electronic maintenance. Maybe that was because my dad was a broadcast engineer. Who knows? Anyway, the recruiter told me about this elite unit called the Army Security Agency. The work they did was all high-tech and top-secret. They never got sent to Vietnam, wore civilian clothes, and carried a .38 revolver instead of a rifle. That sounded good to me, so I signed up. What a sucker I was!

After I finished Basic at Fort Leonard Wood, I did my first AIT at Fort Benning for basic electronics and radio repair, and then a second AIT at Ft. Gordon, Georgia, in advanced radio repair, where I was trained to repair the big R-390 radio receivers and the T-368 transmitters. Once my Top-Secret security clearance came through, I got my orders sending me to the 509th Radio Research Group in… you guessed it, the Republic of South Vietnam. I went over in jungle fatigues and combat boots, just like all the others, and nobody issued me a .38 caliber revolver, either.

After my arrival, I was sent out to the 330th Radio Research Company in Pleiku. The ASA had their own compound within the base on "Engineer Hill." It was a high-security area and you needed a special badge to even get inside. We lived in wooden hooches and slept on cots. No air-conditioning, but we had a mess hall, and the food wasn't that bad.

While we didn't go out on patrols there, we drew guard duty in the bunkers that surrounded our compound. They were equipped with .50-caliber machine guns. The perimeter going out a good distance all around had been cleared and sprayed with Agent Orange, which was very nice to know as the years passed. We also had "Foo Gas" drums

251

buried out there, which was like a napalm bomb that we could set off, and we also had Claymore mines.

The 330th was a Primary Processing Center for radio intercepts, finding, translating, and decoding VC and NVA radio traffic, both Morse code and voice, using Radio Direction Finder equipment to locate the source of the signal, and passing all that up to the 509th Group. Our equipment was in big truck vans, and my maintenance shop kept it all working. There were three of us. Another guy and myself repaired the transmitters and receivers, twelve hours on and twelve hours off, while the third guy was there to repair the teletype machines.

Most of the ASA people in the vans were crazy, but that's what you get from sitting and listening to Morse code all day long. And Pleiku had its moments. We would get rockets fired at us at night and we would run to the bunkers, but the NVA were usually aiming at the ammo dump or the helicopters, not at us.

One time, I was sent TDY, temporary duty, to An Khe to repair some equipment. I believe it was in April of '70. That night, we were sitting in the mess hall watching Sharon Tate in *The Fearless Vampire Killers* when VC sappers started blowing up the helicopters on the airfield. They ordered us into these little Conex containers they were using as shelters. Luckily, we weren't expected to do any fighting, because all we had were M14s as compared to the rest of the Army with their M16s.

Another time at Pleiku, a Huey came in to land on the football field that they used as a helipad. The pilot must've gotten disoriented with all the dust he kicked up, because he hit the goalpost with his rotor blade. That broke off, and the helicopter came down hard. I didn't want to fly with that guy anytime soon.

In May, 1970, my company was moved from Pleiku down to Nha Trang as part of a consolidation and downsizing. It was on the ocean and a lot safer there. I was short when we moved to Nha Trang, and never left the base much. The NCO club would bring in Filipino bands to play, and we would go drinking there. In June, 1970, my time was up, and I rotated back to the States. I re-enlisted and spent twenty-three years in the Army, working for the Army Security Agency. I worked at Fort Hood, Augsburg, Germany, and in Berlin. At Fort Hood, I was the NCOIC of the Sensitive Compartmentalized Information Center from 1982 to 1986. If nothing else, the name was guaranteed to confuse people. I then served a four-year tour in South Korea, which was my last before I retired in 1990 as a Sergeant First Class. I returned to the Fort Hood area, working for another twenty-three years for a contractor, repairing equipment on the ranges.

I have an 80% disability because of Agent Orange-induced Ischemic Heart Disease, and other things. My wife and I continue to live in west-central Texas, where we enjoy taking cruises, and I grow exotic plants, including Plumeria, Desert Rose, and various types of Orchids.

JOHN BERRY'S WAR

**US Marine Corps, E-3 Lance Corporal,
CUPP Program, 2nd Battalion,
5th Regiment, 1st Marine Division,
Que Son and Tam Ky, 1970**

I'm from Phillipsburg, a small town on the Delaware River in northwest New Jersey. It was mostly farm country. In July, 1969, the month they walked on the moon, I enlisted in the Marines. Six months later, after Parris Island and Camp Lejeune, I was in Vietnam, an 03-11, a rifleman assigned to A Company, 1st Battalion of the 7th Marines, and then to G Company, 2nd Battalion of the 5th Marines when the 7th rotated home.

My war was spent as part of a CUPP Team, which stood for Combined Unit Pacification Program. We operated out in the villages in small units of six to twelve Marines and maybe twenty or thirty Vietnamese Popular Forces, the PFs, or local militia. I spent my year in the field, living out in the open, and never went back to a base camp.

We operated in the Que Son and Tam Ky area, about twenty-five miles south of Da Nang, protecting the villages and interdicting the VC and NVA infiltration routes from their base camps in the Que Son mountains to the west. The area was mostly rolling hills and rice paddies, no jungle. My typical day was spent out patrolling and my nights were spent in ambushes, or "kill teams," as they were called. We lived with the people, shared our food with them and ate theirs, and helped them out with medical issues when we could. It was the kind of work where you had diarrhea three fourths of the time and infections from cuts and scratches that never went away.

The PFs weren't well trained, but you had to respect

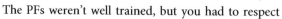

them. Some of the older men had fought against the French and even the Japanese. If they lost and the NVA won, they knew what was going to happen to them. I was a rifleman, but something happened to our radio operator, so they handed it to me to carry. Sometime later, we had a visit from our battalion. When they found out none of us were trained on the radio or had the right MOS, they quickly set up a two-hour class to teach us everything we'd already figured out.

In the photograph, I'm on the left and the guy on the right with the M-60 machine gun is Tom "Pittsburgh" Lawlor, a good friend during my tour. He was nicknamed "Pittsburgh," because that's where he was from. We look like two kids "playing war" in the back yard, but the guns and bullets were very real, and so was the war.

One of the funniest things that happened that year was what we called "Spaghetti Night at An Xaun." Normally, we ate nothing but Cs or Vietnamese food, mostly rice. Once in a blue moon, battalion would send us hot chow in big metal insulated mermite cans. One day, the helicopters arrived and dropped off dozens of cans full of spaghetti and meatballs, French bread, and all the rest. There were only ten of us, but they must have thought we were a whole company. We didn't know what to do with it, so we carried the cans down to the village and shared it with them. They knew what noodles were, but they had never seen spaghetti with tomato sauce and meatballs. Maybe their stomachs couldn't take it, but that night the entire village got sick. In a way it was funny, because we always got sick from eating their food.

In the villages, we were only a squad or a fire team. Our Lieutenant and the Platoon Sergeant usually stayed on a hill some distance away in the center of all the teams. It was my bad luck that about the only time I ended up back there, the hill was attacked by an NVA sapper battalion, the 82nd I heard later, and overrun. The Sergeant had built a wooden building, more like a shelter, out of 105 shell crates. I was used to sleeping out on the ground in a foxhole, but he insisted we all sleep inside.

On the night of December 9, 1970, we had nine Marines and twenty to thirty RFs on that hill. I went to sleep in that makeshift bunker and the first thing I knew was when an RPG blew through the wall and knocked me out. When I came to I couldn't find my rifle and grabbed one that a *Stars & Stripes* reporter had brought with him. He had a head wound and he wasn't going to need it. Later, we heard the PFs had fallen asleep, the NVA had cut their way through the wire, and were on us before we knew what happened. They brought satchel charges and were throwing grenades. I began returning fire and eventually got outside, where another guy and I sat on the ground, back to back, shooting and throwing hand grenades at them. I got hit three times by explosions and shrapnel—from that first RPG, a hand grenade, and finally a mortar round. I passed out and the next thing I knew I was being medevaced out.

One of our guys, Ed Starrett, received the Navy Cross, which is one rung below the Medal of Honor. He was a mortarman, kept firing illumination rounds, and ran around from position to position returning fire. He was badly wounded himself, but he held them back almost single-handedly. Our Lieutenant received the Silver Star, but a lot of guys never got the medals they deserved. There was no one left to write them up.

That night was the end of my war, and I was medevaced back to Saint Albans VA Hospital in Queens, New York. It was a huge place, but it was the closest VA Hospital to where my parents lived in New Jersey. I was there for five months. After I was back on my feet, they made me an elevator operator in the hospital, until I was released. In total, I spent four years on active duty. I'm rated 100% disabled by the VA from the wounds I received that night, including a traumatic brain injury, PTSD, shrapnel in both legs, back, buttocks, left arm, and face. People ask me how I was wounded in the buttocks. I tell them you can't get any important job done unless you stick your ass out once in a while. Actually, it was probably the highest part of my body, since I was hugging the deck. I received the Bronze Star with "V" and a Purple Heart.

You might think that was my worst night in country, but it really wasn't. I had gone out on a "kill team" ambush with a guy named Ávila and two PFs. Unfortunately, instead of running into a couple of VC or even a squad, it was a large NVA unit that came up the trail. They saw us, and we took off running. This went on for hours. We'd lose them for a while and then they'd find us and chase us again. Finally, we reached a Vietnamese graveyard and were so exhausted that we couldn't go on anymore. We hid among the headstones and the enemy passed within twenty yards, but they never saw us. That was when Ávila and I decided that we would never give up. No matter what, we were going to keep on fighting. Maybe that helped me that night up on the hill.

Probably the most interesting thing I've done since 1970 was to go back to Vietnam in 2005 with my wife and two sons, who were fourteen and fifteen. We were living in Japan, so I could make the arrangements myself. The kids were very surprised at how beautiful the country was, but in that climate, the jungle quickly covers everything over. We took a cab and went back to An Xaun, even up to the hill where we had the bunker and I was wounded. I had some old photographs of the Vietnamese we worked with, and tracked some of them down. One of the young Vietnamese who hung around with us was called Tom-Tom. I found him, and after a lot of "Whatever happened to…," I mentioned all the VC he had killed, and he ran away. They were friendly, but you had to be careful what you said. The hill where the battle was had become a tree farm, but it was still littered with Army stuff, even some old boots. One of my sons brought one home as a souvenir.

After my service was over and I was discharged, I went to work for the Penn Central Railroad; and then went back to school, got an MA, and became a Special Education teacher. My wife was in the Navy and I went around the world with her. I taught school and she works for the VA.

SUSAN DRECHSEL'S WAR

US Army First Lieutenant and Surgical Nurse, 91st Evac Hospital, Chu Lai, 1969–70

I grew up in Iowa, became a Registered Nurse in 1966, and worked at the VA hospital in Iowa City, Iowa, for three years. Some of the senior nurses there had served in WW II and Korea, so I decided to do my part, too. RNs received a direct commission in return for a two-year commitment; so, I was sworn in on July 5, 1969 and volunteered for Vietnam.

Nurse Corps Officer Basic is held at Fort Sam Houston in Texas, the Army's medical center. By the end of August, I was the only military female on a United Airlines charter flight headed for Saigon. I was doing fine, until we approached Tan Son Nhut airport and I saw fighter jets off our wing escorting us. We circled for a while, because the base had been under rocket attack. "Oh, my God," I thought, "what have I done?"

The windows on the bus that drove us to the medical command had sturdy wire screens over them. I wondered how big the bugs must be, until the driver told me the screens were to keep grenades out, not bugs. How nice.

When I met with the Chief Nurse she said nurses were needed at Cu Chi and Chu Lai. I knew Cu Chi had a swimming pool, so I said I'd like to go there. She just looked at me. It might have a pool, but it was a much more dangerous place to be. I later found out that the Cu Chi hospital sat on top of a VC tunnel complex. As it turned out, they needed a surgical nurse at the 91st EVAC at Chu Lai.

After we processed-in at Danang, they pointed to the helicopter on the landing pad, which was to fly me to Chu Lai. I had never been in one and wasn't too keen on the idea, but they shoved me inside anyway, and away we went. As the chopper took off and tilted and turned, I hung on for dear life, expecting to fall out the door at any moment, not realizing that really can't happen. After a while, I preferred to fly in the ones that carried guns, rather than the ones with red crosses on the side that made big targets.

Chu Lai was on the coast south of Danang. The Evac Hospital was set back on a sand dune above the beach on the South China Sea, tucked behind the Marine airfield and the headquarters of the 23rd Infantry Division, the Americal, where many of our patients came from. I was a replacement, "filler" for the 91st, which had just taken over from the 312th, a reserve unit that was rotating home to North Carolina. They were the only reserve hospital unit to be activated during the war, and did an outstanding job. We had all the specialties from neurosurgery to thoracic, orthopedic, ophthalmology, and the rest, with a staff of 113 medical officers and 223 enlisted. The year I was there, we treated 9,000 patients, which equated to  twenty-five new cases every day. Obviously, they did not come in an even flow like that, and some days and nights we were pushed to the limit.

All "newbie" nurses were assigned to the Vietnamese POW and civilian wards for two months, to learn the military system. We were not familiar with their culture, values, religion, dietary requirements, or language. They were Buddhists, Taoists, Catholics, and followers of various folk religions, and they didn't trust each other. I saw many patients with malaria, TB, parasitic infections, cholera, and war related injuries, such as from white phosphorus.

Working on the POW ward was a challenge. The MP's had control of the prisoners. They were young, poor, uneducated, malnourished, afraid, angry, and sometimes mean, aggressive, and hardcore. They had been told we would poison them or kill them with our drugs and blood transfusions. Once they learned how humanely we treated them, using the Geneva Convention, most became cooperative. Of course, when they were released, they were transferred to an ARVN prison camp and a very uncertain future.

We gave good care to the civilians, too, but it was unlikely they would get proper follow-up care when they returned to their villages. A lot of pregnant women appeared at our gate believing, incorrectly, that if their babies were delivered at our hospital, they would become US citizens.

After two months in the Vietnamese ward, I was transferred to the US medical wards. After four months working in the Intensive Care Unit, I was moved to the Emergency room. The ER was the ultimate challenge of nursing skills. Emotions were high or low. We were "pumped up" when soldiers fared well. When the outcome was terrible, we were devastated. Wounded soldiers and civilians came to us mostly by medical evacuation helicopters. Some had received care in the field by a medic or at an aid station. Others came directly from the field, were loaded on a helicopter, and flown to us, sometimes unannounced. I always questioned if I could pull it together, and we had to react fast. It was easy to be stressed and anxious.

On high volume days, we practiced triage, which took some getting used to. An ER physician evaluated and categorized each patient. That dictated which soldiers we would treat first. "Immediate" was a life-threatening injury. "Delayed" was non-life threatening, but needed treatment. "Minor" was the walking wounded. And "Expectant" was not expected to live. The patient was in the process of dying, and no amount of intervention could help. I was always worried that a soldier classified as Expectant would die alone. All of the medical staff made special efforts to spend a few moments with them. Physical contact, such as holding and touching, was so vital. For the ones who were terminal, we put them behind a screen and tried to keep them comfortable. As far as I could tell, every doctor and nurse would slip behind the curtain and talk to them. You never asked anyone what they said to them; but for me, I would usually tell them, if your mother was here, here's what she would say to you. It was a very emotional time for us.

I could handle most injuries except for burns. I would pray if someone was burned let it be by napalm as those burns were terrible but treatable. White phosphorus or "Willie Pete" chemical burns were far more devastating. When blown into the skin, this substance continues to burn deep into the tissues and even down to the bone. A neutralizing agent is used to stop the burning by depriving oxygen to tissue.

In the VA hospital back in Iowa, most of my patients were over sixty-five. In Vietnam, most were 18 to 20 years old, and I was only 25. But this was exactly what I signed "up for". They were from all parts of the country, had different backgrounds, educations, and views of that war. I enjoyed their stories. I was amazed by the number of men who said, "If you were my woman, you'd be back home where you belong." I'd usually respond, "If I was, and you were wounded, who would take care of you, if the nurses weren't here?"

In the ER we might have an NVA patient on one table and an American soldier on another. One day, someone yelled: "Susan, watch out." I turned to find a wounded GI standing behind me with a big knife, about to kill my patient. I grabbed his bloody arm, while a couple of corpsmen grabbed him and got him back on his gurney. That was scary.

It was difficult being a woman in Vietnam. The ratio of women to men was 1 to… who knows, a whole lot. After working a 12-hour shift, all I wanted was to be alone, sit quietly in a cool, dark corner, relax, and have a drink. Other nurses felt the same. Some of the men thought we were rude, not realizing we were just "wiped out." No doubt there was a lot of alcohol and drug abuse going on, due to the stress, but everyone was living on the edge. I recognized that I used alcohol to decrease stress. Fortunately, after returning from Vietnam, I resolved my alcohol issues. But did we make a difference? Yes. Would I do it again? Yes.

Here's some of my firmly held opinions from my year in Vietnam:

Snakes!—Kill the snake! Never put a stunned snake in a bag and expect the ER staff to open a bag and identify snake. My friend Irene found a viper in the women's bath-room. She chopped and diced that thing with her machete.

Rockets!—If the NVA can't hit the fuel tanks on the airfield, seems to me their next choice is the big red crosses on the roof of the hospital. It might be a violation of the Geneva Convention, but they didn't care. Besides, the bunkers had smelly water, rats, and spiders.

Rats!—They were big as cats. The rat poison only made them grow bigger.

Mama-sans!—These were local women who were paid to clean our rooms and wash and iron our clothes. Each officer paid $25.00 a month for their services. One women working for four officers earned more money in a month than some families earned in a year. Yes, some of them were VC but they did a good job ironing our fatigues.

Weapons!—Some soldiers arriving in the ER came with their weapons, especially those flown directly from the field on non-medical choppers. Corpsmen and nurses needed to clear them, and then test space fire them into a sand barrel. Hand grenades had to have their handles taped down with wide tape. After a while, several of us had one of the orderlies take us to the range, where we got to shoot M-16s, .45s, an M-60 machine gun, and a grenade launcher. I even fired a LAW anti-tank rocket. It was amazing! Better still was the M-60. Nothing like blazing away with a machine gun to give you a feeling of real power!

The BOQ was a two-story wooden barracks. The nurses had their own section, which had been divided into one-person rooms, with the usual Army standard metal cot and lockers. Every now and then, the Battleship *New Jersey* would be in our area. When it fired its big guns, the perfume bottles on my table would bounce and rattle.

When we came under rocket attack, as we often did, we would all run for the sand-bagged bunker outside. I ran fast, but I looked out for the doctors. They would run right over us if we let them. The rockets would come in groups of three or four, and the NVA found the big red crosses on our roof perfect targets. They paid no attention to the Geneva Convention. Two months before I arrived, Sharon Lane, an Army nurse working the night shift, was killed by a Russian 122-mm rocket while trying to protect her patients. I believe she was the only US servicewoman killed in the war.

I must admit, I continue to be angry and bitter about the war and about the inequal-ities in the draft process. Many young men who did not have the money for college did not receive deferments, and many of them died. It was a TV war. The news was always about body counts. In my opinion, it was run by political hacks. The military leaders were not allowed to do their jobs. Returning solders were not recognized back then, and many became ashamed and disillusioned about their service.

Like many who served in Vietnam, I developed PTSD, which proves that you did not need to be in direct combat or be a man, and it even afflicts officers. When the stress really got to me, I would visit the nursery, pick a baby, and get a quick reality check. It usually helped. After Vietnam, I remained in the Army for twenty years. I married a West Point graduate and we both retired as Lieutenant Colonels. After living in Monument, Colorado for twenty years, we moved to The Villages, Florida. My husband developed early-onset Alzheimer's and died within five years at the age of 65 last May.

BILL KUFFNER'S WAR

US Marine Corps, Lieutenant,
7th Motor Transport Battalion,
Quang Tri, 1969–70

I grew up on Staten Island and attended Marist College, a Catholic school in Poughkeepsie, New York, graduating in 1968. After graduation, I enlisted in the Marines and went to OCS and then Officer Basic School at Quantico. The Marines are different from the other services in that all officers, no matter what their job will be, are sent to the Basic School for twenty-three weeks, where we were all taught to be infantry platoon leaders. "Every Marine a Rifleman." After that, I became a Motor Transportation Logistics Officer, a "Motor T," as it's called. Two weeks after completing training, I married Barbara. Four weeks later, I was on my way to Vietnam.

When I arrived in country on August 20, 1969, I was lucky. I was assigned to 7th Motor Transportation Battalion in Quang Tri, which needed an S4 or Logistics Officer. I was only a second lieutenant, but I was the only guy coming off the plane with the right MOS. So even though that position called for a captain, I got the assignment. Luckier still was that four of the twenty officers in that battalion were fellow Marist graduates, guys I knew, were friends with, and who looked out for me. "Luck of the draw," I guess, but that's how my war started.

Quang Tri is in I Corps, right along the DMZ, which was mountains and jungle—really bad country. Our battalion provided transportation to the 3rd Marine Division, and we ran daily truck convoys back and forth on Route 9 to Vandegrift Combat Base, eighty miles, or five hours to the west, and down to Danang, 150 miles or eight hours south, through the Hai Van Pass. That may sound slow compared to driving on a road back home, but Route 9 was mostly a one-lane asphalt road. The Seabees, did a wonderful job paving it, which made it harder for the enemy to hide land mines, than would be the case with a gravel or dirt road. Even still, every other truck in our convoys was an armored "gun truck" with .50-caliber machine guns up top, port and starboard. That's a lot of firepower, but we took hits anyway, primarily from snipers.

Most nights, from our perimeter, we witnessed fire fights down at the bridge that crossed the river into Quang Tri. Helicopter gunships would circle the area, and when they opened up, they put out an incredible amount of fire. Hard to believe anything could survive an attack like that; but a few nights later, the fighting down there would start all over again.

Our compound was laid out in three sections. The enlisted men's "hooches" were on one side, our trucks were parked in the middle and officer hooches were on the other side. They were little shacks with plywood floors, plywood walls that went up about waist high, screens above that, and a tin roof. Outside along with the walls, there were usually stacks of sandbags and 55-gallon oil drums filled with sand to protect us from blasts and shrapnel. We had eight officers to a hooch, with metal bunks and lockers inside. However, the two most important things were outside—the latrine and our bunker. That's how I lived for six months.

Our base at Quang Tri came under fire from 122-millimeter rockets at least once a week. They weren't very accurate, but we would get five or six at a time. On the night of August 31, 1969, we had seven Marines killed and more wounded. I had only been in country for two weeks, and I'll never forget that night. The battalion area was hit with six rockets, and one made a direct hit on one of the enlisted hooches. It would've been a lot worse, if there hadn't been a large water truck parked between that hooch and the one next to it, and the water truck absorbed a lot of the blast. After it struck, we heard screams and calls for "Corpsman!" Everyone ran to help, but it was shocking to see those dead and wounded kids.

Because of my job as a battalion staff officer, I wasn't out in the bush slogging through the jungle. However, like every other officer, I took my turn posting guard, doing perimeter security, and going out on patrols. I guess that was why we were trained to be infantry platoon leaders.

Some fun things also happened while I was in Vietnam. When 7th Motors relocated from Quang Tri to Danang, the lieutenants got to take our Marines to China Beach for break. I was standing in the white sand with some of the other Marist guys, when we looked up and saw yet another of our classmates walking toward us. The four of us were Marine Corps officers, while he had been drafted into the Army and was a Spec-4 stationed at Phu Bai with an artillery unit. We decided to have a "night on the town," so we pinned a pair of Marine lieutenant bars on our buddy, and went to the Air Force

Officers Club. Sure enough, as we headed out we ran into our battalion commander. Now, Army fatigues don't look at all like Marine Corps fatigues, and Marine lieutenant bars don't look like Army bars, either. The Colonel took one look at him and one look at us, and knew exactly what we were up to. Finally, he smiled and said, "Make sure he doesn't get caught wearing those."

In February, the 7th Motors was given orders to stand down. The unit was going home, and its functions were being turned over to the Vietnamese. The Marine Corps has a rule that all equipment had to be returned to the US in "stateside compatibility," which meant all trucks repaired and fully operable, no matter how much it was a beat-up piece of junk from combat operations. That was a big job. When it was finished, all the equipment and the Marines who had at least nine months in country were sent home to the States on Navy ships. I only had six months in country, so I was transferred to another unit and became the "Crappy Little Job Officer." In my case, that meant being an Accident Investigation Officer until my tour was over. After Vietnam, I was assigned to Headquarters, Marine Corps District in Philadelphia for my remaining fourteen months in the Corps. We supervised Marine Corps reserve units and recruiting offices in the area.

A week before I was discharged, more good luck, as the Marist alumni network helped me once again. One of the guys who had preceded me in 7th Motors and worked in personnel at a Wall Street brokerage firm. He phoned me and told me to come up to New York City for a job interview. I had a BA in history and knew very little about the banking business, but he said our Marine Corps training and experience was perfect for a job opening he had. I got the job, and for the next thirty-two years I held a variety of positions with various large banks such as Citibank, Continental Bank, and others, managing their check processing, branch operations, and international banking, with assignments in New York, Dakar, Athens, and London. It was a great career. I am now seventy years old and finally retired last year.

Like many vets my age, I've experienced several illnesses, such as cancers and Crohn's Disease, which may have been caused by exposure to Agent Orange while in country, or from the contaminated drinking water at Camp Lejeune, while I was stationed there. My VA claims are still "in process."

JUDI HIGBEE'S WAR

Red Cross Recreation Aide or "Donut Dolly,"
Cam Ranh Bay and Tuy Hoa, 1969–70

I grew up in the small town of Cheboygan, Michigan, and graduated from Central Michigan University. In the summer of 1969, I was working as a secretary in downtown Detroit. A man in my church choir who owned a personnel agency, told me about a job order they had just received from the American Red Cross for Recreation Aides in Vietnam. "For the best year of your life...serving others," was the hook. That really sounded interesting! My brother had been in the Army, and my dad wasn't thrilled with his only daughter being in the military, much less in Vietnam. But I was very patriotic and wanted to serve, so I sent in my application.

In July, they flew me to St. Louis for a job interview. That was the first time I had flown in a commercial airplane. After learning more details and getting my questions answered, I felt this civilian job was a good fit and was hired. In September, I had two weeks of training in Washington, DC to be a Recreation Aide. There were forty-three girls in my class and we had a choice of going to Korea or Vietnam—only thirteen picked Korea. After a four-day orientation in Saigon, my first assignment was Cam Ranh Bay Army Support Command.

The job title was Recreation Aide, but everyone called us "Red Cross Girls" or "Donut Dollies." The truth is, we never gave out donuts. That nickname came from the Red Cross workers in Europe during World War II who provided coffee and donuts. The totally different climate in Vietnam made sheet cake and Kool-Aid the standard refreshment in our centers.

Our job was to bring a touch of home to the American servicemen, to boost their morale and bring a smiling face with a bit of fun and diversion to their daily routine. Sixteen bases in Vietnam had a Red Cross unit of six to ten girls each, who operated our "Centers." They were small buildings, like a lounge. They didn't have a gym, and we

266

weren't like the USO, but it was a place where guys could go to get away. We had a piano, ping pong, tables for card and board games, a trading paperback library, comfy chairs and couches to relax and socialize. Every evening there was a special program provided for and sometimes performed by the guys—like a karate demonstration, an artist, or a guitar player. We also threw parties for short-timers, new arrivals, or new dads, and we'd bring out the current travelling recreation program, or use holiday special themes. Of course, there was always sheet cake from the mess hall and Kool-Aid.

We also travelled to fourteen bases around the country with our programs. There were nine of us Red Cross girls stationed at Cam Ranh Bay, and we always worked in pairs. Monday through Saturday a team of us would go by jeep or chopper to visit the troops with an informal, one-hour recreation program. It consisted of different group activities like games, puzzles or quizzes with visual info boards that we carried in a big canvas bag. The most popular ones had to do with football, sports, cars, state flags and food. For football we wore striped referee shirts, played games with the guys like guessing hand signals, called plays, talked about NFL team stats, or any other fun contest we could think up. We visited motor pools, ammunition dumps, offices, day rooms, mess halls, forward units, landing zones, and fire bases.

Occasionally, we went to some very small, remote firebases and landing zones. The officers in charge were very good about releasing guys from duty for an hour so they could participate. Often, we were the first "round-eyed females who spoke English" they'd seen in a long time. Sometimes we'd only get a few guys, and sometimes fifteen to twenty, but we always had a chance to talk with them and laugh and joke. Time permitting, we would serve them lunch in their chow line. They called it "local R&R." No

matter where we went, our visit was good for morale, and the officers knew it.

Despite the anti-war sentiment back home, we received a good bit of support from women in state-side Red Cross chapters. They sewed and filled ditty bags, which we helped distribute before Christmas to every American military person in Vietnam.

Cam Ranh Bay was a big base, and relatively quiet. It didn't feel like a war zone, but when we flew out to the firebases, we could see it up close on the guys' faces. Security was very tight where the Red Cross girls were concerned, and occasionally our "run" had to be delayed due to fighting in the area. We never came under fire, but one time when our helicopter returned to pick us up, the pilot saw some enemy activity in the jungle near the base. He peeled off and called in gunships, who rocketed the wood line. That was a bit scary, but we really felt very protected and safe.

We were required to have college degrees in order to have a GS rank equivalent to a second lieutenant, which they needed to give us officer housing. We lived in mobile home trailers, three girls in each. The conditions were fairly basic, but the trailers had window air-conditioners. We would usually eat a big lunch in the mess hall and have a small dinner in our trailer.

The 18th Engineer Brigade at Dong Ba Tin was about ten miles from Cam Ranh. Word got to their Chaplain that I could play the organ and he immediately came to our center to request I "share my talent at his two chapels." How could I resist? For the next three months, at 0700 every Sunday morning, the chaplain's assistant picked me up in a jeep for the drive to DBT to be the organist for their chapel services. My 'payment' was lunch with the officers at their mess.

Halfway through my tour, I was transferred to Tuy Hoa, a smaller Air Force base up the coast. It was so small that we walked everywhere, and I became a lean 125 pounds. A week of temporary duty at Cu Chi gave me a great opportunity to bring a smile and a 'touch of home' to the guys who had been fighting in the jungle.

One day I won't forget was when we dropped in at the small Navy base at Nha Trang with one of our recreation programs. Afterward, I got talking to one of the Navy guys who seemed depressed. He was concerned that his wife wouldn't understand what he was going through and it would ruin their relationship. We chatted, and I told him to open up when he got back home and tell her, as best he could, what he saw and how he felt. From his reaction, I think my words helped. It was little encounters like that which made the whole Vietnam experience worthwhile.

In 1969 there were about 128 of us "Donut Dollies" in country. Each month we traveled 30,000 miles making 2,700 visits to 114,000 servicemen. In total, 627 of us served in Vietnam from 1965 through 1972.

My tour ended in 1970. It was an unparalleled time of my life. I was clueless when I left home, and returned with a defining view of the war and the world that was experienced by very few—with the wonderful feeling of having done a job that had a meaningful impact and was very much appreciated. Of course, it put me and the other girls at the center of attention, with all the cat calls, waves, and smiles, but I loved meeting so many awesome American GIs, and I loved providing a touch of home for them.

After my Red Cross tenure, I married a man I met in Cam Ranh Bay, had a very successful career as a Certified Medical Transcriptionist, divorced, met and married John (see his war story on page 8).

We have loved traveling the world since 2001. Our first big international trip was a two-week tour of Vietnam with John's mom. We saw newer motorbikes on the streets of Saigon than we saw thirty years before, but a lot less exhaust air pollution. Otherwise, there wasn't much change. Americans are very welcome there and the Vietnamese are very appreciative of the American involvement in their country's history. We have been retired since 2010. I no longer play the organ, but the music continues with singing and ringing English handbells.

J. B. HEATON'S WAR

US Army, Sergeant, Quick Response Team,
41st Signal Battalion, 1st Signal Brigade,
4th Infantry Division, An Khe and Qui Nhon,
1969–71

My Grand Daddy gave me a rifle as soon as I could walk, which was pretty normal where I grew up in Alabama and north Florida. When I was eight years old I had a .22, and I got so good with it that I would use the .22 shell casings for targets. By the time I hit Basic at Fort Benning, I had developed quite a reputation as a marksman. On the rifle range, I maxed out the scores on the M-14. They gave us one hundred rounds and I had to hit the target with eighty of them to qualify. I did that, and gave them twenty rounds back.

You'd think I'd have ended up in the Infantry, but I didn't. I worked for a year after high school, went to college for a while, and when I went in the Army in June, 1969, I enlisted to get into the Signal Corps. After Basic at Fort Benning, I was sent to Fort Gordon and came out a Communication Center Specialist, 72-B and later a 72-F, which was a Data Communications Terminal Specialist. Five months later, I was at the 41st signal Battalion headquarters, part of the 1st Signal Brigade, at Qui Nhon on the central coast in II Corps. We provided communication support to the 4th Infantry Division.

I worked in the communication center, until I was picked for the battalion's Quick Response Team. There were twelve of us, with a lieutenant in charge and two sergeants. They changed my rank from Specialist-5 to Sergeant E5, since I would be commanding a squad. We called ourselves the Go-fer Squad, because we got stuck with all the odd jobs that they couldn't figure out anyone else to give to, like escorting convoys, picking up and delivering classified communications equipment, being a reaction force if we were attacked, and helping anybody who needed help. We didn't go out on search-and-destroy patrols like the infantry, but we were heavily armed whenever we left the base. I carried an M-14, which is what I had fired on the range in Basic. I preferred it to the M-16.

We were in the Central Highlands, which I would compare to the Smokies back home. The mountains were bigger than hills, but not like the Rockies. The valleys had a lot of tall grass and rice paddies, not true jungle, but very thick. Our squad frequently had to go up and down Highway 19 from Qui Nhon to An Khe and Pleiku to escort convoys or deliver things. Another time, we had to deliver some top-secret equipment to Cam Ranh Bay further down the coast. We went by helicopter, and the pilot must've been bored, because on the way back he decided to wave hop up the shoreline, a foot or two above the water, and buzzed a couple of ships. Me? I just wanted to get back to my base without him getting us killed.

We frequently stayed at An Khe, which was a large base and the second home of our battalion. There, we stayed in tents that held four to five men, and they had a mess hall. Other than that, when we were out in the field we ate C-rations and the better LRRP meals which began to arrive at the very end of my tour.

One night at about 2:00 a.m., a team of a dozen VC sappers with satchel charges waited for the duty officer at the An Khe fuel dump to come around in his Jeep to inspect. As soon as he opened the gate, they came in behind, killed him, and put satchel charges on one of the big fuel tanks. The explosion blew off one of the valves and set that tank and several others on fire. It was a big blaze. One of our armor-plated gun trucks rushed to the scene and killed most of them with its .50-caliber machine guns, but too late.

Another time, during the day, I was standing watch in a guard tower on the perimeter, when some sappers got into the ammo dump. When it went off, the concussion blew me to the other side of the tower. I got to my feet, looked out and saw a big mushroom cloud rising into the sky, and immediately thought, "Oh my God, they've really done it this time!" thinking the VC had detonated an atomic bomb. I soon realized it wasn't; but there were a lot of other guys who thought the same thing, until we were told it was only the ammo dump going up.

I didn't want to stay in the Army any longer than I had to, so I extended in Vietnam for six months to get an early out when I got home. Instead, they sent me to Germany. We had nothing to do over there. My job was to go out and start the truck engines every day. Finally, out of the blue, they sent me orders to go home, and I was discharged.

When I got home, at first, I didn't do much of anything except grow long hair. For a while, I had a job installing air-conditioning in mobile homes, and then worked as a cargo foreman at the port of Jacksonville. We finally moved to Oregon, where my wife is from, and I got a job with the post office. I worked there for the next twenty-seven years until I retired.

I've been diagnosed with PTSD and some service-related hearing loss, but I still enjoy playing golf and hanging out with several veteran's groups, when we aren't traveling.

PAUL CASH'S WAR

US Army, 1st Lieutenant and Convoy Commander,
545th Military Police Battalion, 1st Cavalry Division,
Tay Ninh, 1970

I'm from Chillicothe, Ohio, on the river an hour south of Columbus. I went to Ohio University and graduated from ROTC as a member of the Pershing Rifles Honor Society in June, 1968. There was a six-month delay and I couldn't go on active duty until January, 1969; so I was able to work for Goodyear Tire in Akron, hoping to get my foot in the door. They had 25,000 employees back then, but only 5,000 now. So much for a foot in that door.

I was assigned to the Military Police, and sent to Fort Gordon for Officer Basic. After an initial assignment with the 559th MP Company at Fort Monroe, Virginia, I received orders to Vietnam. My original orders were to the 716th MP Brigade in Saigon, but when I arrived in country they reassigned me to the 545th MP Company. They had lost several officers, and the personnel depot was told to grab the first MP lieutenant who got off the plane and send him up there. That was me. I was initially sent to Phouc Vinh, the 1st Cav Division Headquarters, and was later sent up country to the 3rd Brigade in Tay Ninh.

At that time, the base was partly 1st Cav and partly 25th Infantry Division. We supported both for normal military police duties and convoy defense, with one platoon assigned to each brigade. Typically, we would escort a convoy that was leaving Saigon or Long Binh and going to Tay Ninh or Phouc Vinh, or the other way around.

I was a first lieutenant and we would have two officers assigned to each convoy. One would be the convoy commander and ride in the lead jeep, while the other officer flew overhead in an OH-6 Cayuse observation helicopter, checking out the route and the surrounding countryside for ambushes. I'd say 40% of my time was spent in the lead jeep, 40% in the helicopter, and 20% at Tay Ninh on routine MP duties; but I spent enough time in the air to get three Air Medals.

In addition to the lead jeep, we had other MP jeeps interspersed in the convoy, all of

which carried M-60 machine guns. We did not have any large, armor-plated "hard trucks," or V-100 armored cars that were used in other parts of the country for convoy defense, because the Cav had Cobra gunships flying around that we could call in. Maybe that's why we didn't run into many ambushes, perhaps a half-dozen, no more. When we did, the standing order was to never stop the convoy—push on through, and let the jeeps return fire.

Our quarters at Tay Ninh had been home to a Philippine Army unit, years before. It had some very unique underground, squad-sized bunkers with sand-bagged, igloo-shaped mounds above ground. We were close to the airstrip, but because they were underground, we didn't get much noise and they were cool inside. And we didn't need to run to a bunker when the enemy dropped in 122 mm rockets on us. We were already in one.

Most of our enlisted men were eighteen- to nineteen-year-old kids, and it never ceased to amaze me how quick-thinking, brave, and resourceful they were. Two of our guys on patrol came across some South Vietnamese kids who had wandered into a minefield. Two of them were hurt, and our guys got down on the ground and crawled between the mines, finding them with their bayonets and marking them with strips of cloth from their shirts, just like you see in old World War II movies, until they reached the kids and got them safely back out of there.

Anytime we flew, the pilot would routinely check to ensure that we weren't going into an area where artillery would be firing. One day, we headed up a valley when I noticed silver objects flashing down out of the sky all around us, explosions below us, and pieces of tree trunks and branches flying up all around. The area had been checked; but we found ourselves flying right through an artillery barrage. When we landed, the cockpit and skids were filled with leaves and tree branches.

The top picture is our MP unit with some captured Chinese .50-caliber machine guns. They were very nasty against helicopters. The second photo is our company area during the monsoon. The third photo is what the ground looks like after a B-52 strike.

Agent Orange? I was on the road one time in the lead jeep, when one of the spraying airplanes flew right over us. No one told us anything about that stuff, and the spray got all over us. It was a hot day and it felt so nice and cool that we loved it.

All the guys felt great when we ran our first truck convoy into Cambodia to support the troops who went in there. No more sanctuary. The US was fighting back, and we were all in favor of that. When we were up there, they dropped off some *Stars & Stripes* newspapers. The cover showed the protests at Kent State. That got us angry. Here we were, trying to do our jobs and they were doing that. Everyone had strong feelings about the protesters.

Midway through 1970, I was sent out by Huey to pick up a Prisoner of War at a remote firebase. He had been captured by one of our infantry units, and I was ordered to bring him back to the 1st Cav Division HQ at Phouc Vinh. The guy I picked up was in a military uniform, but it wasn't NVA. I am 6"2'. He was a couple of inches taller than I was, and he did not look Vietnamese, either. I handcuffed him to me and

after we took off, he began talking. He spoke perfect English and addressed me by my rank. I was surprised. I asked him how he learned English so well. He smiled and said he had attended Stanford and lived for several years in the United States. I suspected he was Chinese, but he would only admit that he was an advisor to the NVA. When we arrived in Phouc Vinh, before I turned him over to the officer waiting for him, he thanked me for the courtesy I had shown him. He said he would never forget this occasion, and if we ever met again he would show me the same. He then said that he expected to be back home in a few days, and I doubt he meant North Vietnam. Then he said goodbye.

No one said a word about it afterward. I figured it was politics. I suppose he could have been a US intelligence asset of some kind, but I don't think so. Whatever, he knew the US military would release him. For political reasons, our government would rather not admit that China had people on the ground in South Vietnam, advisors or not.

I served in Vietnam for almost twelve months before being sent home before Christmas, 1970, with two Bronze Stars, three Air Medals, and a Vietnamese Cross of Gallantry. I returned to Ohio University and earned a master's degree in economics. I worked for Mars Candy and several other corporations, before I switched fields to HR and became an independent management consultant. Now 70, I live in Columbus, Ohio, where I continue to run my consulting business. I've been diagnosed with Agent Orange-related heart issues, skin disease, and diabetes, probably from those nice aerial showers they gave us on the road to Tay Ninh.

RAY PETRINO'S WAR

**US Army, Spec 5 and Company Clerk,
Alpha Company, 301st Engineers,
101st Airborne Division, Camp Eagle,
1970–71**

I'm from the Bronx. I had graduated from CCNY with a BS in chemistry, was married, and I had a job deferment from the draft because of the work I did for my employer. One day, someone in the personnel department called me and said someone screwed up and they hadn't filed the form they were supposed to file to renew my deferment. Great, I thought. Two weeks later I got my draft notice, was sworn in in September, 1969, and packed off to Fort Gordon for Basic and Fort McClellan in Anniston, Alabama for infantry AIT.

My whole class, including me, were given an 11-Bravo MOS, infantry rifleman, and we all came down on orders to infantry units in Vietnam. However, the Army had screwed up in not giving me a secondary MOS having to do with my chemistry degree. My congressman intervened and that held up my deployment for two weeks. I still went to the 101st Airborne, but they sent me to Company A of the 301st Engineers instead, not to a line infantry unit.

Camp Eagle was southeast of Hue, near the coast. I arrived there in January, 1970, and remember reporting to the Quonset hut where the company headquarters was. I could hear the helicopters coming and going, and the Captain told me not to put my bag down, because I was going to be on the next one. While he was doing something else, I got talking to the company clerk and learned he was real short, his tour about over. He was looking for a guy to take over his job, and take care of the men in the company as he had done. For some reason, we hit it off, so he picked up the phone and called the Sergeant Major at battalion. The next thing I know the phone on the Captain's desk rang. I heard him talking as he turned and glared at me, none too happy. As everyone in the

Army knows, not even a Captain is going to argue with the Sergeant Major, so I stayed, did a good job, and the Captain ended up giving me two promotions.

The main thing our engineering company did was clear Landing Zones for the infantry and artillery and build roads all across I Corps. In addition to big equipment, we used a lot of C-4 and "Det Cord," a rope-like explosive we wrapped around trees to blow the trunks and cut them down. Believe me, it beat using a saw. The engineers would usually be the second ones in after the Pathfinders, so it was very dangerous work. Who would have thought that all that college typing I did back at CCNY kept me out of that and may have saved my life, not that anywhere in Vietnam was completely safe, not even Camp Eagle. We got rockets every now and then, and every few weeks, the Captain would drag me along in his jeep to visit the units. We were usually in hills, in deep jungle, going through small villages. They weren't very safe, and we were one of the first units that went into Cambodia.

By 1970–71, the war was being fought with the draft. Drugs and race issues were big problems, especially in rear area base camps like where I was. I drew guard duty on the perimeter at least once a month, but I never slept. I saw too many guys walking around stoned, even my friends, and I didn't trust anyone. Being twenty-four years old, one of the older guys, and married, a lot of the younger nineteen- and twenty-year-olds would come up to me for advice. It seemed natural at the time. Now, it seems ridiculous, but that was how it was.

Today, kids don't understand that we had no internet, no cell phone, no e-mail, no texts, chats, or Face Books, none of that. Maybe you could stand in a line to try to get a pay phone, but that was it. My wife and I wrote each other letters every day. You know the kind, with paper, envelopes, and stamps. But the mail wasn't all that reliable. We would put a number on each envelope, so they'd be read in the right order. After a while, we bought two small cassette recorders and we'd send each other recordings every day or two. I would record one side of the tape for my wife and the other side of the tape for my parents. That helped.

I stayed in Vietnam for sixteen months, until April, 1971, so I could get an "early out" and be discharged as soon as I got home. Even though I wasn't in serious combat, I did enough and saw enough, that I never talked about the war for decades. I never saw the movies, never read any books, and never talked to anybody until I joined some of the Vietnam Vets groups in Florida. If people weren't there, they wouldn't understand anyway.

When I got home, I went back to school on the G.I. Bill, got an MBA, and later a second Master's Degree in advanced accounting. I got a position with a car auction company as Group Controller, and stayed there for twenty years. I spent the last 16 years of my career as assistant general manager at the Manheim Palm Beach Auction in Florida.

Like many other Vets, I must have gotten too close to Agent Orange and developed diabetes, kidney disease, and neuropathy. The VA is treating me for diabetes, but turned me down for kidney disease and neuropathy, even though there were never any of those in my family. I'm appealing, but it's ridiculous that so many guys need to fight for that. Meanwhile, I stay active playing golf, bowling, and with fantasy sports.

DEAN VETTER'S WAR

US Air Force Captain, Navigator, and Bombardier, Flying 180 B-52 Missions over North and South Vietnam, Cambodia, and Laos from 1970-72

In November, 1962, I was twenty-two years old, in college, and about to be drafted; so, I enlisted in the Air Force. This was the height of the Berlin crisis and they sent me to a small, old Air Force base in Greenville, Mississippi to become a personnel clerk. You knew it was a lousy place to go, because the base commander was only a Lieutenant Colonel and he drove an old Nash Rambler.

I used Operation Bootstrap to finish my college degree and they sent me to Officer Training School, bombardier training, and then training on the B-52. After that, I was stationed at various places from Hawaii to Barksdale to Dayton, flying the D-model B-52. Halfway through, I was promoted from Navigator to "Radar Navigator," who was really the Bombardier, but the Air Force didn't want to call it that anymore.

People ask what it was like to fly a B-52 strike. I did 180 of them, and they were all pretty much the same. Flying from Guam was a twelve-hour day, roundtrip. Flying from Okinawa or Thailand was eight hours, roundtrip. In the first year or two, the missions involved a lot of planes, but they soon realized it was more effective to send the planes in groups of three. This wasn't like an old WWII B-17 bombing run, where the Bombardier looked down through a Norden Bomb sight, put the crosshairs over the target, and pushed a button. We never knew what the target was, never saw it, and had no idea what we were bombing. Still, we usually could tell the area.

Flying from Guam, it was five hours to the Philippines, where we would have an aerial refueling before proceeding to the IP or Initial Point. That was where command of the airplane passed to the "radar bombing site," which meant our headquarters was flying the plane. Eventually, there would be a countdown, a light would come on, and I would push the button to drop the bombs, but it was all based on GPS, not seeing the target. After the bombs were gone, control of the plane would revert to the pilot, and we would head back home.

I don't think I was ever on a bombing run over South Vietnam. We bombed the jungle border areas of Cambodia and Laos, where the NVA base camps and the Ho Chi Minh Trail supply routes were located, and we bombed military targets in North Vietnam.

We would laugh at some of the "old guys," as we called them. They were the pilots and copilots who would go to sleep right after we took off, despite all the noise, the engine roar, and the other loud sounds that happened inside. The pilot and copilot were up in the cockpit and I was down below in our navigation compartment, but the airplane was on autopilot the whole way. Somehow, they always woke up before we got to the IP. Maybe they had an alarm clock.

We would fly for six weeks from each of Guam, Thailand, and Okinawa. That would be a total of three to four months. Then, we would rotate back to the States for a break before we were sent back over again. Our families stayed at the stateside base where we were assigned, because the Air Force didn't want to keep moving families around. Our usual work rotation was that we would fly three days in a row, then have one or two days off, and then spend a day in the plane, ready to go, as the "hot spare," in case one of the others had mechanical problems.

We had been bombing North Vietnam all along, but when the peace talks broke down in 1972, Nixon ordered everything into the air. We called it "Going north." We had seventeen B-52s shot down on the first two or three days, largely because of the tactics we were ordered to use. They wanted the bombing to be so accurate, that we were not allowed to use any evasive measures—just fly straight over the targets. Most of those planes were shot down by SAMs, which have a proximity explosive charge that basically shoots shrapnel and metal all over the sky, so the damage depended on how close it got. Those seventeen airplanes each had a crew of six. That was over 100 guys, about half of whom died, and the other half became POWs.

There were also a lot of planes returning that may not have been shot down, but they had serious damage. At the beginning, the squadron maintenance guys would give the crew members a plaque upon which they had mounted some of the shrapnel they dug out of the plane. Fortunately, our plane was never hit.

When we bombed Haiphong Harbor, they told us if we see any foreign ships in harbor, we shouldn't drop our bombs. Nobody explained how we were supposed to know what country the ship was from, from way up there, but I don't think anyone held their bombs. Certainly, we didn't. The last thing you'd wanted to do was fly back home with a full load. Then, they called a Christmas Truce and we stopped bombing. All that did was to let the North Vietnamese reorganize, rearm, and bring in more SAMs. I think that was when Jane Fonda was there.

On the missions to Hanoi, I remember removing my watch, my wallet, and all my Velcroed patches and insignias and putting them in a bag which was to be left on the plane, if we were shot down or had to bail out. As I put my wallet in the bag, the reality of it suddenly struck me, "What are you doing?" But we were young kids and under a lot of pressure. We all drank a lot. I remember one day when I was Navigator, that me and the Bombardier did our entire preflight check using Donald Duck voices. Later, a friend of mine at headquarters warned me, "You know, they record all that stuff. Good thing nobody was listening except me."

In the early years, they would have little parties and award ceremonies to give you your medals. As time wore on, by 1971–72 when you got home, your CO would just reach in his desk and hand you a stack of boxes with a comment such as, "Oh yeah, these came for you." Like most other guys, I was a dummy, and was probably in denial. I did my job, I stayed very busy, and I was pretty insulated. I never paid much attention to the politics of it all, or what was really going on. But as we kept doing that, over and over again, the number of guys with alcoholism and nervous and psychiatric problems kept increasing.

As I said, I flew 180 bombing missions, and then went back to Wright-Patterson in Dayton, where I became an instructor and then worked on various kinds of missiles. I also got my first of two master's degrees and was sent to Rapid City where I became part of the crew on one of the three "Looking Glass" airborne battle staff command-and-control planes. If there was ever a nuclear attack and the other headquarters became inoperable, we would take over command of the missile silos. In March, 1986, I retired as a Lieutenant Colonel after 24 ½ years on active duty. After that, I worked for several defense contractors on maintenance issues and even opened a small store in one of the main malls in Dayton, where we sold NASCAR and automotive-related gifts. Now seventy-seven, I stay busy playing golf and participating in various Vietnam Vet groups, neighborhood associations, and church activities.

LANCE POTT'S WAR

US Army, Spec-4, B Company,
1st Battalion of the 501st Infantry,
101st Airborne Division Phu Bai, 1971

Like a lot of guys, I tried college, but wasn't ready for it and got drafted. I was from Independence, Missouri, Harry Truman's town, and went in the Army in August, 1970. After Basic at Fort Campbell, Kentucky, and AIT at Fort Polk, Louisiana, the garden spot of the Army, I was an 11-C mortarman. They offered me flight training, OCS, and the NCO Academy, but I wasn't interested in any of that. All I wanted was to get in and out. Five months later, in January, 1971, I was at the "Repo Depot" in Long Binh. From there, they flew me north in a helicopter to the 101st Airborne Division in Phu Bai near Hue, up in I Corps, for three to four days of "in-country orientation," and then on to my unit, B Company of the 1st of the 501st Regiment at Phu Bai.

A few days later, I was sent out on my first patrol and they handed me a PRC-25 backpack radio. After that, I was the radioman, for which I hadn't been trained; and never fired a mortar, for which I had. We were an air-mobile division and I made twenty or more Combat Assaults in a Huey, enough to get an Air Medal or two. The funny thing was, I had always been deathly afraid of heights. Somehow, however, flying a few thousand feet up with a full load, a rifle, and my legs dangling out the door of a Huey, didn't bother me at all. Go figure.

On that first patrol, there were six or seven of us newbies, and they put us in the rear. The first three guys in the line hit a boobie trap; they went down, wounded by shrapnel and medevaced out. It was apparently from a GI grenade the VC had put in a C-ration can on a string, with its pin pulled out. We found a second one, too. We had a "mine dog" with us, but it hadn't reacted. The best we could figure was it was trained for mines, but not for hand grenades. On the other hand, we had a very poor company commander, and one day the dog bit him in the crotch. It might not be able to find hand grenades, but we liked the dog just fine after that.

We would go out to the field for thirty to forty days at a time and get resupplied every four days or so, sometimes with hot food flown in, and mail. Our first month, we went on patrol around Firebase Tomahawk, forty miles southeast of Hue on Highway 1. Our whole battalion went there two or three times. Usually one company would stay at the firebase while the others would operate four to five kilometers out on search and destroy operations.

The next place we went was an old ARVN firebase which was on the beach one kilometer south of the DMZ. The land was mostly scrub brush and sand, with big rats everywhere. They would be all over us and our stuff at night. After a while, someone devised an expensive rat trap, consisting of a blasting cap from a Claymore mine and some bait under an ammo can. Boys will be boys, but it blew the hell out of the can and the rat. While we were there, half the unit would go out on patrol each night and set up an ambush, while the other half stayed in the fire base and tried to sleep. One of our guys at the base was killed by shrapnel when a supposedly "errant" ARVN mortar shell hit us. You never knew who you could trust.

They then moved us to Danang for thirty days for perimeter security. The Marines were leaving, and the ARVN hadn't taken over yet. That was the best duty I had in Vietnam. We slept in hooches, had showers and hot food. That's where I turned twenty-one. We flew down there and back in big Chinook helicopters. They had twin engines, front and back, and carried thirty guys. I couldn't hear for three to four days afterward. Of course, the VA later said my hearing loss was not service-related.

While I was there, we had no big battles. We probably lost more guys from booby traps, accidents, and "friendly fire" than we did from hostile fire. Most of the contact was simply that someone shot at us, and we opened up.

The 101st had a firm policy that we were not to fraternize with the locals. I never even met one. Only when we took over from the Marines in Danang did we have Vietnamese maids to do our laundry and clean the hooch.

When we went out on patrol, we never walked on a trail, on a ridgeline, or on a dike. You could always assume those were booby trapped. When we went into an NDP, a Night Defensive Perimeter, we'd set out mechanical ambush devices, usually Claymore mines. We never seemed to have enough trip wire, so we'd make our own, using two plastic C-ration spoons, back to back, with the lead wires through them, and a piece of plastic separating them, which was connected to the trip wire. The leads were connected to a 9-volt battery, and when the strip of plastic was pulled out, or "tripped," they detonated. One night we were hunkered down near Khe Sanh, when one blew up. Our CO wanted us to go out in the jungle at night and check it out, but we refused. At daylight, we looked and found two dead NVA.

For the last third of my tour, I became the battalion radioman and worked "twelve on and twelve off" in the Tactical Operation Center with another guy. One of our jobs was to get hourly "sit-reps," or situation reports, from every unit. There were no computers or recorders, so we had to write detailed notes in a ledger on every fire mission, troop movement, and contact. After a while, I got to know all the unit RTOs, and passed on most of their medevac pick up requests.

I came to believe that PTSD comes from things you see, and can't "un-see."

I've been to one or two company reunions since I got out, but I never got into that stuff like some guys did, who never seem able to get out of the 1970s. My year in Vietnam wasn't the most defining days of my life. To me, it was something I just got through.

When I got out of the Army, I finished the apprentice program and went back to my job laying carpet. For eleven years, I served as a union Business Agent. After that, I went to work for the Federal Government in the Bureau of Apprenticeship, overseeing job training programs and grants to local agencies. From there, I worked at the US Department of Labor for twenty-four years.

I'm now 67. I have tinnitus, which is a persistent ringing in my ears caused by the quinine in the medicine they gave us for the treatment of malaria. I have also been diagnosed with PTSD. Oher than that, I haven't been diagnosed with any of the other serious service-related disabilities.

GARY MILLER'S WAR

US Navy, E-5 Corpsman and Pharmacist,
USS New Orleans, Landing Platform Helicopter,
Yankee Station, 1970

I didn't do very well in school, but I managed to graduate from high school in Storrs, Connecticut, in 1967. After a year knocking around doing construction, I decided to enlist in the Air Force. I didn't want any part of getting drafted into the Army, but the Air Force seemed okay. Unfortunately, they couldn't take me right away, so I switched to the Navy. I wanted to go into submarines, as my father had, but I didn't have enough rank yet. I tested well, and Corpsman and Pharmacist schools were open, so I took that and went in, in June 1968. Corpsman school was fourteen weeks long, one week of which was pharmacy. My first assignment was on a destroyer in San Diego, which I didn't like at all. When an opening popped up for a pharmacist on the *USS New Orleans*, I transferred and stayed there for the next two years.

The *New Orleans* was a "Landing Platform-Helicopter," which looked like a small aircraft carrier. We carried 2,000 Marines and helicopters, whose job was amphibious assault. Two different Marine battalions alternated going out with us. One was the 1st of the 9th Marine Regiment and the other was the 2nd of the 9th. Our ship had a Navy crew of five hundred, with two operating rooms, a laboratory, an x-ray room, dental clinic, pharmacy, a sick bay, eleven Corpsmen and a doctor. The Marines had their own Corpsmen, but they were mostly trained for combat

and did not have our equipment, clinics, pharmacy, or doctor. When we were out to sea, we usually worked twelve on and twelve off. When we were in port, the Marines would go to their own bases and we would only take care of the Navy crew. My primary training was as a Corpsman, and I would revert to that work when they didn't need a pharmacist.

Basically, we ran a small hospital. In the morning, we would have sick call for two hours, and then I would spend an hour or two filling prescriptions. Our doctor was a little bit "surgery happy" so in the afternoon we would usually do one or two and I would have to scrub and stand in as the First Assistant Surgical Nurse. I became very impressed by the progress the military had made in treating serious wounds and burns. They got some amazing results.

When we were out at sea, we would put into port every two weeks or so, usually at Subic Bay in the Philippines. From March, 1970, to November, 1970, we were on a deployment off Vietnam. They sent the Marines ashore to Vietnam couple of times, but nothing exciting happened and we did not end up with many combat wounds.

One of the things I remember most and am proudest of was a training exercise we did in the Philippines. There was a very isolated, very poor island, with a small village. We did an exercise where the Marines went ashore and pretended to capture the place, and we set up a field hospital in the City Hall. As a humanitarian gesture, for the next week we provided medical services for all the people in the village and on the

island, and we saw a lot—all sorts of illnesses and infections. I gave out a lot of medications, which I'm sure helped those people, but the truth was we had a lot of meds that were going out of code and would only end up being thrown away anyway. So, it was good for everyone. When the week was over, the Philippine government threw a party and a steak dinner for us. Naturally, it was the Captain who got invited, but he was nice enough to invite all the Corpsmen to go with him.

I also remember several times when we had to rescue crewmen on passing freighters who got sick. One was a really fat guy who had a blocked bowel and the doctor had to operate. The seas were rough and there was no place to land our helicopter on the freighter's deck. They had to pick him up in a basket, which wasn't easy. One of the other Corpsmen had tried to give him an IV and ended up tearing an artery. We had blood all over the place by the time we got him stabilized and into triage.

Our ship was home-ported at San Diego. When we weren't out to sea, we lived in apartments in the city and would only have to report on board for duty every four or five days as the Duty Corpsman. I was lucky when it came to quarters on the ship. We had some overflow crew space in various places, and I was able to grab one of those for myself. Below decks, the ship was air-conditioned, and we had mess halls with fairly good food.

Toward the end of my enlistment, I found out that UCLA had special program for veterans who had done poorly in high school. That was me, and one hundred and fifty other guys. The Navy let us go to college full time for a semester, although we had to report in every two weeks and keep our hair cut. That gave me some decent grades, and when I was discharged I was accepted to Eastern Connecticut University, where I got a BA in biology on the G.I. Bill.

I graduated in 1977 and ended up teaching high school science—chemistry, biology, and general science in Willimantic, Connecticut, next door to Storrs where the University of Connecticut is located. I later went on to get a master's degree in environ-mental science which was just getting popular at that time.

Unfortunately, when I worked in the Navy pharmacies and labs back then, I became exposed to several chemicals that have proved to be very dangerous. I am 68 now, fighting leukemia, bladder cancer, and other service-related issues, but I continue to play golf, attend veteran's meetings, and remain interested in environmental issues.

KENT HOLWELL'S WAR

US Army Warrant Officer 3 and Huey "Slick" Pilot,
187th Assault Helicopter Company, "The Crusaders."
25th Infantry Division, Tay Ninh,
1970–71

I grew up on a farm north of Minneapolis and enlisted in the Army in September, 1968, just after I turned seventeen. I wanted to fly helicopters, and that's what the Army wanted too. The war was at its peak, and they were rushing classes through Fort Rucker so fast that I ran into a problem. When I graduated, I was supposed to be commissioned as a warrant officer, but I was only seventeen. You had to be eighteen to become an officer, so they sat on my paperwork for a week before they let me have my wings and my CW-1 bars.

Nine months later I was in Tay Ninh as part of the 187th Assault Helicopter Company, the "Crusaders," flying slicks and supporting the 25th Infantry Division. We also had gunships and Cobras, but all they did was fly around in circles and look for things to shoot up. To me, flying a slick was much more interesting work, particularly in the Central Highlands around the Parrot's Beak and the Cambodian border.

We had twenty-four slicks, eight Cobras, a command helicopter, and a maintenance helicopter in our company. We would usually do air assaults and insertions early in the morning, going out in flights of six or eight, flying low and fast at treetop level. The lead ship would be navigating, but he would get his instructions from the command helicopter up above. The most important ship was the Trail. It was his responsibility to keep the formation very tight and to pick up the crew if anyone was shot down. If that happened, you grabbed the machine guns and got the hell out of the aircraft. We flew over triple-canopy jungle most of the time, and the reason we flew in tight formations was so that the enemy on the ground could only have time to shoot at the group, not get a clear shot at one machine as we flashed overhead at ninety miles an hour. When you were alone, you made a distinct target, and were much more at risk. We would bob and weave, making it appear we were going to one LZ, only to go on to another. Sometimes it was an old LZ and sometimes one where the Air Force had just dropped a couple of 500-pound bombs.

The most important things I carried were our maps, covered with acetate that you could write on with a grease pencil. I would also write the frequencies we might need and the map coordinates on the inside of the Plexiglas in front of me, so that everyone on board would know, and there would be no mistakes if we got shot down or things got hairy. Those, and our unit standards and SOPs, we came to know by heart.

When a new pilot arrived in the unit, he served as a copilot for maybe four months. During that time, he flew with different pilots every day, until he memorized the maps and the ground around our area of operations. After that, the Chief Instructor Pilot would give him check rides, and the Aircraft Commanders would vote whether he was ready to join them. Sometimes that took five months, and sometimes three, depending upon how many casualties the unit had taken. The Aircraft Commanders had their pecking order, too. The most senior was called the "high-time guy," and he was usually designated as the Trail Pilot.

In the afternoon, we would fly single-aircraft missions. They were usually "ash and trash" runs in support of the infantry units, resupplying them with food and ammunition, dropping off mail, taking guys back and forth to the hospital, or whatever. The CO would divide up our "blade time" between the different infantry units. As I said, we were much more likely to get shot down in the afternoon, when we were flying alone, than in the morning when we were flying in a tight formation. All in all, I was shot down three times, usually from AK-47 or light machine gun fire. We all did. It was part of the job. One day my helicopter had forty bullet holes in it, but it was still flying. Somehow, they missed the important parts. Usually when you got shot down, the Trail or one of the other ships would come right in and pick you up. Several times we crashed in the jungle and had to run to a clearing or LZ to get picked up. In one case, the Cobras came in behind us. One of them shot the hell out of the jungle behind us while the other strafed a path up ahead for us to follow on a straight line to the LZ, where a slick dropped in to pick us up.

When Nixon finally turned us loose to go into Cambodia, we ferried in a lot of troops and brought out tons of weapons that had been captured. At least that made us feel good.

Twice when I was the copilot I had aircraft commanders shot or wounded and I had to take control of the aircraft. One guy had some bad shrapnel wounds in his legs. The crew chief tipped his chair back and treated him while I peeled off, and flew straight to the hospital. I caught a lot of hell afterwards because I had broken formation and never should have done that. Again, a single aircraft makes itself a target.

The base we flew out of wasn't all that bad. We had hooches, a mess hall, and even hot showers, because someone had stolen a hot water heater from somewhere. Unfortunately, we were at the far end of the supply road from Saigon. By the time the trucks got to us, almost everything good had already been traded away. Much of the food was powdered, and we never had milk. They took the water from the Saigon River, and it stunk. I wouldn't eat or drink it. That meant we got by on a lot of cheese and crackers, popcorn, and corn flakes with RC Cola.

The infantry provided our perimeter security, but the biggest threat came from little kids who the VC sent through the multiple concertina wire fences with satchel charges. These were skinny little kids, maybe ten or twelve years old, and they could get through without a scratch. It was unbelievable. One night, they got in and blew up half of our helicopters. They got in, but they didn't get back out. It wasn't very long before we got new slicks to fly.

We transported the Korean infantry from time to time. They were mean. One day, we went in with eight ships to pick them up at an LZ, but they were all lined up for six ships, which would have made the Huey too heavy. As they piled in, I tried to explain to one of their officers that one or two men from each group should go back to one of the others. I finally got him to understand that we were too heavy to get up, so he pulled out his pistol, shot one of his men in the head, and dumped his body outside. That was the way they were.

My all-time worst day was March 3, 1971, when we lost twenty-one of twenty-four aircraft from two companies on a combat assault into the Parrot's Beak. We were in our usual tight formation, inserting a full ARVN infantry company into a small LZ, and I was in one of the first three ships in. The intelligence and planning had been done by the ARVN and the Op was being run in our Command Ship by a new American Lieutenant Colonel we'd never seen before. He was sent down from Division for a couple of days—no doubt some staff officer with no combat assault experience looking for flight time on his record. It was a fiasco. No sooner did we set down than we came under heavy fire from bunkers all around the LZ. It was either poor intelligence, and we had dropped right on top of an NVA regimental base camp, or they knew we were coming. With the ARVN, it could have been either one; but their guys were getting mowed down before they could get out the door.

In a dense formation like that, there's little time to react. We dropped off the infantry, who were supposed to fan out and take control of the LZ, while we quickly took off; because the next three ships were coming right in behind us, followed by the next three, and the next three. Our three lead ships were the only ones to make it back out. All the others were shot down as soon as they landed. The Command Ship should have called them off as soon as he saw the intensity of the ground fire, but he didn't. He kept sending them in; and to compound the folly, he sent in Medevac aircraft, too. They had no guns, and simply added to the number of downed helicopters clogging up the LZ.

Eventually, we gained control of the battle by bringing in Air Force fighter bombers, more gunships, and artillery, enough to allow us to evacuate our flight crews from the scene. They had stayed in the middle near the downed aircraft. Amazingly, we did not lose a single man. The ARVN troops, on the other hand, who had attempted to work their way to the perimeter, some 240 in all, were annihilated and none of them got out alive. When our last men were out, the Cobras were sent back in to destroy all the wrecked machinery. Naturally, there was a big investigation by both the US and South Vietnamese. I never heard how it came out, but I doubt they ended up blaming spies and double agents at the ARVN headquarters, nor an incompetent US Lieutenant Colonel, whom we never saw again.

That was about the time when they started sending ARVN pilots to fly with us, because we weren't getting any American replacements. That was a fiasco. They were poorly trained cowboys. When things got hot they'd break formation, do whatever they wanted to do, start chattering away in Vietnamese, and "keying the mic" by holding the transmit button down. That blocked the frequency, and made communication impossible. I was there for the beginning of that transition. As I got short, I'd refused to fly with them. I had done my bit.

Toward the end, we all got job offers from the CIA to fly with Air America, which I had no interest in doing. The first time I saw them was when I landed at Kontum. There were a half-dozen guys dressed in black, with no insignias, sitting in lawn chairs in front of a line of unmarked helicopters that had .50-caliber machine guns mounted in the doors, drinking beer. Our mechanics had always said that a Huey couldn't take a .50, but the Air America machines had them and twin engines. We had never seen anything like that before. The job looked interesting, but at the end of the day they didn't have the backup or support that we had. If they got shot down, which happened quite often, the best they could do was to get on one of our frequencies and call for help, "off the books," so to speak.

One day, I sprayed Agent Orange. I didn't know what it was then, and they sure weren't telling anyone. If you came back looking "healthy" with nothing obviously wrong with you in your exit physical, the VA simply cut you off from any future treatment. It wasn't until eight years ago that I was finally tested and had my benefits reinstated.

I rotated out in April, 1971, was discharged, and never looked back. I had received a Silver Star, Bronze Stars, and air medals, but we were in so much stuff that I can't remember which days they were for. Back home in Minnesota, I went into the concrete ready-mix business, and built my own experimental aircraft and helicopter. After I retired to Florida, I built my own swimming pool and added some other major house renovations myself.

KEN MANLEY'S WAR

US Army Specialist 5 and Morse Code Interceptor, 265th Radio Research Company, 101st Airborne Division, Camp Eagle, 1970–71

I graduated from high school in Fort Worth, Texas, in 1969 and got a job on a cattle ranch in east Texas. That's me on the right in both photos. My ambition had always been to have my own cattle ranch; but a Draft Notice kind of interfered, and I found myself in Fort Leonard Wood, Missouri, that August. After Basic, I was sent to Fort Devens, Massachusetts, for Morse Code Radio Interceptor School. It sounds old fashioned, but the VC and NVA did most of their radio communications in Morse code.

On June 2, 1970, I arrived in Phu Bai near Camp Eagle, assigned to "the 265th Radio Research Company" at the "8th Radio Research Field Station," attached to the 101st Airborne. Everything we did, even the existence of the unit itself, was secret. Only the highest officers at Phu Bai or Camp Eagle knew who we were, what we did, or had heard of the unit. Even today, we are rarely listed as one of the component units in the 101st during the war.

We worked two ways. Our base station had power-ful receivers to intercept the longer-range VC and NVA signals. Those were always in Morse code and encryp-ted; but we had a sophisticated operation with linguists, code breakers, and analysts to decipher them. However, the enemy also had very low power Chinese transmit-ters for local radio traffic, and those couldn't be picked up by our base stations. They didn't think anyone could hear them way out west in the mountains near the Laotian border, so many of those transmissions were not encrypted, and were voice transmissions in the clear. But to hear them, we had to get a whole lot closer,

which meant sending teams out in the bush, usually to small firebases in the mountains, where we could sit and listen. Our team usually consisted of a linguist, an analyst, and an interceptor, which was me. We could deal with the simple transmissions, and would send the higher-level coded ones back to base. As a result, we picked up a lot of stuff about VC and NVA locations and troop movements, which allowed our Air Force, tactical air, and field artillery to hit them. Other times, we learned of impending attacks. We had our skeptics, but it didn't take many hits to turn them into believers.

I enjoyed being out in the field. One time, my team spent three weeks on an ARVN firebase. We were the only Americans there and worked with a Major Tranh, who spoke some English. He had also been in the Viet Minh fighting the French, and maybe the Japanese before that, for all I knew. Officially, he didn't know what we were doing, but of course he did. One day we picked up some intercepts that told us that the 324th NVA Regiment would hit the firebase the next day, so I told him, "Major, a usually reliable source..." which was our standard euphemism about the intercepts, "says that this fire-base will be hit tomorrow."

He looked at me, smiled, and shook his head. "No, I think not," he answered.

I pressed the point and told him our source was usually right.

"Perhaps, but not in this case. You see, the Commander of the 324th is Colonel Nguyen. Tomorrow is his daughter's birthday and he will be celebrating. Perhaps he will attack the next day, but not tomorrow."

The Major was right. They didn't attack the next day, they attacked the day after.

Another time, we were on a hill in the A-Shau Valley and picked up a new, strong signal coming from a hillside across the valley. A strong signal meant it was likely a headquarters, probably a regiment. We called in artillery and air strikes to take it out several times, but they must have been in a cave, because the signals didn't stop. A couple of days later, a helicopter showed up with some guys and a couple of big crates. They hauled their equipment out, aimed it at the cave mouth and several other known points for a few minutes, packed up, and left. They were top secret too, but we found out that was the Army's first experimental laser rangefinder, and they had precisely plotted the location of the cave. Shortly after that, the side of the hill erupted with naval gunfire from one of the battleships and a B-52 strike. Then, the cave disappeared. I happened to be listening to one of the enemy's Morse code radio transmissions when it happened. In mid-sentence, I heard a loud screech, and the signal suddenly stopped, which meant their radioman died with his hand on the key.

We used different radio receivers, but my favorite was an old Chinese radio. It was a beautifully engineered HF receiver, powerful, but so small that it fit inside a .50-caliber ammo can. Most of the time we were on remote firebases. On occasion, the infantry guys would come across an enemy commo wire and we would tap into it, but sooner or later the NVA would figure out there was a tap on the line. Eventually, the Army developed a passive listening device that you could lay down next to a cable without it being detected, and later upload the signals to an airplane. Whatever, it all helped to save lives.

For the two months before Tet in 1971, we were on Co Pung Mountain working with the ARVN "Black Tiger" Ranger Battalion. It was a hot area. We would get mortared almost every day and have ground probes and rocket attacks at night. The Black Tigers fought their way back into Hue after Tet, 1968, and were one of the very best ARVN units. There were some US units that didn't accept our warnings, but the Black Tigers always did. We told them we had picked up signals from a troop concentration down in the valley and their commander took half the unit down on a sweep that led to a major battle.

Another firebase where we set up had the most primitive living conditions of any of the places we went. It had been an old NVA or Viet Minh artillery base, and there were tunnels everywhere. When we were there, we set up in a dry wash on the top of the hill, covered it with PSP to keep the sun off, and ate C-rations the whole time.

All in all, it was great work and I was very proud of what we accomplished. I know we saved lives. When I rotated out in May, 1971, they sent me to Fort Hood. A year later I was ordered back to Vietnam, but at the last minute the orders were changed to Udorn Air Force Base in Thailand, near the Cambodian and Vietnamese borders. We had a detachment of thirty-five guys there and much more sophisticated gear to work with. Better still, we had an air-conditioned building and slept downtown in a hotel. After that tour, I was sent to the 10th Special Forces Group in Fort Devens, Massachusetts, where I was promoted to E-6. I ended up staying in the Army for ten years, and my last assignment was at the US Army Security Field Station in Augsburg, Germany.

I got out, but continued to work in the aerospace and defense industry with General Dynamics and Hughes Aircraft, doing various things. I live in Texas, play golf, cook, and am the barn manager for an equine therapy program for vets. I have a 50% disability with heart issues, due to Agent Orange and PTSD, but given where I was, I consider that lucky.

ERIC BROWN'S WAR

**US Army Captain and Gunship Platoon Leader,
the 57th Assault Helicopter Company,
52nd Aviation Battalion,
An Khe and Pleiku, 1970–71**

I was an ROTC student at "The" Ohio State University, when the Army decided they needed more helicopter pilots. They offered to give us our commissions and send us to pilot training early, before we graduated. I jumped at it, figuring I could always come back and finish up my degree on the G.I. Bill later. I got my Lieutenant's bars and went on active duty in March 1968 as an Engineer Officer. However, the path to Vietnam was not exactly a straight one. After Officer Basic and Jump School, I was sent to Fort Greeley Alaska, to the US Army Arctic Test Center, to test equipment in a "cold-weather environment."

So, it was early 1970 before I was finally sent to flight school. By then, they had shortened and condensed the program. By June, I was "in country," assigned to the "Cougar" gunship platoon of the 57th Assault Helicopter Company at An Khe in the Central Highlands, where I stayed for the next three months. The area was hilly, with deep valleys and mountain passes. Two-thirds was dense triple-canopy jungle. The rest was flat scrub land. I flew both C and M-model Huey gunships in various configurations. All had door guns, while some had miniguns, some had a 40-millimeter grenade launcher in front, and most carried 2.75-inch rocket pods.

For the most part, we supported the 4th Infantry Division and the 7th of the 17th Cavalry Regiment. We flew them out, picked them up from insertions, and provided weapons support. I was a

Captain by then and flew missions into Cambodia and Laos. "Official" or not, we were supporting Special Forces units who were working along the Ho Chi Minh trail. I flew gunship missions twice with them, keeping an eye out in case they got in trouble. Mostly we just hung around if they needed us, but once we went in and opened up on some NVA positions.

By the summer of 1970, the war had definitely wound down, but you still had to be careful. Just to remind us they were still there, the NVA rocketed us fairly often. But there were no serious battles in or around where we worked, and I'm not sure my helicopter was ever hit by ground fire. However, one of my good friends was flying a slick and must have had some type of catastrophic engine failure. His aircraft suddenly went nose-down and flew him right into a hillside, killing him and burying the machine six feet into the ground.

The facilities at both An Khe and Pleiku were halfway civilized. We had wooden hooches and slept on metal cots. We had a latrine with running water, showers, and a mess hall with pretty good food, although most of the pilots ate at the officer's club. We had Vietnamese women who did our laundry, provided all the KPs in the kitchen, and even burned the barrels under the latrines every morning—and probably mapped the compound for the VC while they were doing it.

After three months, I was pulled up onto the 52nd Combat Aviation Battalion staff, our parent unit at nearby Pleiku, to be on the S-3's Mission Control Center staff. We planned day-to-day operations and scheduling missions. Our battalion commander was Engineer Corps, and he decided he wanted all engineer officers around him. That's how I got the job. In addition to doing plans and operations, I also flew normal combat missions, but there really weren't all that many at that time. We had a big refueling station with six 125,000-gallon gas tanks that could refuel six helicopters at once. When I became Battalion S-4, one of my jobs was to fly fuel samples down to Qui Nhon for testing, to ensure we were getting good fuel for our aircraft. We also got quite a few USO shows and TV and movie stars up at An Khe and Pleiku, and I was frequently tasked to fly them around to the firebases and outposts.

Towards the end, while I was on the battalion staff, there were a lot of aviation units scattered about that were being closed down and had excess aircraft. It was the beginning of the big drawdown, and many staff pilots like myself were tasked to fly the extra helicopters to units that might need them, or back to one of the depots where they were being shipped home or turned over the Vietnamese.

What I remember most about Vietnam was the heat, the rain, and counting down the days until I went home. When I did, at the end of my year, I received a Bronze Star and some of the usual Vietnam and staff metals, but I've developed no service-related or Agent Orange-related disabilities, so far. On my return to the US, I was sent to Fort Dix where I worked in the training command. Between various courses and several assignments at Fort Carson in Colorado, I was allowed to go back to Ohio State to finish my degree in 1975.

I got off active duty in 1977, and joined the Ohio Army National Guard. In 1985, I became a full-time member of the Guard, retiring in November, 1995. I then spent eleven more years with the Ohio Department of Corrections and the US the Department of Housing and Urban Development in Colorado, before I completely retired.

CRAIG TONJE'S WAR

**US Army Specialist 5th Class and Huey Crew Chief,
A Company, 227th Aviation Regiment,
1st Cav Division 1970–72**

I'm an Ohio boy, from Toledo. After graduating from high school in 1967, I spent an indifferent year and a half at Ohio State before I was invited to pursue other interests and enlisted in the Army in the summer of 1969. After basic at Fort Jackson I was sent to Fort Eustis, trained as a Cobra Crew Chief, and sent to Fort Hood, Texas, for six months.

In August, 1970, I arrived at Lai Khe in III Corps and was assigned to A Company of the 227th Air Assault Regiment, part of the 1st Cav Division. I was trained on Cobras, but frequently flew on Hueys, depending on what was needed. We later moved to Camp Holloway in II Corps, but the work was the same.

My most interesting day was March 31, 1971, right after we moved. My regular aircraft was waiting for maintenance and I was asked if I would fly door gunner on one of the slicks to ferry some VIPs up to Kontum for a briefing. While we were waiting for them, we were told that an ARVN firebase outside Dak To, was being hit hard. There were ten American advisors stationed there, and they had been attacked before daylight. A satchel charge had already taken out three of the Americans, and it was escalating into a major battle.

We landed at Dak To, could see the battle raging on the hill nearby, and were told the good guys were running out of ammunition. As everyone in the Army knew, Rule #1 was never volunteer, but we quickly agreed to fly the ammo over, if it could be sling loaded under the helicopter, so we could drop it and get out of there. The firebase was being hit from three sides, but there was a gap on one side we could use. We flew in that way and dropped the load, taking fire the entire time. When we got to back to Dak To, we checked out the aircraft. It had some bullet holes here and there, but nothing serious;

so we set off with a second load, accompanied by another Huey from our company. We had to go in the same way as before, because there wasn't much choice. Unfortunately, this time, having had some practice, the bad guy's aim was better. Our pilot was shot and killed, and we went into a tight spiral, crashing on the hillside, about fifteen meters outside and below the wire.

Three of us were relatively unhurt, but our pilot was dead. At that point, we were as worried about the ARVN firing down at us as we were of the NVA firing up, but I was wearing my "Captain America" flight helmet, which I hoped would help. As we ran for the wire, the lieutenant in charge of the advisors, Brian Thacker, yelled down and told us there was a gate about thirty meters around the perimeter, but we chose to go straight up, laying our field jackets across the wire and scooting across. We managed to get through and make it inside to their command bunker. As I sat there, I realized that my ankle ached, and figured I might've broken it in the crash. There were mortars coming in everywhere and small and medium arms fire as another helicopter tried to come in and get us out, but it crashed too. Soon, there were seven aviators crowded into the command bunker as our Air Force, the Vietnamese Air Force, artillery, and Army gunships began pounding the surrounding hillsides. Even still, the bunker was hit by a flamethrower at least twice and we had to put out the fires by throwing sand from the floor on them. It was harrowing.

As we expected, it wasn't very long before the ARVNs caved. They began running out through the gate into the jungle. Not wanting to be left alone up there, we had no choice but to follow. I still wasn't sure if my ankle was broken, but I took off running with everyone else. It's amazing what a great painkiller adrenaline can be. When we hit the tree line, I stumbled and lost my glasses, leaving me both lame and semi-blind! But as I turned and looked back, I saw that same Lieutenant Thacker on top of the firebase firing his M-16 and holding off the bad guys until we reached the tree line and got away.

We were following a long line of ARVNs running in the direction of Dak To, chased by the NVA, who kept getting ahead of the column to set ambushes. Finally, toward dark, we heard a Cobra overhead, used our emergency radio to make contact, and our last flare to mark the enemy positions. He began unloading on them and directed us to a clearing where we could be extracted. Fortunately, we got there just as a slick came in. There was too much vegetation for him to land, but he hovered long enough to pick us up. The others managed to climb up, but the best I could do with my bad leg was grab onto one of the skids, kick one of the ARVNs away, and swing the leg over the bar. One of the crew grabbed my arm and tried to pull me inside, but I was kind of stuck. The guy was yelling at me to get in, while I was yelling back at him that I was doing just fine, thank you, and that they should get the hell out of there, which they did, with me hanging onto the skid under the helicopter all the way back.

At camp Holloway, I was taken to the clinic. The Doc told me my ankle wasn't broken but it had swollen up to the size of a cantaloupe by the time they took my boot off. The next day, we were told that we had run about fifteen kilometers from that firebase. It was also determined that it had been hit by two regiments of NVA regulars. Before the night was over, Firebase Six and the surrounding area was leveled by a B-52 strike. A week later, the ARVN went back in and reoccupied the place. To everyone's shock, a few days after that, Lieutenant Brian Thacker emerged from the jungle, where he had been hiding. He had been classified as MIA, but must've had some very good jungle survival training. He was later awarded the Congressional Medal of Honor for saving us and a lot of other people that night.

I remained in-country and flying until March 31, 1972, when I rotated back to Fort Lewis, and was discharged. I returned to Ohio State and graduated in 1974 with a bachelor's degree in history, before moving to Florida. I'm now sixty-eight. Since 1977 I have been an independent, certified real estate appraiser in Fort Myers. I've been diagnosed with PTSD, but I've been active in several veteran's groups, including the 1st CAV Association, the VFW, the American Legion, and I've served as President of my Vietnam Veterans of America chapter.

In 2000, I went back to Vietnam and stood on the remnants of what used to be the runway at Dak To, at the very spot where we stood that day watching the fighting going on at Firebase Six. I could see it all over again, just as I had then. But the jungle is now all gone, clear-cut for lumber, leaving only grassy mountains. The ridge around Dak To looks about the same as it did back then, as does the point of land where the firebase stood. After I got all the chills and emotions under control, I realized that I was okay! I often see and relive that day, but it continues to come out the same. I survive.

HARRY LUMPKIN'S WAR

**US Army Captain, Mission Supply Officer,
1st Transportation Battalion, *USS Corpus Christi Bay*
Helicopter Repair Ship, Vung Tau, 1971–72**

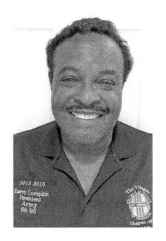

One of the larger ships operating off the coast of Vietnam belonged to the US Army. It was the *USS Corpus Christi Bay*, formerly a Navy World War II anti-submarine ship, the *USS Albemarle*. It looked like a small aircraft carrier, but we used it to repair and rebuild helicopters, so they didn't need to be sent back to the States or be scrapped. It was anchored at Vung Tau, at the mouth of the Saigon River, south of the capital. We had a crew of six hundred repair technicians and one hundred and twenty-nine Merchant Marine sailors. It had a helicopter pad in front, a flight deck in the rear, and an air-conditioned hangar deck below with thirty-two repair shops. I was in charge of supply and had "Red-Con" claim on any repair part in country. If pressed, we could completely rebuild a Huey in forty-eight hours. Our shops were very busy, and at one time or another, almost every helicopter in-country spent some time onboard.

I was an ROTC graduate from Morgan State, Regular Army, Quartermaster Corps. I'd gone to Airborne School at Fort Benning and spent a year with the infantry at Fort Hood. I arrived in Vietnam as a Captain in February, 1971, by which time things were winding down.

One day I'll always remember was when we built a church. A young GI who had spent time helping a local missionary near Vung Tau had been killed. His family raised the money and sent over a pre-fab church, so he'd be remembered. What they didn't have was people to put it up. I heard about it, got some volunteers from the ship,

04 OUR VIETNAM WARS
and we did it. When we were done, we sent some photographs back to the family. Lots of Vietnamese came to the opening. After the country fell to the North Vietnamese a few years later, I wondered what happened to the church and all those people. But on that day, we all felt very good about what we did.

Another time, we were returning by Huey from Tan Son Nhut with some Red-Con parts when we heard a distress call. An American unit was under attack and the gunships that had come to provide support were almost out of ammo. They had to leave, and the unit needed help, quick. I was in back, and my pilot asked me, "Okay, Dai Wi?" which was Vietnamese slang for the boss, "What should we do?" Naturally we diverted and went in, with me on one M-60 and the Crew Chief on the other. Our pilot was an old 1st Cav major, and knew how to fly. We began circling the unit, looping and swooping, sometimes with the helicopter heeled over on its side as I fired belt after belt into the bush. I had never seen a machine gun barrel get that hot. Pretty soon, we also got low on ammo. As other aircraft arrived, we left.

The whole time we were in that fight, we were screaming back and forth in the mics, shooting at one target after another, completely unaware that it was all being picked up back on the ship. When we landed, all the guys came out and started patting us on the back and congratulating us. I had felt no fear the entire time, not until I got back to my cabin. I quickly closed the door, began to shake, and almost threw up.

A USO group featuring the Dallas Cowboys Cheerleaders put on a show on our ship. We were supposed to fly them on to their next stop, a firebase in the bush, but the Army decided to call it off, because that area had become too dangerous. The Cheerleaders would have none of it, however. They didn't care how dangerous it was, they came to see those kids out there and they were going, which they did. After that, I've always support-ed the USO.

Toward the end of my year, it was decided that the ship would head home, so I was ordered to stay aboard. We left Vung Tau in March, 1972, and headed for Japan with one hundred helicopters, all wrapped in plastic, and began to clean the ship for its return to the States. As that work was underway, the North invaded the South, and we were ordered back to Vietnam, to Danang this time. It had almost been overrun. As soon as we got there, we began ferrying the helicopters to the units there, until we got a call and were told to stop. The VC and NVA were blowing them up as fast as we sent them in, so we were told to return south to Vung Tau.

We were the only American unit for miles around, all the way up to Saigon, but we fell quickly back into our old role of repairing helicopters. Unfortunately, there weren't very many around anymore, and nothing is worse than a bored GI, especially one who had expected to be home. We were frozen there, and no one could tell us why, or when we would leave. That was a major leadership challenge, since bored troops led to increases in drug abuse and disciplinary problems. What the officers knew, but could not reveal, was that the ship had been designated to be the floating headquarters for the US command, if Saigon was overrun. We were told not to engage the enemy unless fired upon, and not to repair any South Vietnamese helicopters. One could only assume the US wanted to leave as little useful equipment behind as possible if the country fell. It did, but there was no need for a floating US headquarters. Finally, just before Christmas, 1972, we pulled out and went home.

One problem that continues to haunt me had to do with my friend Tom. We became great friends in Officer Basic and Ranger School, as did our wives and kids. He was white, I'm African-American, and we were called "Salt and Pepper." He went to Vietnam before I did, and was badly wounded, paralyzed from the chest down, and wasn't going to get any better. His wife finally called me for help, because he shut her out and wanted a divorce. I went there and talked to him, but I couldn't change his mind. He had grown bitter, and was determined not to ruin his wife's life or his kids'. Finally, he left the house, moved in with a brother, and disappeared. It was a real tragedy, and showed me that not all Vietnam casualties have their names on the Wall.

I remained in the Army and among other assignments served as General Colin Powell's logistics briefer during the Gulf War, later as a professor at West Point developing systems to measure female integration into the Academy, and finally was placed in charge of the drawdown of all US units from Europe. When we began, there were over 1 million service members and dependents located there, plus facilities and equipment. With a staff of 1,500, I had five years to get that down to 65,000 people and eliminate 486 installations. Then, the five years was reduced to three, and we still got it done.

After twenty-six years, I retired as a Colonel. I had a series of wonderful assignments. My wife and kids enjoyed the Army too, although we moved twenty-three times, almost once per year. I earned two master's degrees, while on active duty, and was awarded two Bronze Stars, a Civic Action Medal 1st Class, the Defense Superior Service Medal, and the Legion of Merit, of which I'm very proud, as well as other awards, including a Resolution by both Houses of Congress for outstanding leadership and service, commending our work on the drawdown in Europe. After Europe, I put in my papers and retired, taking a job with the UN in Rome and Switzerland, developing systems and accountability for the UN Worldwide Food Program, reducing the theft and abuse. When that three-year assignment was completed, I was hired as COO of a defense contractor doing IT work in DC.

After Vietnam, I had given serious thought to getting out of the Army, but one incident made me choose not to. When I was out at locations away from the ship, I would often pass low-ranking African-American enlisted men. They'd see me, make a fist, and bump it on their chests several times. That was a new one to me. Good or bad, I had no idea what it meant; so, I finally stopped one of them and asked. He told me, "It means they're so pleased to see a Black officer that they'll die for you." That sunk in. I was the only African-American officer around, so I got assigned to handle all the race problems, but I did not resent it. I realized that I was their voice, and that was motivation enough for me to stay in. There was a need for more minority officers to ensure the conversation was fair.

Now seventy, my wife and I have retired to Florida where I remain active in veteran's groups, serving as President of our local Vietnam Veterans of America Chapter. I've been diagnosed with Agent Orange issues and have a 50% disability from that, as well as a bad back and knees.

DENNIS STOREY'S WAR

US Army, Spec 4 and Communication Specialist,
124th Signal Battalion, 4th Infantry Division,
Kon Tum, 1971

I grew up as a Navy brat, bouncing around the Pacific from San Diego to the Far East as my father moved from duty station to duty station. In 1971, when I was seventeen, I decided to join the Army Reserves. Needless to say, my father was less than thrilled with the choice. But I scored very high on the standardized tests, and was sent to Fort Gordon to the Signal Corps to be a radio operator with orders to the 4th Infantry Division at Fort Carson, Colorado. What the heck, I thought; the war was winding down, the 4th Infantry was returning home from Vietnam, not going over. I figured that between Basic Training, AIT, and an initial stateside assignment, they would kill most of that first year or two anyway.

Fool me, they had condensed Basic to three weeks, AIT was condensed to another three weeks, and part of the 4th Infantry was staying in Vietnam as a Consolidation Team with the remnants of the 25th Infantry Division. So, I went on active duty January 1, 1971, and on March 1, EIGHT WEEKS later, I arrived in Kon Tum as a communications specialist, working in an old signal van on the Cambodian border. Unbelievable!

While I was supposed to be a radio operator, they handed me a rifle and I became part of a group training the ARVN to take over defense of the border. There were about two hundred of us working with South Vietnamese units, basically serving as advisors. I had never been trained for that, or for the infantry, beyond what we learned in our own "3-Week Basic Lite," and now I was teaching it. We spent most of our time patrolling in the jungle in the Central Highlands near the border. I knew from the place names that this was the same geographical area where some of the worst fighting of the war took place in the late 1960s.

I had an ARVN squad assigned to me, and I worked with the same Vietnamese soldiers every day, going out with groups of ten to thirty, and trying to teach them standard combat stuff and patrolling. I ate with them and slept with them. Fortunately, I was a little guy, about their size; and as several other Americans joked, I was too short to get shot. Fortunately, while we had some firefights, there wasn't much action going on then.

The one thing I learned most during that tour was the importance of teamwork and depending upon others. A lot of the ARVNs really cared about what we were doing, but they were very poorly led and most of them were very young. One of them was fourteen, as I recall. Worse still, most of them had grown up in Saigon and knew even less about the jungle than we did. Their officers and NCOs were hopeless. They wouldn't accept our advice or help, and many of them were playing both sides. You couldn't trust them.

After eight and one-half months, they pulled the plug on what we were doing and sent us home. So, after thirty days in Hawaii, by mid-November, I was back at Fort Carson. The drawdown was continuing, and I was given an early out and discharged in December, 1971, after less than one full year on active duty. There I was, eighteen years old, with my military service over and having served a tour in Vietnam, if you can believe that.

I enrolled in the University of Southern Mississippi and earned a BA in biology with a major in chemistry under the G.I. Bill, and later got a Master of Science at Mary Washington College in Virginia. The job market wasn't the best, so I reenlisted in the Army in 1976. I had grown up with guns, and I qualified as a sniper this time around, was promoted to Sergeant E-5 and sent back to the 1st Battalion of the 24th Signal at Fort Carson, where my career took some strange twists. After three years at Fort Carson I was transferred to SHAPE headquarters in Holland and got more and more into information technology and Special Ops. I spent five years in the Delta Force in the late 1970s, and then went to the Signal Intelligence Field Stations in Augsburg and Berlin, doing signal intelligence with the Special Forces.

I then went to the Management Information Office at the Pentagon. After twenty-one years in uniform, I retired and went to work for Booze Allen. While there, I completed a BA in Computer Science at Strayer University. The discipline that the Military taught me enabled me to complete my education and become a successful Computer Security Engineer at Booz-Allen. I remained there for the next twenty years doing IT, communications, and intelligence contract work for the CIA.

Completely retired now, I enjoy golf and working on my family's history. I serve as the Public Affairs Officer and member of the Board of Directors of the Band of Brothers, a local nonprofit Vietnam Veterans group in my community, which now has over 410 members.

Author's note: the second story in this book, Ernie Burzamato's, is about a seventeen-year-old Marine Corporal sent to Vietnam in 1956 to teach and advise South Vietnamese militia around Danang. The symmetry with Dennis Storey, a seventeen-year-old Army Spec-4 being sent to do the same thing near Kontum in 1971 shows how little we had learned in fifteen years.

BRIAN BLACK'S WAR

**US Army 1st Lieutenant, Mac-V Advisor
to the ARVN 33rd Ranger Battalion,
3rd ARVN Airborne Group, 1971–72**

My father was a career Army Officer in the Corps of Engineers during World War II and Korea. In 1981, he retired and worked on engineering projects overseas, mostly in Latin America, until 1990. My mother served in the Royal Canadian Air Force during World War II. I was raised overseas, and grew up learning foreign languages and developing a passion for soccer. I graduated from a German high school, and spent a semester at the University of Heidelberg. Returning to the States for college, I graduated from TCU, earning BA and BS degrees and a Commission in the Army from their ROTC program.

In July, 1970, I was posted to Fort Benning and completed the Infantry Officer's Basic Course, Airborne, Ranger, and Pathfinder Schools. Later assignments included Jungle Warfare and Long-Range Recon Patrol, or LRRP, training in Panama, before arriving in Vietnam in early 1971. I was originally on orders to be a Platoon Leader in the 82nd Airborne Division at Xuan Loc, but somewhere in the process, the Army noticed that I could speak French and my orders were changed. Instead of a Platoon Leader in the 82nd, I became an Advisor to the 33rd ARVN Ranger Battalion.

We operated out of two firebases in III Corps near the Cambodian border. Most of the South Vietnamese officers and NCOs spoke good French, but far fewer spoke English. While I could speak Spanish, Portuguese, German, and even some Russian, I spoke no Vietnamese, at least at the beginning, so French came in handy.

The 33rd ARVN Ranger Battalion was a crack, well-trained and well-led unit. They had been fighting the Viet Minh, the VC, and the NVA for almost twenty years. In many respects, I was the student, at least during the first three months. I served as a liaison, coordinator, and trainer, amongst other duties, and became very attached to the men there.

I spent that year eating, sleeping, and fighting along-side them in the Central Highlands, along the Cambodian border, and west of Pleiku around Black Virgin Mountain. Frequently, we'd be on one side of the mountain, while several of the NVA's best regiments were on the other side. We had five American advisors assigned to the battalion, with one assigned to each company. In that year, I took no R&R and rarely visited any American firebases, as we worked our way up and down the border.

My main job was to train the ARVN units on Long-Range Recon Patrol techniques, and go out with them. The terrain was dense, triple-canopy jungle and hills. We would be dropped in by helicopter, usually an ARVN Huey, in eight to twelve-man teams, and be out for three to five days, sometimes longer, before we were picked up. Our usual destination was the Ho Chi Minh Trail. We would find a spot and set up an observation post for forty-eight to seventy-two hours, and observe the movement of North Vietnamese men and equipment headed south. We were almost always above 3,000 feet elevation, and humping eighty-pound rucksacks. The duration of the mission was usually limited by how much water, food, and ammunition we could carry, not to mention radios, machine guns, and other items. It was exhausting work, and the most difficult thing I've ever done physically and mentally.

This was somewhat late in the war, long after the big American battles in the Ia Drang Valley, A-Shau Valley, Hamburger Hill, Khe Sanh, and Tet in '68, and it was a year after the Cambodian incursion. Most of the major American ground combat units had been withdrawn or were on their way out, and there was very little American tactical air support or artillery available for us or the South Vietnamese.

People often ask what the Ho Chi Minh Trail looked like. This was 1971, and most of it was a very serviceable gravel road. The bridges tended to be hastily-built wood plank or bamboo affairs. At that time, North Vietnamese were sending convoys down the road with fifty and even seventy vehicles in them. These were mostly old Russian "Kamaz" trucks, a copy of the American 2 ½ ton truck, or the Chinese copy of the Russian copy, but they carried an unbelievable number of weapons and supplies down that gravel road. The bottlenecks were when bridges were knocked out, the road bombed, or when they crossed into South Vietnam, had to offload their cargo, and carry it the rest of the way on bicycles or on their backs.

I rotated out in March, 1972, after eleven months, because the regiment of the 101st Airborne to which I was officially assigned, but had hardly ever seen, was returning to the States. I decided it was not a good time to try to begin a career in the Army and got out in 1974 as a Captain. I attended the American Graduate School of International Management in Phoenix. There were thirty-nine Vietnam-era vets in my class. One former Air Force pilot had even been a POW for a short period. We supported one another and became life-long friends. The closest we came to combat in Arizona was when we played beach volleyball vs the Navy and Marine vets.

We were all depressed for days after watching Saigon fall in April, 1975. It felt as if we had been punched in the gut, thinking about all the sacrifices that had been made by so many good people. I had a particularly tough time, feeling that our ARVN Brothers had been betrayed, and that we had sold them out!

My background and military service proved to be very advantageous when interviewing for jobs during the last semester of grad school. I spent the next forty years working for companies that manufactured heavy construction equipment, setting up distribution channels, and doing both civil and mining engineering studies in Latin America, the Middle East, and Asia. It was very satisfying work. In 1976, I met my future wife at Caterpillar in Illinois. We have two beautiful daughters and two fine grandchildren. I am both Blessed and a Very Fortunate Man.

I'm now sixty-nine years old, retired, and live in suburban Houston. Like a lot of other vets, I've experienced Agent Orange-related issues. Now, I like to spend my time reading history and archaeology, and doing Christian outreach work in the local prisons. Like many other vets, I haven't talked much about the war or my experiences, until recently.

A. J. WELCH'S WAR

US Army, Captain and Cobra Helicopter Pilot,
1st Cavalry Division, Ben Cat and Bien Hoa,
III Corps, 1971–72

I went to high school in Iowa, graduated from the University of South Carolina, and entered the Army in October, 1967. After OCS and the Armor Basic and Maintenance Schools, I was sent to Germany to an armored cavalry unit. In 1970, I received my orders to Vietnam and flight school, became a helicopter pilot, and transitioned to the Cobra.

In April 1971, I arrived in Viet Nam and spent the next year flying in three different units—B Troop in the 1st Squadron of the 9th Cav, H Troop in the 16th Cav, and F Troop in the 9th Cav. They told us the war was winding down, but no one told the enemy. I had been promoted to Captain, and one of my assignments was to lead the Aerial Weapons Section. Initially, we were based at Bear Cat, directly north of Saigon, and then relocated to Bien Hoa. Our troop typically had nine Cobras, with two pilots each, plus the crew chiefs and other maintenance men, for a total of thirty-five to forty men.

The Cobra helicopter was a two-seat aerial weapons platform. It could carry many different weapons in many configurations, depending on the mission. The gunner sat up front and worked with the maps and the nose turret, which normally had a 40-millimeter grenade launcher or a mini gun. The pilot was in back and controlled the rockets and other guns. That usually included two nineteen-shot 2.75-inch rocket pods inboard under the "wings," plus two more outboard nine-shot rocket pods with "nails," or flechette warheads. That was called a "Light Hog." Or, it could have four nineteen-shot pods with miniguns and or grenade launchers, which was called a "Heavy Hog," used by the Aerial Rocket Artillery. There was one other configuration which I preferred. It had rocket pods on the starboard side and a 20-millimeter Gatling Gun on the port side. Any of those did a lot of damage. On occasion, we would "borrow" some 20-millimeter armor-piercing Gatling gun rounds from the Air Force. Those did a great job penetrating bunkers. But no matter how it was configured, the Cobra carried a lot of firepower.

The Air Cav's mission was to aggressively seek out the enemy and we typically operated in Hunter-Killer teams. Our normal tactic was to have a Loach (Little Bird), a small, observation helicopter, fly low, search out the enemy, and draw fire. Up above, around 1500 feet, the Cobra would circle, ready to pounce when that happened. Up in I Corps they used a Loach with a team of Cobras. We would usually have at least three Slicks or Hueys carrying infantry available to go in for follow-up on the ground.

Our area of operations was the rocket belt around Saigon, where the NVA and VC most frequently fired the Russian and Chinese-made 122, 107, or 140-millimeter rockets at our bases. They weren't terribly accurate, but they didn't have to be against large targets. In our Hunter-Killer system, the scouts were referred to as White, the gunships Red, and the infantry Blue. The usual scout-gunship configuration was called a Pink team. The Loach carried a pilot and an observer with an M-60 machine gun. The cynics referred to this tactic of having them fly around to draw enemy fire as "recon by sacrifice." They  didn't have much armor, except for the seat, and it took a lot of guts to do what those guys did.

When people mention Bob Hope and the Christmas shows he put on in Vietnam, I quickly tell them that I saw one in 1971. Unfortunately, I was in my Cobra up at 1,500 feet providing air cover.

As with most helicopters or fixed wing units, I did not fly the same machine every day, because they had to rotate in and out for maintenance. When your name came up on a mission, you took whatever aircraft was available.

On the surface, we had it pretty good. My wife shipped me an air-conditioner, and I had a fifteen-foot-long bar in my hooch. My roommate and I would get up in the morning, have a hot breakfast in the air-conditioned mess hall, fly around in our air-conditioned helicopters—the Cobra was the only helicopter with any air-conditioning—and be back at base by around 5:00 p.m., in time to hit the bar in the air-conditioned Cav Club across the street. We would go out in the morning, laager at a firebase or an airfield, look for trouble for about two and a half hours, return, refuel, and do it again. It sounds easy, but the job came with a lot of stress and nervous tension. One day while doing what I thought was a routine Hunter-Killer operation, we targeted some bunkers and inserted the infantry blue team only to find out that we had put them almost right on top of the 33rd NVA regimental headquarters. It developed into a major fire fight and we had to call in other brigade assets to extract our "Blues."

The one thing I will always remember from my tour was that we lost no Cobra pilots in my unit while I was there. Unfortunately, when I went on R&R we lost two men the first time, and then three more when I went on a second trip. But the worst day was March 17. I had some time off coming and went down to Saigon to meet with some Australian friends, and one of the other guys took my place flying a slick full of infantry. One of the troops in back was apparently playing with a white phosphorus grenade, and it went off. All eleven men on that helicopter were killed. That's why when I go to the Wall in DC, I'm there visiting friends.

I flew one of the last aircraft to leave Bear Cat before it was turned over to the South Vietnamese Army. As we took off, we could see a convoy at least two miles long of Vietnamese trucks coming down the road and heading for the gate. When we happened to swing by at 8:00 a.m. the next morning, everything was gone except the berm. They had scavenged and picked the place clean.

I remained in the Army for a total of thirty-three years, twenty-seven in command slots, including everything from an Air Cav Aviation Platoon, an Armored Cav Troop, a Brigade Headquarters Company, a Special Forces Military Intelligence Company, a Division Headquarters Company, an MI Battalion, and a Training Support Brigade. I retired from the Army in 2001 with the rank of Colonel.

Three months later, I took a job as a military contractor in Germany. I became the Site Leader and it was our job to develop scenarios to validate the performance of our troops going "downrange" to Kosovo, Iraq, and Afghanistan. Finally, I completely retired in 2013, after a total of fifty years working in and around the military. Unfortunately, that was the same year that I was diagnosed with Agent Orange-related Parkinson's Disease, no doubt a result of my service in Vietnam.

Today, I say that my main hobbies include going to doctors, and participating in three different veteran's organizations as well as the Knights Templar organization.

ERIC PERLMAN'S WAR

U.S. Air Force, Sergeant,
F-4 Phantom Avionics Repairman,
Danang, 1971–72

I grew up near Oyster Bay on Long Island. I wasn't much of a student, graduating in the bottom third of my high school class. I went on to Nassau Community College, but that didn't go very well either. I promptly flunked out. With the draft breathing down my neck, I enlisted in the Air Force in March, 1969. I was eighteen years old and after Basic at Lackland, they sent me to the Inertial Navigation Avionics Repair Course. Figures. After my dismal high school and college performance, they send me to the longest and one of the hardest tech schools the Air Force had, almost a year at Keesler Air Force Base in Biloxi, Mississippi, nowhere near Long Island.

After a stint at Homestead Air Force Base in Florida, I got orders to Vietnam and was assigned to the 366th Field Maintenance Squadron in Danang in July, 1971. When I landed at 1:00 a.m., they opened the doors and that heat and humidity hit like a wet blanket.

I was the kind of guy who was always getting in trouble. I was horrible doing bench repairs inside, in the shop, but I was the best guy they had for solving problems out on the flight line. I worked exclusively on F-4 Phantom D and E models. We had three squadrons with eighteen jets in each. We usually worked from midnight until noon, with four days on and one day off. But when a job opened for a statistician in the office, I grabbed it. It was in an air-conditioned building and got me away from the NCOs, whom I couldn't seem to get along with.

316

That lasted seven months until one of the NCOs I had worked for at Homestead arrived and told them they were out of their minds not having me out on the flight line. Shortly, a "GIB" in an F-4, that's the "Guy In Back," which is what we call the navigator-bombardier, couldn't get his avionics system working and wanted to abort his mission. The last thing any maintenance squadron wanted was an "abort" on its record, so I got called out of the office and sent to the flight line. The F-4 was parked under one of those concrete arches for protection. I got his system restarted and the F-4 took off on its mission. I turned to my Sergeant and asked why he called me out. He told me I might be a little guy and only be twenty-one years old, but I had a big mouth. He knew I could get the problem straightened out, because I wouldn't take any crap from that navigator or the pilot. So, I was back working on the flight line.

I felt sorry for the Army and Marine guys who were out in the hills protecting us, but I couldn't complain about the living conditions we had. I lived in what was called "gunfighter village," which was right across the street from the Base Exchange. We had air-conditioning in the offices and shops, and hot food in the mess halls. In the year I spent there, I never missed a hot shower or a hot meal, and I never left the airbase.

The war was winding down, and there weren't many repairs to make. Because we weren't busy, I soon became bored out of my mind. About all there was to do were movies, hanging around the barracks, drinking, drugs, and all the rest, which was not good. One day I ran into another guy who, like me, was one of the three Jews on the base, and he talked me into taking some college classes. I had no idea they even offered those on base, but those classes kept me out of the bars, and I had plenty of time to study. Technically, it was the University of Maryland—Southeast Asia Campus, if you can believe that. We had a real professor teaching English lit and a guy in fatigues with no insignias whatsoever, who had to be CIA, teaching political science; but that was okay. I ended up earning 15 hours of college credit.

Let's face it, there aren't very many guys who can say they got a full semester of college credit while serving in Vietnam during the war.

No doubt the most memorable day I had in Vietnam was the day Nixon ordered the bombing of North Vietnam. I think it was December 18, 1972. Peace talks had broken down, and he turned everything loose including the B-52s, and all the F-4s at Danang. The base came alive. It was electric. We were using two runways and you can't imagine the sound three squadrons of F-4 Phantoms made when they took off, side by side, one group after another, all headed north. It wasn't all that far of a flight, and the last planes were just getting into the air when the first ones were coming back around to land. That was a proud day.

Toward the end of my tour, we started getting more incoming rocket and mortar fire at night. In June 1972, when my time was up, they sent me down to Tan Son Nhut in a C-130 to process out. We were taking off down the runway just as rockets came in. The pilot floored it and we almost went vertical. I remember hanging onto the straps, looking down at the ground through the rear ramp as it closed, and almost throwing up.

I still had time left, so the Air Force sent me to Patrick Air Force Base at Cocoa Beach, Florida, to an air rescue squadron. They had helicopters, not F-4 Phantoms; and I knew nothing about helicopters. Naturally, I got in still more trouble and they finally called me in and told me that since I had some college, if I could get myself accepted to one, they'd let me out early. So, I went home on leave and went back to Nassau Community College. I assumed the Air Force meant I had to go back full-time and I was afraid if I came up short they'd pull me back in, so I signed up for anything I could get into, one of which was an accounting class. I knew nothing about accounting, but ended up liking it. Eventually, I transferred to SUNY Albany, the State University, which had a top-notch accounting program. I graduated with a BA in accounting in 1975 and went on for an MBA in finance at CW Post University in 1980.

When I received my bachelor's degree, I knocked on a lot of doors and got very frustrated trying to find an accounting job, to no avail. The accounting firms made one excuse after another like I was too old, or this or that, but I suspected it had to do with my having been in Vietnam. A lot of guys had that problem. Grumman, who had repair contracts for the avionics equipment I worked on, offered to send me back to school for an electrical engineering degree, but I didn't want to become an engineer and turned them down.

One day, the unemployment office sent me on a job interview for a state job. There was a big scandal then about nursing homes, and New York had set up a Special Prosecutor's Office to audit nursing homes for Medicaid fraud. I went to work for them as an Auditor Investigator. Since then, I have worked for several corporations as controller and CFO. I eventually went on to get professional certification as a certified financial planner, all of which flowed from that first accounting class I took to get an early-out from the Air Force. I now live in Florida, but continue to do financial planning for my clients in New York.

BILL BROWN'S WAR

US Army First Lieutenant and Executive Officer,
HHC, 124th Transportation Command,
Cam Ranh Bay, 1971–72

I was an ROTC Transportation Corps Lieutenant, married, with a one-year-old son, and a master's degree. I went to the Army computer systems school and spent two years in Germany, designing automated supply and inventory systems that saved the Army a lot of money. As Vietnam approached, I knew a colonel who knew a colonel who was supposed to get me a computer job at the big logistics center near Saigon, doing the same thing I did in Germany.

Unfortunately, my airplane landed at Cam Ranh Bay, not Saigon, and I found myself assigned to the 124th Transportation Command. We ran the port. At its peak, several years before, it had stevedore units, harbor masters, three boat companies, and fourteen different types of truck companies. Not when I got there, however. Many of the once-busy supply and maintenance buildings were empty, half the truck companies were gone, and the port was shipping stuff out, not bringing it in.

Fortunately, since I had barely seen a truck in two years, Personnel had the good sense to assign me to the Headquarters Company. We already had one first lieutenant, an E-6 supply sergeant, and two clerks to run the place. I became the CO and the other lieutenant became the XO. A week later, we got force-fed a West Point captain fresh off the plane who needed "command time." He became CO, I became XO, and the other lieutenant became... the other lieutenant. A week after that, the door of our Orderly Room flew open, and in walked an 82nd Airborne Infantry first sergeant on his third tour. He

wanted to be out in the bush shooting bad guys, but his beloved Army sent him to "a goddamned Transportation unit." He was furious. After he'd spent a night in his own hooch, with electricity, a maid, clean sheets, and hot water, and walked around the corner to the mess hall and a nice hot breakfast, he said, "You know, Lieutenant, this is my third tour, I'm thirty-nine years old, and maybe this isn't such a bad deal after all." Indeed.

On Thanksgiving, we invited a local Catholic orphanage for dinner in our Mess Hall. They had maybe 200 kids, all mixed race, maybe 1/3 Vietnamese and Caucasian, and 2/3 Vietnamese and African-American. I nudged our African-American Mess Sergeant and asked, "When was your first tour?" He jumped. "No, no, LT, weren't me. Least wise not all of 'em." We might joke, but Asian countries are very mono-culture. Those mixed-race kids were going to have a very hard time after we left.

One day, a guy was assigned to us whose unit stood down and he walked in with his M-16. The First Sergeant went nuts. "They can't just let you walk away with a rifle," he growled. "Well, they did," the new guy said and laid it on the counter. Top had the Supply Sergeant lock it up in the Arms Room, but Property Books are sacred things. Rifles are strictly recorded by serial number. The Supply Sergeant's tour was soon over. When that happens, everything gets inventoried. Seems he had the right number of rifles, but one serial number was wrong. Top finally came up with a story that we pulled guard duty with another unit and the rifles must've gotten mixed up; but I'd bet anything that he told the Supply Sergeant to toss the new one in the Bay, and the dummy took one of ours by mistake. That delayed his return home by a week or so.

Every month, one company would get tasked to set a night ambush. When our turn came, I was stuck taking them out. There was a huge scrap metal yard on the bay, and we were told to set up our ambush there, to stop any infiltrators coming in by boat. So, there I was, with fifteen clerk typists and supply clerks loaded down for World War III, with war paint on, all nestled down among the wrecked trucks and Conex containers, just waiting. Sure enough, about 3:00 a.m., we saw two small boats coming in. I popped a flare to get a better look, and my bozos opened up. I finally got them to stop shooting as two helicopters came in and swamped the boats. Turns out, it was a small gang of thieves, who were looking to see what they could find in the scrap. Fortunately, my guys hadn't hit a thing; but as dawn broke, they sauntered back into the company area with grins and chest bumps, as if they had single-handedly defeated Ho Chi Minh. Later, it dawned on me that the scrap yard was owned by AB&T, a big commercial scrap metal contractor, and all that stuff was being shipped to Japan. Nice to know we were keeping the world safe for new Toyotas, I thought.

We were hit with 122-millimeter rockets every few weeks, but that was about it. When we did get hit, I figured they had been aiming for the Air Force Base and couldn't shoot any better than my clerks. With a Korean Division in the hills to the west of us, we felt plenty safe.

Down on the pier one night, two chuckleheads on guard duty decided to shoot at fish in the water. Naturally, a bullet bounced up and hit the other guy. Fortunately, he didn't die. Another time, one of our truck convoys had a crane riding on the back of a flatbed truck. Something came loose, so this moron climbed out to the end of the crane to hook it back up. He fell off, broke his neck, and died. Combat deaths were one thing, but I'm glad I wasn't the officer who had to write his mother and explain that one.

At Cam Ranh Bay, boredom and drugs went hand in hand. On any given night, I figured 40% percent of our guys were drunk, 40% were high on pot, 10% were high on hard drugs, which was heroin; and 10% were on... who knows? They were either "Jesus freaks," were on nothing, or were doing something so weird we never did figure it out.

The heroin came in a small, clear-plastic screw-top cylinders called a "cap," like something might put contact lenses into. It came from China and was very pure. If you shot it in your arm with a syringe, it would kill you. Instead, the users put it in a Kool cigarette and smoked it—only in Kools, which only addicts smoked. That's why we really didn't need drug tests. All you had to do was look in their eyes and see a pack of Kool cigarettes rolled in their shirt sleeve to know what they were doing.

The Army administered random urinalysis drug tests. The first time a kid came up positive, he could go to the Drug Treatment Center for a week of counseling, and subsequent testing. It was like a clinic or hospital. But, if he came up positive a second time, he went to the Detox Center, which was like a maximum-security prison, would be flown home on a medevac flight, not a "Freedom Bird" like everyone else, and given a General Discharge.

Seeing the drug problem, I thought I could do some good, so I volunteered for a one-week training course, and became a Drug Counselor. The next month, they pulled a urinalysis test on our whole company. I probably set the all-time Cam Ranh Bay record by talking nineteen guys into turning themselves in to the Treatment Center in one day. Boy, was that cool, or what! Despite my naïve enthusiasm, it accomplished very little. Over the next few months I processed thirteen of them for General Discharges. Most had major problems before they ever put on a uniform and should've never been in the military. One kid from California had been arrested for dealing drugs, and the Judge told him it was enlist or three years in jail. Several had IQs of less than ninety. And one guy had been a carpenter's apprentice in San Diego. He told me his union didn't care. He'd be back in his old job in a week, and making a lot more money than I was. The whole thing left me very cynical about trying to help drug addicts. As one of them told me, "I'll get off the stuff when I want to get off, and there's nothing you can do or say that will make any difference." He was right.

Fortunately, I got an early out after six months, went home to my wife and one-year-old son, and became a civilian. While I was interviewing for a job, even as a white, former officer with a master's degree, one prospective employer had the nerve to tell me, "Oh, don't worry, we won't hold that military stuff against you." Imagine how much harder it was for a black or Hispanic kid from the inner city.

When I did get a job, I was the only one in that large city office who had been in the military, much less in Vietnam. They never warmed to me, nor I to them; and I think you hear that same experience from a lot of vets. It was the "don't ask, don't tell" of our generation.

Personally, I think they were the ones with the problem, not me. I wasn't in combat, but I went where the Army sent me and did my job. The other guys in the office had skated by and avoided the draft one way or another, knowing many guys had not or could not. I believe it left them with some serious guilts. They were ones who didn't do their service and they knew it. The last thing they wanted was to have a guy like me walking around reminding them of that, so they avoided me as if I had the plague. That was why Vietnam wasn't something they wanted to hear about from any of us, or any-thing they would ever understand.

GARY CHAPMAN'S WAR

**US Navy, Command Master Chief and Hospital Corpsman
Neurosurgery Ward, Oakland Naval Hospital and
the "Operation Homecoming" Flights for POWs
from Hanoi, 1973**

I'm from Deer Lodge, Montana, a small town near Missoula. After high school, I attended the University of Montana for a year before enlisting in the Navy. Obviously, there was no seafaring tradition in Montana, but my Draft Number was 3, so I decided to join the Navy because of their medical training. I went on active duty in January, 1972. After Boot Camp and Corpsman training, I was sent to the Oakland Naval Hospital. It was a big facility, with a large Prosthetic Lab, a Neurosurgery Ward, Research Labs, and Clinical Investigations Labs, which dealt with diet, diseases, and things like that.

This was the height of the Watergate crisis in Washington, which got much more publicity than Henry Kissinger's negotiations with the North Vietnamese in Paris or the signing of the Paris Peace Accords on January 27th. Part of that agreement was the return of the 591 American POWs the North Vietnamese held, largely Air Force and Navy airmen who had been shot down on bombing missions.

In early February, 1973, I was suddenly ordered to pack a bag, along with quite a few other doctors and corpsmen, and standby. This wasn't terribly unusual, but we weren't told where we were going other than we would not need any civilian clothes. We were bussed to Travis Air Force Base near Sacramento, an hour away, where we boarded an Air Force C-141-A. That's the big Lockheed Starlifter. The rear cargo compartment of those planes was huge and could be modified to carry seats, hospital litters, or a mix of both. There were no explanations, but onboard was a full complement of medical personnel and supplies, and we immediately took off. We landed at Clark Air Force Base in the Philippines, stayed there for less than twenty-four hours, and soon flew on to Hanoi, landing on February 12th.

We were very busy inside the airplane and could not see what was going on outside through the small windows. Afterward, I learned that three American airplanes had landed in Hanoi that day, but I'm not sure which of the three I was on. Each plane picked up approximately forty prisoners each, while a smaller C-9 went to Saigon to pick up the Viet Cong prisoners, who were released at Loc Ninh. In total, fifty-four flights went to Hanoi between February 12th and April 4th.

The turnover of prisoners by the North Vietnamese followed an elaborate set of procedures which had been negotiated in Paris. Unbeknownst to the US government, the POWs had sworn a strict pact that they would only leave according to the number of days they had been held in captivity, with the longest-held POW leaving first. They didn't believe what the North Vietnamese told them, and refused to cooperate with any other release scheme. Apparently, that caused some initial confusion and delays. The problem was resolved when they were visited by US officers and told that all prisoners were coming home, and that this wasn't just a North Vietnamese ploy to release a few.

While we were on the ground in Hanoi, we were not allowed to leave the airplane, so technically I did not set foot in North Vietnam. The prisoners were brought to the tarmac by the North Vietnamese, lined up in formation, and marched aboard wearing some odd brown-denim uniforms the North Vietnamese had given them. They all walked aboard, or in a few cases were carried. There had been very little contact between the prisoners and the US government, so no one knew what condition they were in or what to expect, medically speaking. As they came aboard, each man was identified, quickly examined by our staff of doctors and corpsmen, and given medicine or treatment for any immediate issues or illnesses they had. Other than those first-aid type treatments, our job was to get them back to the Philippines, where they would be given thorough exams at the big Naval Hospital at Subic Bay.

The first airplane, dubbed "the Hanoi Taxi," is now in the Air Force Museum at Wright Patterson in Dayton. I think that was the plane I was on, but I can't swear by it. Mine was one of the three, and we were very busy attending to the men. In total, of the 591 POWs, 325 were from the Air Force, mostly from bomber crews, 138 were Navy, mostly fighter-bomber pilots, 77 were Army, 26 were Marines, and 25 were civilians. In addition, there were 69 Viet Cong prisoners held in South Vietnam, and 3 held in China.

After the release, the US government maintained there were another 1350 MIAs unaccounted for. By 2015, that list still contained 516 names.

Our return flight to the Philippines was busy, but uneventful. Most of the POWs had substantial physical issues resulting from their long captivity, but they all proved to be more resilient than expected. When our plane arrived at Clark Air Force Base, the POWs passed to the care of the hospital staff there, and we returned to our previous assignments. I only made that one run to Hanoi, but by the time I returned to Oakland, the former Neurology Ward where I worked had been remodeled and converted into a POW ward, as had the South Male Enlisted Barracks, where I had lived.

In subsequent years, I went on deployments as a Corpsman aboard the *USS Enterprise*, had temporary duty many other places, and met my future wife in the Navy Lab School. I changed fields from Neurosurgery to Clinical medicine, studying diet and other things. I remained in the Navy for twenty-eight years, retiring as an E-9 Command Master Chief. My wife stayed in for forty-three years, earned her BS, MS, and PhD as a microbiologist dealing with infectious diseases while in the Navy, and recently retired with the rank of Lieutenant Commander. I'm now sixty-four, and continue to be active traveling and attending the meetings of various veteran's organizations.

BOB PORTER'S WAR

US Navy Lieutenant JG and Supply Officer,
***USS Hancock*, Yankee Station**
off the Coast of Vietnam, April-May 1975

I grew up in the small, central Texas town of Brownwood, about one hundred and fifty miles west of Fort Worth. After getting a degree from Baylor University in banking and business, and having a draft number of 52, I thought the time was right to join the Navy and "see the world." In 1972, I completed OCS and was commissioned an Ensign. When I filled out my "dream sheet" after Supply Officer's School, I asked to be assigned to an aircraft carrier on the West Coast, preferably Northern California, and to my amazement that's what I got. In January 1973, I went aboard the *USS Hancock*, an older Essex Class World War II design, which had been refitted with an angle deck for Korea and refitted again for Vietnam.

The *Hancock* was only 45,000 tons, half the size of today's big nuclear carriers, but it carried an Air Wing with five Squadrons of jets, and a crew of 3,700. As a junior Ensign, I oversaw the Officer's Mess for my first year. My quarters were in the Junior Officer's Bunk Room with fifteen to twenty others, far forward, one deck below the Flight Deck, just aft of the Anchor Chain Room. When the ship was running night ops and the jets warming up and taking off right over our heads, you could hear and feel it; and the catapult would bounce us out of our beds. When I made Lieutenant JG, I moved to a two-man room with an upper and lower bunk, a desk, a closet, a lot more privacy, and a better location.

My three-year enlistment was up the first week of May, 1975. In late March, I was in the last month of my final cruise, looking forward to going home and hanging up the uniform. We were carrying the normal complement of five squadrons of attack jets when we were suddenly ordered to put in at Hawaii. The fighter jets and all their support staff were quickly put ashore. Several squadrons of big, Marine CH-46 and 53 helicopters,

Stallions, Super Stallions, and Chinooks came aboard, filling the flight deck, while the hangar deck, just below, was cleared out. I had been following the news and was aware of the pending collapse of South Vietnam. When the Hancock left port and steamed west, it was easy to figure where we were going.

We put in at Subic Bay and picked up a huge amount of food, cots, tables, chairs, and bedding, before we headed west again, toward Vietnam. For several weeks, we steamed around, apparently killing time. There was a rumor that we would go to Australia and wait, but ended up putting in at Singapore which was much closer. Much of the crew had been allowed to go ashore that first afternoon for some R&R, when the ship suddenly got orders to return to Vietnam. They attempted to get everyone back aboard, but that was impossible. Those that didn't make it were left ashore and flown out to the carrier the next day at sea.

One South Vietnamese city after another fell in April, and they say 100,000 North Vietnamese troops had surrounded Saigon by April 27th. It was on April 29th that the official emergency evacuation of US personnel, dependents, and a considerable number of Vietnamese was ordered. It was called "Operation Frequent Wind."

We had been on Yankee Station for several days, and when I went up on the flight deck and looked around, there were American ships everywhere, all around us to the horizon. The big Marine helicopters on our deck took off in waves, went to various pickup points in Saigon and other cities, and began ferrying people out to the *Hancock* and other ships. This went on for several days. Some even left via Huey from the US Embassy roof as you can see in the photo.

I was involved in the reception process. When the passengers got off the helicopters, they were patted down for pistols and other weapons, cash, drugs, and contraband, deloused, and escorted below by supply corps personnel to the Induction Station on the hangar deck. Their identity papers were checked, they were issued a pallet, a blanket, and a pillow, and given a place on the deck to bed down. Eventually, we had 2,000 refugees on board our ship, and the hangar deck was not air-conditioned.

Some of the evacuees on our ship were US citizens, some were advisors, but most were Vietnamese, who were now political refugees. A chow line was set up and we fed them on a rotating basis by section. With that number of people, about the time we finished running them all through one meal, it was time to start the next one. It was almost continuous feeding. This went on for days.

In addition to the official airlift that had been organized by the Pentagon, there was a sizable and ongoing unofficial airlift and boatlift. Thousands of other South Vietnamese, mostly high-ranking or influential civilians or military, anyone who could get their hands on a helicopter, a small plane, or a boat, tried to get out of the country. For four days, there was a constant flow of boats and helicopters headed out to the US fleet. The smaller American Navy ships picked up the people in boats, but the *Hancock* had a continuous problem with unauthorized helicopter landings.

As everyone back home who watched the 6 o'clock news saw, these were primarily American-made Huey helicopters, which had been given to the South Vietnamese Army months and years before. They were not American, per se; and were pretty much old and beat up. They came in by the dozen in a long line back to the coast, and all were overloaded. They would ask for permission to land, and be denied. With the flight deck already taken up by the big Marine Corps helicopters, and the hangar deck full of refugees, we simply had no room. That didn't stop them. They would come in and land anyway.

After they did, we would take the people below, search them and process them, while the mechanics stripped the helicopter of its avionics, guns, and anything else of value. Then, our deck crew would push the helicopter overboard, by hand if necessary. We had a big forklift aboard which we called "Tilly." That's what we used to push some of them overboard, and made the cover of *Time Magazine*. I was up on deck, and watched it being done; but as the captain reminded us, our mission was about people, not equipment. We saved a lot of lives and saved the helicopter components that might be of value, but the hulk of an old ARVN Huey didn't make the cut.

As we learned later, the North Vietnamese did not try to interfere with the evacuation, for fear of giving the US an excuse to attack or perhaps send troops back in. About 100,000 South Vietnamese refugees had been flown out of the country before then, and another 7,000 made it out to the boats in one fashion or another.

Toward the end of the first week of May, the evacuation had largely run its course. My enlistment in the Navy was almost up, whether the evacuation was over or not. I said my goodbyes to the crew and ship and was airlifted to another carrier, the *Coral Sea*, and flown on to Subic Bay and Clark Air Force Base for my return to the US. The *Hancock* finally left Yankee Station and went to Subic Bay as well, where the American nationals were unloaded, and then to Guam where the South Vietnamese were processed as political refugees.

When I was discharged from the Navy I went back home to Texas and faced the choice as to whether to go back to the bank in Waco, where I had worked and had done an internship, or join my father in the family independent insurance business. My grandfather had founded the firm, which my father now ran. I decided that was my best career path and joined him. My younger brother later joined us as well.

I'm now sixty-nine years old, and my wife Sally and I continue to live in Brown-wood, Texas. I am still working in the insurance business, although I'm spending more and more time following my favorite pursuits of bow hunting, fishing, and traveling.

XXX

I hope you found this book and its incredibly fascinating stories as interesting to read as I did to put down on paper. If so, the credit belongs to the 100 veterans who agreed to open up and talk about their experiences from fifty years ago. My goal was to cover all the years, the units, and the locations where we served, but even 100 stories doesn't begin to do that job. Nonetheless, I hope they can help educate people on what we experienced. I also hope that they can be therapeutic to the tens of thousands of other veterans who need to understand that they are not unique, and they are not alone.

To continue to tell this important story, many of my interviewees have suggested that I not stop, try to cover even more years, jobs, and locations, and write a second volume. So, if you are a Vietnam Vet and would like me to add your story to our narrative, send me an email at Billthursday1@gmail.com and I'll be in touch.

Bill Brown

If you enjoyed the read, I would appreciate your going to the Our Vietnam Wars Kindle Book Page on Amazon Kindle and posting a rating and comment. Just click on the blue words "Customer Reviews" under the book title and my name, and follow the prompts. It is very simple to do, and it really helps other readers find the book.

ABOUT THE AUTHOR

With the addition of <u>Our Vietnam Wars</u>, I'm the author of ten books available exclusively on Kindle. The first nine are mystery and international suspense thrillers,

A native of Chicago, I received a BA from The University of Illinois in History and Russian Area studies, and a Masters in City Planning. I served as a Company Commander in the US Army in Vietnam and later became active in local and regional politics in Virginia. As a Vice President of the real estate subsidiary of a Fortune 500 corporation, I was able to travel widely in the US and now travel extensively abroad, particularly in Europe and the Middle East, locations which have featured prominently in my writing. When not writing, I play bad golf, have become a dogged runner, and paint passable landscapes in oil and acrylic. Now retired, my wife and I live in Florida.

In addition to the novels, I've written four award-winning screenplays. They've placed First in the suspense category of Final Draft, were a Finalist in Fade In, First in Screenwriter's Utopia—Screenwriter's Showcase Awards, Second in the American Screenwriter's Association, Second at Breckenridge, and others. One was optioned for film.

The best way to follow my work and learn about sales and freebees is through my web site http://billbrownwritesnovels.wordpress.com,which has Preview Chapters of each of my novels, interviews, book reviews, and other links.

Burke's Revenge can be found at http://amzn.to/2ob7qnX

Burke's Gamble can be found at http://amzn.to/2lORmXJ

Burke's War can be found at http://amzn.to/2muFG9C

Cold War Trilogy can be found at http://amzn.to/2mmTweV

The Undertaker can be found at http://amzn.to/2l9Chfg

Amongst My Enemies can be found at http://amzn.to/2lTovlu

Thursday at Noon can be found at http://amzn.to/2ljs1SI

Winner Lose All can be found at http://amzn.to/2lTqRke

Aim True, My Brothers can be found at http://amzn.to/2lPbj0t

DEDICATION

First and foremost, this book is dedicated to the 2,709,918 men and women who served in Vietnam, the 211,454 who were wounded, and the 58,220 who died there. Second, it is dedicated to the 100 vets who cared enough to open up and tell me about their lives, experiences, and very personal memories.

I also want to thank the best set of proof readers a writer can have: my wife, Elisabeth Hallett in far-away Montana, my friend Loren Vinson in California, and my new proofing friends, Wayne Burnop in Texas, John Brady in Louisiana, and Reg Thibodeau. I also want to thank Hitch, Barb and the staff of Booknook Biz in Phoenix and Toronto for their usual marvelous advice and help with processing and conversion of this manuscript and its photographs into Kindle-Speak. And I want to thank Todd Hebertson at My Personal Art in Salt Lake City, for the outstanding cover art he has provided for my books.

Table of Contents

Our Vietnam Wars

Copyright © 2018 by William F. Brown

Cover Design and map by Todd Hebertson of My Personal Artist.

Photography by William F. Brown and the veterans in the stories, used with their permission.

Digital Editions produced by Booknook.biz.